ON THEIR WAY REJOICING

The history and role of the Bible in Africa

ON THEIR WAY REJOICING

Ype Schaaf

The history and role of the Bible in Africa

translated by Paul Ellingworth
with an epilogue by Kwame Bediako

THE PATERNOSTER PRESS
CARLISLE, UK

ALL AFRICA CONFERENCE OF CHURCHES

This edition published 1994 by Paternoster Press
PO Box 300, Carlisle, Cumbria CA3 0QS, UK
in association with
All Africa Conference of Churches
Theology and Interfaith Desk,
PO Box 14205, Nairobi, Kenya
Tel: 443580/1   Fax: (2542) 443241

British Library Cataloguing in Publication Data
A catalogue record for this book
is available from the British Library

UK ISBN 0–85364–561–2
AACC ISBN 9966–886–84–2

Typeset by Photoprint, Torquay, Devon
and printed by
The Guernsey Press Co Ltd, Guernsey, Channel Islands

Contents

Foreword

When he contacted me with a view to publishing a French edition of his book, Ype Schaaf promised me that he had the desire, even the duty, to present to the African people their history.

In reading the text it is apparent that the history of the Bible in Africa is closely linked to the destiny of the inhabitants of that continent. If the tendency exists to set Scripture against the oral tradition or if they are treated as separate entities, we must not forget that above all the Bible is a successful example of the documentation of the oral traditions. This explains, I believe, why the Africans reserve pride of place for biblical narratives and in particular those of the Old Testament.

What is more, God reveals himself to be the final source of comfort for victims of suffering and uncertainty and exploitation through the Bible. He offers promises that the African can find nowhere else than in the pages of the Bible. This books gives birth to hope even where the forces of evil seem hellbent on causing chaos.

Would not human logic want God's Word to be self-evident to all cultures with a universal application, and adaptable to all times?

The Bible formulates and communicates God's message to mankind using the language of men who lived in communion with the Creator God. However, the Bible is unique in that although it forms the basis for the lifestyle of many groups, it is far from being a propaganda tool. The moral weakness of men who have been called into a relationship with a holy God is not hidden, evidenced by the accounts of disloyalty of some of these men. Furthermore, this collection of books has not been sheltered from criticism or protected from prolonged attack. Indeed with the passage of time it has survived, indeed has penetrated into all parts of the world. Many people have relied on its teaching, proving it to be powerful to overcome the challenges of their time and culture. For example, the Bible was fundamental in enabling the German people under the direction of Martin Luther to succeed in overcoming linguistic divisions and forming one united nation.

But the Bible can also be compared to an ocean in which people can be lost and drowned. Its actual usage in Africa does not seem to be totally positive because many read it not to reinforce their unity, but to enforce division. Ethnic groups still do not read the Bible to meet each other as brothers and sisters united by the blood of Christ. On the contrary, denominationalism, tribalism and regionalism characterize the life and co-existence of different members of our societies. Nevertheless, the Bible is to Africa a treasure which no one can take away from us. It is at our disposal to be read and interpreted in conjunction with our problems and essential obstacles.

The Bible is for us both a symbol and the means of the continuing work of the God who exposed himself to the mercy of humankind with the aim of obtaining their salvation. The Bible contains a message of life and of hope for the future which Africa needs so much today. Let Africans congratulate, therefore, the author who has helped us to benefit from this thrilling history.

André Karamaga

Introduction

History, or rather the story of the ancestors, plays an important part in African life and thought. Europeans robbed Africans of their history for centuries by reducing it to an account of all the white incursions on the African continent.

For a long time, African missions, African churches and African Christians had no history. The story of the ancient Christian churches in Africa was little known, and all that was available about the growth of missions consisted of money-raising propaganda, or commemorative volumes put out by missions or Bible societies, which read like lives of saints. When Africans themselves began to look at their past, each produced his own history of Africa. Some African scholars were so concerned to rehabilitate Africa that they tried to prove that Egyptian civilization had its source in tropical Africa. Philosophers or anthropologists romanticized the life of peoples who had no writing. Historians and sociologists projected their secularized thinking onto Africa. Muslims exaggerated the role of Islam. Studies in French largely ignored English-speaking Africa, while writing in English tends not to understand the situation in French-speaking Africa. As for the history of the church and Christianity, Roman Catholic and Protestant versions each have their own distinctive features.

This book tries to describe how the Bible came to Africa, how it was translated and distributed, and how its message came to influence culture, politics, religion, education, and African society as a whole. We shall also mention other influences, such as the Qur'an and modern ideologies.

This book is written by a European who worked for the Bible Societies in Cameroon and Gabon in the 1960s, and who then travelled throughout Africa for six years as information secretary for the United Bible Societies. Ever since, Africa has held him in its grip.

It goes without saying that it is for Africans themselves to write the history of the Bible in their continent; this book is only a preliminary journalistic introduction.

It is dedicated to those who work to translate and distribute the Bible in Africa, so that in that Book people may meet their Lord, and 'go on their way rejoicing', like the Ethiopian in the Book of Acts.

The book is divided into two parts. Chapters 1 to 26 give a historical description of two thousand years of Bible translation and distribution. Chapters 27 to 38 are a thematic discussion of the role of the Bible in Africa. This arrangement inevitably entails some repetition between the two parts of the book.

My last thirteen years working as a newspaper journalist have left their mark on this book; each of the chapters may be read on its own as an independent article, while taking its place in the wider historical or thematic context.

I have discovered, while writing, that for Africa, it is impossible to speak of the history of the Bible without setting it within the history, not only of the missions, but also of political, economic and cultural developments.

In the historical part, I have used the old names as long as they remained in use, and for recent times the modern names; that is, for countries:

Basutoland	Lesotho
Bechuanaland	Botswana
Belgian Congo	Zaïre
Dahomey	Benin
Gold Coast	Ghana
Northern Rhodesia	Zambia
Nyasaland	Malawi
Soudan (French)	Mali
Southern Rhodesia	Zimbabwe
South-West Africa	Namibia
Upper Volta	Burkina Faso
Tanganyika and Zanzibar	Tanzania

and for towns:

Léopoldville	Kinshasa
Lourenço Marques	Maputo
Salisbury	Harare

The word 'western' is generally used to refer to the culture of Europe, the United States and the former Soviet Union. In place of the negative colonial expressions 'native', 'tribe' and 'tribal', I have normally used 'national', 'people' and 'ethnic' respectively. Although the French, with their superiority complex, refer to European 'languages', but call Yoruba and Swahili 'dialects', this book uses the linguistically appropriate term 'language' for what Africans speak. South African languages present a special problem: the white Boers have borrowed the Dutch word for 'African', 'Afrikaans', for their own language, whereas Africans in South Africa are said to speak 'Bantu', that is, 'human', languages!

In this book, all inhabitants of Africa are called Africans: not just black Bantu, Sudanese or Nilotic peoples, but also white South Africans, and millions of Africans of Semitic and Hamitic descent in the north. Many North Africans, indeed, have a kind of double loyalty, feeling themselves to belong both to Africa and to the Arab world.

Finally, the reader will notice that Cameroon is rather often quoted as an example. There are two reasons for this. First, although only 5% of the population of Africa lives there, 15% of its languages are spoken there. This means that for questions of language and translation, this country serves as an example for situations elsewhere. The second reason is that although I have visited 26 African countries over the years, I have lived and worked for four years in Cameroon, and in no other African country.

Ype Schaaf

About the Author

Ype Schaaf was born in 1930 in Leeuwarden in the Netherlands. He studied theology at the University of Groningen and in 1959 was ordained as a minister in the Netherlands Reformed Church. From 1959 to 1963 he organized Bible Society work in Cameroon and Gabon, and was one of the founders of CLE in Yaoundé, Cameroon, the Christian publishing house for French-speaking Africa. From 1963 to 1968 he was the United Bible Societies' secretary for promotion and information in Africa, then until 1972 deputy general secretary of the Netherlands Bible Society. Since then he has been active in Christian broadcasting and journalism in the Netherlands and is now editor of the interconfessional missiological journal *Wereld en Zending*. He has written books and articles and produced radio and television programmes, on Africa and the developing world.

The photographs and illustrations in this book were provided by the Netherlands Bible Society and the United Bible Societies (UBS).

This edition contains an additional chapter by the Rev. Dr Kwame Bediako, Founder Director of the Akrofi-Kristaller Memorial Centre for Mission Research and Applied Theology, Akropong-Akuapem, Ghana. He is a director of the Oxford Centre for Mission Studies, and Duff Lecturer and Research Fellow of the Centre for the Study of Christianity in the Non-Western World, New College, Edinburgh.

Part One

1

The People of the Book

Ptolemy II, who ruled Egypt from 285 to 247 BC, and his counsellor Demetrius, had a scholarly interest in the law of the God worshipped by the Jews in Jerusalem. So they established relations with the high priest in Jerusalem. In response, the high priest sent 6 x 12 translators with scrolls to Ptolemy's court, where they were well received. But the Egyptian ruler could not understand the Jews' sacred books in Hebrew. A detailed and interesting discussion took place, and the scholars translated the books of the Old Testament into Greek in 6 × 12 days.

This translation, called the Septuagint or 'seventy', was read aloud to the Jewish congregation in Alexandria, accepted by the believers, and then presented to Ptolemy.

All this happened in Egypt, in Africa, around 260 BC.

The oldest strip cartoon in the world comes from Ethiopia. It depicts on linen or vellum how the Ethiopian Queen of Sheba went to Jerusalem to meet the wise King Solomon, of whom she had heard so much. The queen was deeply impressed by his wisdom and his wealth. The king, for his part, was captivated by her beauty. When the time came to enter a more intimate relationship, the Queen of Sheba sent her slave woman to Solomon's bedroom. The king discovered the ruse, and beckoned with a large finger to the beautiful queen herself. The picture of their meeting leaves little to the imagination. The Queen of Sheba returned to her own country of Ethiopia laden with gifts. Some time after their journey, both the slave woman and the queen gave birth to children. The last emperor of Ethiopia claimed direct descent from this union between King Solomon and the Queen of Sheba. This was the reason for his official title 'Lion of Judah'.

But that was not the end of this graphic novel. The child grew up and asked his royal mother who his father was. When he heard about the wise King Solomon, he too wanted to go to Jerusalem. He goes and is brought up by his father. Finally he returned to Ethiopia as king. He took with him the greatest treasure he had found in Israel: two stone tablets bearing the Law of Moses.

On the silent road which leads south from Jerusalem to Gaza, there comes a chariot, in which an important man is riding. He is *aithops*, that is, dark-skinned. He is the finance minister of the Candace or queen mother of Meroe, a kingdom on the Nile to the south of Egypt. The 'treasurer' has been to the temple in Jerusalem to pray to the God of the Jews. In his own 'Moorish' kingdom, he had learned of the God of Abraham, Isaac and Jacob. On the way back, he is reading one of the Jews' sacred books, the prophecies of Isaiah. This happened around 40 AD. This story is told in the eighth chapter of the Book of Acts.

In the countryside around Lake Chad, there live a number of farming peoples, called Kirdi by the cattle-raising Fulani, the dominant group in the region. One of these peoples is the Massana. Beginning in 1919, an American Lutheran missionary called Revne preached the gospel to them. In the 1940s, he worked with Massana evangelists to translate the New Testament into their language. When he began on the Old Testament, he made a strange discovery. The Massana had exactly the same sacrifices as those described in the Bible in the Book of Leviticus.

He talked about this with his colleague, a Swiss called Hans Eichenberger, who was working as a missionary with another Kirdi people, the Matakam, who live in the mountains separating Nigeria and Cameroon. Eichenberger told how the Matakam say they came to live in these mountains. It is a story about a king's son, a promised land, and a bull stuck in a river bed. Many of the same features are found in the story of Moses in the Old Testament.

The Septuagint, the ten commandments in Ethiopia, the sacrificial practices of the Massana, and the stories of the Matakam, are all examples of Jewish influence in Africa. Before Christianity came, Africa knew the God of Abraham, Isaac and Jacob.

The reason for this is that 'people of the Book' settled in Africa before the birth of Christ. 'People of the Book' is what Jews were called in the Roman Empire.

The Old Testament tells us how, in 721 BC, Samaria, the capital of Israel was captured and destroyed by the Assyrians. Deportations of the Jews followed. In 587 the Babylonians occupied Jerusalem, the capital of the other little Jewish state, Judah. Fresh deportations followed, now to 'the rivers of Babylon'. The Jews swarmed out; under pressure, and perhaps later also voluntarily, they settled everywhere they could survive. They did not travel as traders. That happened many centuries later, under the impact of pogroms in Europe. The Jewish 'displaced persons' from pre-Christian times were farmers and handworkers. Among their specialities were weaving and painting cloth. In the four centuries before the birth of Christ, they established themselves throughout the Near East, in Egypt, North Africa and Sudan, as far as Ethiopia. Wherever the Pax Romana, the

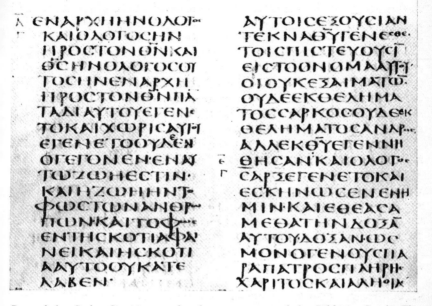

Part of the Codex Sinaiticus, a fourth-century copy of the Bible in Greek. The Septuagint, the Greek translation of the Old Testament made in Alexandria, was the first missionary Bible.

Roman peace, reigned, around the Mediterranean, and also around the Black Sea and in the whole of southern Europe, there were Jewish colonies also. In the time of Christ, the number of Jews in Syria, North Africa and Egypt is estimated at about a million, in Palestine itself at half a million, and in the rest of the Roman Empire another million.

The Jews in the diaspora lived and worked wherever life was materially and spiritually possible for them. As far as the latter is concerned, they desired and sought freedom of public worship. They left Jerusalem and the promised land, but they took with them the Book which states that they are God's chosen people. Even in the 'far country', they taught their children at Passover time the story of the exodus from Egypt. Even in the 'far country', they built their synagogues, in which they prayed and read the Law and the prophets. Jerusalem remained their capital. They made annual gifts to the Holy City, and many went at Passover time on pilgrimage to the temple.

In the far country, the Jewish migrants learned to speak Greek, the language of trade and culture in the eastern part of the Mediterranean basin. Because the prophet Isaiah had spoken to them of the one who was to come to be the light of the Gentiles, they did not shut themselves off in their synagogues from the people among whom they lived. In the third century BC, in Alexandria, Egypt, the five books of

Moses were translated into Greek. The rest of the Old Testament followed. In this way, Ptolemy II got the sacred books in a language he understood. This 'Septuagint' became the Bible of the Jews in the diaspora, and later the Bible of the first Christians. This means that the first missionary Bible was made in Egypt: it was the translation of the Old Testament from Hebrew into Greek. The same translation was the biblical frame of reference for the Gospel writers and for the primitive Christian church.

Through the Greek translation, the hellenistic world became keenly interested in the Book, and in the religion of the God of Abraham, Isaac and Jacob. The hellenistic world had already discovered that the people of the Book were God-fearers; but through the Bible translated into the Greek they understood, they came to know about monotheism, and simple worship without images; about Israel's Law, and its austere ethics. Jewish scholars in Alexandria went a step further. They built a bridge between the Bible and Greek thought by expounding the books of the Old Testament in a Greek allegorical manner.

Did the Jews, the people of the Book, in the last centuries before Christ, follow the Nile as far as Aksum, in what is now Ethiopia? Could that have been how the story of Solomon and the Ethiopian Queen of Sheba came to be told in Aksum?

Sheba itself is now called Yemen and forms part of the Arabian peninsula. In those days it was a fertile country and Jews settled there from an early date. What is more, the religious practices of the Ethiopian Orthodox Church today show clearly that the Ethiopians knew the Old Testament before the New Testament gospel reached the roof of Africa.

Not long ago, there lived in a remote part of north-west Ethiopia about 30,000 Falasha who called themselves *Beita Israel*, the House of Israel. They are black, and claim descent from Jews who had come with Menelik, the son of Solomon and the Queen of Sheba, who came with her from Jerusalem to Aksum. They know neither Hebrew nor the post-Chistian Jewish wisdom of the Talmud. They have the Book in Ge'ez, the holy language of Christian Ethiopia. They keep the sabbath strictly, and read the Law and the prophets in their *mesquid* or synagogues. Under Haile Selassie they were a kind of second-class citizens, but the later Addis Ababa regime has interfered so much in their traditions and customs that a large proportion of them have emigrated to Israel.

Half-way between Alexandria and Aksum, the 'people of the Book' also had their synagogues in Meroe, the capital of Kush, the 'industrial' kingdom in Sudan, near the Egyptian frontier. In the eighth century BC, Kush had freed itself from the Egyptian pharaohs, and in 725 BC, during the great reigns of Kasita and his son Pianki, the kingdom of Kush conquered Egypt and experienced its greatest expansion. Egypt's 25th dynasty was called the 'Ethiopian' or 'dark' dynasty.

In 663 BC, the Assyrians, who had occupied Egypt, used iron weapons to conquer the Kushites, who like the Egyptians had only bronze weapons. A century later the Kushite kingdom moved further up the Nile and made its capital in Meroe, which became the centre for iron smelting and working, under the inspiration of the old Assyrian enemies. In Meroe, too, Jewish migrants built their synagogues. Traces of Kushite influence have been found in Uganda, and even around Lake Chad and in the Yoruba area of Nigeria. The historical remains of this kingdom are still largely buried under the ruins of Meroe, and of Musawarat and Naga in Sudan. Part of them have been excavated, thanks to the great archeological rescue operation involved in making a great lake above the Aswan dam, on the frontier between Egypt and Sudan. The eunuch in the Book of Acts was chief treasurer of the Candace, the queen mother of the kingdom of Meroe. A bizarre system of appointing a new king had given the queen mother great, even divine, power.

The people of the Book, Jews and their associates, were to be found before the time of Christ not only in Egypt, Meroe and Ethiopia, but also throughout North Africa, from Alexandria to Tangiers.

After the Muslim conquest of North Africa, in the seventh and eighth centuries, the Jews were tolerated by the Muslims, for Abraham and Jerusalem hold a significant place in the Qur'an.

It was only in 1967, when Israeli Zionism became confused with Judaism in many Arab countries, that most of the Jewish communities of Tangiers, Tunis and Cairo disappeared. In Morocco, however, where Jews had always had a special place, some Jews still live today.

In the seventh and eighth centuries, the period of the great Arab conquests, not all Jews simply submitted to the Muslims. Some time in the eighth century, the Berbers in Algeria had, in their struggle against the Muslims, a Jewish woman, Kahena, as their military leader. It is also said that in the same period, groups of Jews fled through the Sahara to black Africa. There is even a theory that, at an earlier time, it was Jews who founded the kingdom of Ghana in Mali. Some people even believe that the Fulani (Peul), the pastoral people who now live in eight West African countries in a belt between Senegal and Lake Chad, are of Jewish descent. It is true that the Fulani have something semitic about them, as do the Choa Arabs, the Arabs who have become dark-skinned, and live beside Lake Chad.

Is it among these Jews who fled through the Sahara that we can find an answer to the question of how the Matakam and the Massana in North Cameroun came to have stories and sacrificial practices which are so strongly reminiscent of the Old Testament?

Muslim scholars have yet another theory. The first Arabic historian of the south was called Wahb-ibn-Moenabbeh. He began to write in

738, and he says that the interior of Africa was populated by peoples descended from Kush, the son of Ham and the grandson of Noah. The people of the Sudan, in the area which we now call the Sahel, who descend from Kush are the Qaran (perhaps the Groan, who live to the south of Lake Chad), the Zaghawa (who can still be found in the Wadai and west of Darfour), the Habbesya (Abyssinians from Ethiopia), the Qibt (Copts) and the Barbar (Berbers). Two hundred years later, El-Mas'oedi, the greatest of all medieval geographers, confirmed this migration theory in a book completed in 947. Indeed, as already stated, there are peoples to the south of the Sahara who have had relations with those north of the great desert. Around Lake Chad bronze was worked, using the same techniques as in Kush. The holy ram from Kush also plays a part in a number of west African forms of worship; and there are shapes and objects which prove that there must have been significant communication between Kush, Lake Chad and the whole of West Africa.

2

The People of the Way

A Ghanaian prayer says: 'Lord, I will bring Mary, Joseph and the child to Africa, by ways which neither Herod nor even the colonialists will find.'

This Ghanaian Christian is thinking of the story Matthew tells in the second chapter of his Gospel:

> 'After they [the wise men] had left, an angel of the Lord appeared in a dream to Joseph and said, "Herod will be looking for the child in order to kill him. So get up, take the child and his mother and escape to Egypt, and stay there until I tell you to leave." Joseph got up, took the child and his mother, and left during the night for Egypt, where he stayed until Herod died. This was done to make what the Lord had said through the prophet come true, "I called my Son out of Egypt".'

Today, guides in the church of Saint Sergius in Old Cairo show tourists a half-submerged crypt, and tell them: 'That is where Joseph and Mary lived with the child.' It is significant that Africa, from which so many people have so often fled or been taken away, is mentioned in the Gospel story as the place to which the refugee Jesus of Nazareth fled.

But that is not all. In 1968, the martyrdom of Mark in Egypt was commemorated and before the ceremony, the Coptic Orthodox patriarch sent out an invitation, part of which reads as follows:

> 'Shortly after the ascension of the Lord, Mark came to Egypt. He was of African descent. He was the writer of the oldest Gospel. He founded the oldest church in Africa in Alexandria, the city in which he died as a martyr in the summer of the year 68.'

Is that true? Was Mark of African descent? The man who carried Jesus' cross certainly was, for he was called Simon of Cyrene, and Cyrene was a town in what is now called Libya. Did Mark live and suffer in Egypt? There is no conclusive historical proof. Yet Egyptian Christianity is very old. The oldest fragments of John's Gospel which we possess, dated AD 175, were written on papyrus found in the bellies of stuffed sacred cats in Egypt.

The 'people of the Way', as Christians are called, came early to Africa. In the famous church history of Eusebius (c. 265–339) he records a report that Mark came to Egypt in AD 41. The Coptic Orthodox Church has indeed a list of bishops going back to 41. But the period of office for each bishop in the entire first series is given as twelve years, and that is strange. The first historically certain bishop was Demetrius of Alexandria (189–232).

Or did the Christians come, not from Palestine, but by the well-used shipping routes from Rome to Alexandria?

Was it perhaps that the church in Egypt soon came to be considered heretical in the West, so that its history was ignored?

It is evident that the Christian church on the Nile is very old. Why should the patriarch who sits in the seat of St Mark not be right in saying that Mark died as a martyr in Egypt in AD 68?

In the time of Christ, Egypt was divided into two completely different regions. In the Nile delta, already overpopulated at that time, a farming people tried to live off the fertile mud which the Nile brought down each year. They were called Copts, from the Egyptian *qyytios* via the Greek *aiguptos* and the Latin *coptus*. Osiris, a god who had overcome evil by rising from the dead, played a great part in their lives. Believers could participate in his resurrection by performing the same magic rites by which Osiris himself had overcome evil. Moreover, the other old gods of Egypt were by no means dead. At the end of their human lives, the good and the evil they had done were weighed in a kind of balance, in the course of very elaborate burial ceremonies.

The centre of the other Egypt was Alexandria. Trade and industry were important here, with weaving and dying, and also learning. Alexandria had a famous library, scriptoria for copying books, and schools of philosophy where Neoplatonists and Stoics taught. In this hellenistic Greek Egypt, the Jews played a great part as weavers and handworkers, and as scholars and copyists. They were well known as 'people of the Book'. It was in Alexandria that the Septuagint, the Greek translation of the Old Testament was made. There, too, Philo and others had tried to build philosophical bridges between the Book and hellenistic thought.

Among the Jews and their associates in this centre of hellenistic culture, the gospel of Jesus, the gospel of the Way, made a great impression. As early as the second century AD, Pantaenus founded in Alexandria the first centre of Christian scholarship in the world: the Catechetical School. His successors Clement and Origen made great efforts to combine Christian thought with Greek philosophy, in order to bring the 'foolishness of the gospel' to the hellenistic Greek elite.

Clement was active in Alexandria from 190 to about 215. 'The logos', he wrote, 'the word, leads mankind to communion with God by revealing himself step by step: first by philosophical thought, then in guiding the people of Israel, and finally in personal revelation in Jesus Christ.'

Clement thought that his philosophical system was too difficult for ordinary believers. He therefore distinguishes 'believers', that is, people who passively accept what has been revealed, from 'gnostics', people who 'know', those who in following Christ rise to perfect freedom from fleshly bonds into spiritual communion with God.

Origen lived from 185 to 254. He is the founder of biblical exegesis, the systematic explanation of the Bible. His book *On First Principles* was the first Christian dogmatics. He also built up a system for 'gnostics'. By means of allegorical exegesis, he developed the Christian gospel into a Platonic Greek system. Historical Christianity thus became for him the foundation and symbol of the eternal history of God and the soul. Origen particularly impressed the Greek elite. His thought has had a permanent influence on all eastern churches.

In Alexandria, in the sphere of this meeting of Christianity and philosophy, the so-called Gnostic Gospels were written: the Gospel of the Egyptians and the Gospel of the Hebrews.

Despite the great gulf between the Greek cities and the Egyptian countryside, the 'people of the Way' also took the gospel to the farmers of the Nile delta.

In 202, under the emperor Septimius Severus, a severe persecution of Christians in North Africa made many martyrs in Alexandria and Thebes. Thebes is a region on the Nile, about 750 kilometres from the coast; so there must by then have been Christians there. Clement fled from this persecution to Asia Minor. Bishop Heraclas (231–247) consecrated twenty bishops, while a hundred bishops attended the Synod of Alexandria in 320. In 248–249 and 303–304 there were again great persecutions. The last was so severe that even non-Christians protested.

The 'people of the Book', the Jews, were mistrusted by the Romans because of their exclusive faith in Jahweh, but the 'people of the Way', the Christians, were a danger for the Roman Empire. The Roman state ideology was personified in the emperor and in emperor worship. Christians' refusal to sacrifice to the emperor, because they believed in only one Way, was thus an attack on the fundamental concept on which the Roman Empire was built.

The church historian Eusebius testifies to the courage and faith with which Christians both in Alexandria and in the country went to their deaths. But Osiris and the other old Egyptian gods were tough. In burial ceremonies, Christian convictions and old practices became mixed, and it was not until 535 that the Temple of Isis on the island of Philae, on the Nile, was closed. Then the whole of Egypt had become Christian.

The Alexandrian builders of hellenistic Greek Christian systems gradually lost ground in the face of Egyptian Christian leaders from the countryside.

In the third century, a Coptic literature began to develop: the language is Egyptian written in Greek letters plus six new characters. Nationalism played a part in this development, together with a growing opposition between the elitist faith of the Catechism School and the convictions of the simple country dwellers. Christianity was becoming Egyptian.

In the second half of the third century, a man called Antony went to live in the desert near the Nile. He was the first Christian monk. In ancient Egypt, human beings became gods and lived in magnificent temples; God did not 'become flesh' as a simple carpenter's son. The poor praying monk was the Christian answer to the great temples for deified human beings. In 320 Pachomius founded the first monastery in Tabannisis. Basil of Pachomius drew up rules for living which concentrated on work and Bible study; that is, on striving for deeper spiritual life through complete concentration and separation from worldly things. The success of the monastic movement was so great that in 365, a law on civic responsibilities was passed to prevent too many people from devoting themselves to meditation at the expense of their duties to the community. The monasteries made Egypt in the fourth century a favourite place of pilgrimage. In the monasteries there grew up a Coptic literature including tracts and commentaries, but also fantastic saints' lives and children's Bibles. In 250 Antony heard the gospel read in a church. He knew no Greek, but the translation of the Bible into Egyptian had begun.

At the end of the third or the beginning of the fourth century, the sacred books were translated into Sahidic, the Coptic of Upper Egypt. The Old Testament was translated from the Septuagint. Soon after, there followed the Bohairic of the Nile Delta, and Bashmuric. Later the Bohairic Bible became the official translation of the church of Egypt.

Egyptian individualism also played an important part. In the sixth century, almost every village in Egypt had its own bishop, and there were quarrels everywhere.

Alexandria became the centre of a great theological controversy which spread all over the Christian world. The issue was the dogmatic relationship between God the Father and Christ the Son. The central figures were Arius and Athanasius. The Councils of Nicaea in 325, and Chalcedon in 451, tried to solve the problem. Athanasius won with his doctrine of the two natures: Christ was truly God and truly man. But the Egyptian monks and bishops did not accept this formula. Alexandria lost more ground, and the Egyptian Christians became monophysite, that is, they believed that Christ had only one, divine, nature. The 'people of the Way' went their own Egyptian way: monophysite, nationalistic, individualistic, distancing themselves from Rome, Carthage and Antioch. Basic to this whole development was the use of the language of the people in worship, in the often fantastic literature, but above all in Bible translation.

After 600, Egypt came under the eastern Roman Empire, which had Constantinople as its capital. The emperor made a fresh attempt to impose the teaching of Chalcedon on Egypt, but failed.

Then, in 640, Egypt fell to the Arabs. They were received almost with open arms, because their occupation meant the end of Orthodox pressure from Constantinople. The Muslim Arabs maintained the existing Christian administrative structures, and guaranteed freedom of worship.

A century later, forced conversion to Islam began, reaching its climax in the fourteenth and fifteenth centuries with persecutions of Christians.

Yet Christians still remained the 'people of the Way'. Even today, seven per cent of the population of Egypt belong to the Coptic Orthodox Church. The Copts are still monophysite. They are recognizable by the Coptic cross tattooed on their wrists, and also by their Christian or ancient Egyptian names: Istafanous, Ramses, Osiris. Even today there is the Bible in Bohairic, now the sacred language of the church of the followers of Mark.

3

The Latin Bible from Africa

In the time of Christ, there lay between Egypt and Tangiers, along the north coast of Africa, a number of prosperous Roman provinces. Their population consisted of four groups:

1. The original inhabitants, blond Berber peoples in the country, in the Atlas mountains, and bordering the Sahara.
2. In Carthage, Tunisia and a number of other places on the coast, descendants of the Phoenician, or Punic, seafarers.
3. Roman emigrants, including many retired professional soldiers, living in the towns but owning farms everywhere. They had made North Africa the granary of the Roman Empire.
4. In Cyrene, home of Simon, in Libya, and in many other towns, groups of Jews, people of the Book.

Did Christianity come from Rome to North Africa? Probably. In any case 'people of the Way' lived there from about AD 130. They found their converts among Jews and their associates, and especiallly among Romans. In July 180 the first twelve martyrs in Carthage were killed. They came from Scilli in Numidia, a Roman province covering parts of what are now Algeria and Tunisia. Ten of them had Roman names, and two were Berbers. Around 200, despite the persecutions, there were seventy bishops in North Africa.

While the Christians in Rome were still speaking Greek, the message of the 'people of the Way' was brought to North Africa in Latin, the language of the Romans there. The Roman lawyer Tertullian started in Carthage by writing books and treatises in Latin against the philosophers and other opponents of Christianity. He used concise and direct language, full of legal terms. So in Africa, in Carthage, church Latin was born around 200. In the third century the Bible was translated in North Africa into this language. We still have parts of it in the so-called Vetus Latinum or Old Latin version. Jerome later used this translation as one of his sources in making the Vulgate, the Latin translation which was to remain for centuries the official translation of the Roman Catholic Church.

Alongside Tertullian, the defender of the faith, Cyprian was the organizer of the church in North Africa, and Augustine was its great theologian. The *lingua franca* of the 'people of the Way' was Latin; Augustine, however, bitterly complained that so few of the clergy spoke Punic. Augustine himself had a Roman mother and a Punic father. The Berbers were scarcely touched by Christianity.

In North Africa, too, Christians suffered for their convictions. Cyprian is one of many martyred in 57. The last great persecution of Christians was in 303–304. After the persecutions, the so-called *lapsi* were a great problem. These were the people who during the persecutions had temporarily abandoned Christianity in order to save their lives. Another problem were the *traditores*, people who had given the sacred books to the Roman persecutors. After the persecutions under Diocletian, Emperor Galerius issued an edict of tolerance in 311. Then conflicts broke out when a bishop was accused of having been a *traditor*. Eventually, the church readmitted *traditores* and *lapsi*, but a puritan group, the Donatists, opposed this policy. This caused quarrels which went on for a century in synods in North Africa and Rome. The number of bishops grew to over 500, because each party wanted to increase its strength by more consecrations. The situation became so bad that each party at times persecuted the other. Finally, at a conference in Carthage in 411, the Donatists were condemned. At that conference, 286 Catholic and 279 Donatist bishops were present. The Donatists became divided among themselves. Augustine, who at first had tried to build bridges, played an important role in their condemnation.

Apart from the conflict with the Donatists, another movement came into the African church in the third century. This was Montanism, which had originated in Asia Minor, now Turkey. Montanism was a strict kind of Pentecostal movement, with its own teaching about the millennium and the Lord's imminent return, and rigorous and severe ethics. Montanus, the founder, felt himself to be the bearer of the Spirit, and ascetic women prophets called Priscilla and Maximilla travelled with him. The movement had anti-ecclesiastical features, but later set up its own organization in which Pentecost was the central festival. In Africa, Tertullian came under its influence.

There are various reasons why these two rigorist movements, Montanism and Donatism, appealed to Christians in Africa.

In the controversy with the Donatists, there was an element of tension between ways of thought determined by Rome, and the wish to be regionally African.

When, after their condemnation, the Donatists ran into difficulties in the towns, they contrived to increase their influence in the country, and in places to gain a hearing among the Berbers. How important, in this situation, was a rising anti-Roman group consciousness among the lower Punic and Berber strata of society? In both movements,

Montanism and Donatism, personal commitment and faith played a central part, whereas Rome thought much more in terms of church organization and structure. In the background was even the fear of Roman secularization. African Christians felt called to be holy.

Then, in 429, North Africa fell to the Vandals from Europe. They came originally from Germany, and settled first in France as part of the emigration of the Gothic peoples. In 439 they conquered Carthage and set up a Vandal kingdom in North Africa. This survived for almost a century, when their last king was forced to surrender to Belisarius, the general of the eastern Roman Emperor Justinian. At some point in their wanderings, the Vandals had become Christians, more precisely, followers of Arius, the man from Alexandria who, in the controversy about the nature of Christ, maintained that God the Father was in some way greater than Christ the Son. The Vandals tried to impose their Arianism in North Africa, thus increasing the confusion.

Many Roman colonists fled to Europe. Others went to the oases in Libya and to the Atlas mountains. They also brought the gospel (at last) to the Berbers. Then peace returned, until the first Arab invasion in 647. In 697, the Muslims captured Cairo, and by 710 the occupation of North Africa was complete.

Two more details of the struggle deserve mention. A Berber Christian leader called Koceila was conquered after having resisted the Arabs, and was converted to Islam. In another Arab raid, the Jewish woman Kahena led the Jewish-Christian resistance to the Berbers. Although defeated, she remained a Jew, but advised her two sons to become Muslims.

Little is heard at this time about the Romans and Punics. Many of them probably fled to Europe, and the Arabs considered the Berbers as the most important group to be won over. Under Arab rule, Christians obtained freedom of worship on payment of a tax, but as in Egypt, forced conversion to Islam followed. In 1053 there were only five bishops left in North Africa, and at the same time, there were still churches in use in Tlemcen in Algeria. In the fifteenth century a small group of Christians remained in Tunis. That was the end.

Church Latin and the first Latin Bible translation came out of North Africa. There were 500 bishops in Africa, and hundreds of thousands of 'people of the Way'. Today there remain only a handful of monuments. Why?

Did the division and the conflict between rigorists and compromisers have anything to do with it? Both factors certainly played a part, but I believe the most important cause to be something else. For too long, the church in North Africa was a movement by a socially higher class which had no real communication with the people. For too long, the church remained a movement of Roman town dwellers and farmers, who had occasional contacts with the Punics, but not with the Berber peoples. The Roman élite understood Latin, and so did some of the

Punics, but the Berbers probably did not. The church's use of Latin in effect limited Christianity to Roman emigrants.

Under the Vandals, and later the Arabs, the Romans fled to Europe, and much of the nucleus of the Christian church disappeared. Christianity reached the Berbers too late for a great religious movement to develop among them. And the Berber leaders saw the choice between Christianity and Islam as political.

The Berbers themselves became so deeply Muslim that they formed the core of the army which Islam later brought to the Pyrenees in Europe. They are the people who spread Islam in the Sahara and in countries south of the Sahara.

Did the Romans who fled to the Atlas mountains leave behind them the vestiges of Christianity which still remain: monogamy among the Kabyle, the organization of corporate life among the Mrabit in Algeria, and the Christian cross of the Taureg?

Is this the way by which the gospel also penetrated in the middle ages to the kingdom of Ghana, in the Sahel? Scholars speak of Judeo-Syrian groups who went that way.

We do not know, but it is certain that the 'people of the Way', with their use of Latin in the Bible and worship, remained for too long foreigners in the Berber country of North Africa.

4

The Eunuch and the real Ethiopia

In AD 320, the last descendant of the Candace from the Moor country, mentioned in Acts 8, was buried in a brick pyramid near Meroe in Sudan. The king of real Ethiopia, then called Aksum, pillaged Meroe in 330. The kingdom of Meroe, which succeeded that of Kush, was thus crushed between Egyptian enemies to the north and the increasingly powerful kingdom of Aksum to the south.

The inscriptions recording this pillage speak of brick-built towns, towns of straw houses, and rich booty. The Romans called this area to south of Egypt Nubia. In the sixth century there were four kingdoms: Nobadae between the first and second cataract on the Nile; Blemmyes in the desert to the east; Makorites to the south of Nobadae, and Alwa around Khartoum.

We do not know whether the eunuch took any further the message about the 'people of the Way' which he had heard from Philip. In 542, a man called Julian sent a message through Theodosius, the monophysite patriarch of Alexandria, to the eastern Roman Empress Theodora, asking permission to take the gospel to Nubia. Theodora's husband, the Emperor Justinian, would have preferred an orthodox mission, but Theodora intrigued so skilfully that the monophysite Julian was allowed to travel to the kingdom of Nobadae. In 543 Julian arrived in Nobadae. He complained about the climate and heat, but stayed a few years, and converted the rulers of Nobadae to Christianity. The rulers of the other kingdoms were also interested. Twenty years later, Theodora again deceived her Orthodox husband and sent Longinus to Nubia. He arrived in 568 after an eventful journey. Longinus built a church for the Nubians, ordained priests, and taught them the liturgy and precepts of Christianity. Later, an ambassador from Nobadae reported to the court in Constantinople: 'We were Christians in name, but we did not know what that meant until Longinus came among us.' Around 600, Nubia thus consisted of three Christian kingdoms: Nabatia, Makouria and Alodia.

The Nubians put their language into writing, on the basis of the Greek alphabet, but influenced by Coptic and Meroean. In that script, there grew up a Christian literature and perhaps even a translation of the Bible. It is remarkable that the few specimens of this literature which remain are translations from Greek rather than from Coptic.

During the great salvage operation which took place in our times in connection with the building of the Aswan Dam, fine remains of Nubian Christian culture were found.

Ten years after the occupation of Egypt, the Arabs conquered Dongola, the capital of one of the Nubian kingdoms. A treaty was signed by which Nubians agreed to barter slaves for corn. Nothing was said about religion. Muslim traders began to infiltrate the Nubian kingdoms, but Islam grew very slowly. An Armenian called Abu Sahib travelled there at the beginning of the thirteenth century and wrote that in one of the kingdoms there were 400 churches and many monasteries. In 1275 Dongola was reoccupied and the Nubian prince replaced by an Egyptian. Only in 1316 was the first Muslim king enthroned. At that time the people were still Christian. The last report of Christians was a call for help from oppressed Christian groups which reached Portugal via Ethiopia in the sixteenth century.

All that now remains of 1200 years of Christianity in the kingdom of the dark-skinned eunuch is a few brick-built churches, graves and wall paintings near Faras, and a handful of manuscripts. Nubia stood at the beginning of a long caravan route to Lake Chad. The remains of Christian influence in the kingdoms around Lake Chad, among the Hausa in northern Nigeria, and even in medieval Ghana in Mali, may also have come from Nubia. That the Nubians held out so long against Islam is certainly due to the fact that in their spoken and written Christian witness, they used the language of the people. The final defeat of Christianity had also strategic causes: in the flat areas around the Nile, the Nubians were much more vulnerable than the Ethiopians on their mountains and high plateaux. But that is another story.

The real Ethiopia was much further south than Nubia.

In the third century there were two kingdoms on the Red Sea: Arabia on one side, and Aksum, now Ethiopia, on the other. They maintained good relations with one another. Jewish emigrants lived in both countries. Greek was spoken at the court.

There are three stories about the introduction of Christianity into Aksum.

1. Two children, Frumentius and Aedesius, travelling with their uncle, were shipwrecked in the Red Sea and arrived at the court of the king of Aksum. They were given positions of trust by the king and allowed to practise their Christian faith. Around 350, they returned to Egypt and there Frumentius asked Patriarch Athanasius of Alexandria to send priests to Aksum. Athanasius responded by consecrating Frumentius as bishop and sending him back to Aksum. Frumentius, known as Abba Salomo in Aksum,

The picture of the apostle Peter stands behind that of Petros, bishop of Faras in Nubia from 974 to 999.

brought the gospel to the country. The king of Aksum, Ezana, was converted to Christianity after the conquest of Meroe.
2. The king of Aksum was at war with the Hamitic kingdom in southern Arabia. He promised that he would become a Christian

if he was victorious. After his victory, he asked the Byzantine Prester John to bring Christianity to his country. John became around 350 the first *aboena* or patriarch of Aksum.

3. According to the tradition of the Orthodox Church of Ethiopia, nine saints brought the gospel at the end of the fifth century. Each of them is said to have built a monastery. They were called Alef (Behza Monastery), Sehma (Sedenya Monastery), Za-Mikohel Aragawi (Dabra Damo Monastery), Afsa (Jaha Monastery), Garima (Madera Monastery), Pantalewon (Aksum Monastery), Liganos (Dabra Qanasel Monastery), Gubu (Madera Monastery) and Yemata (Garalta Monastery). Some of these names are of Syrian origin.

Between the fourth and the sixth century, the Bible was translated into Ge'ez, the language of the people, although the court spoke Greek. The translation gives the impression of having been made from Syriac. Aksum became a monophysite Christian country; the *aboena* or head of the church recognized for centuries the authority of the patriarch of Alexandria.

When the Muslims occupied Egypt, Ethiopia was isolated from European Christianity. The monks and priests built up on the roof of Africa a church with its own distinctive features: the Bible in Ge'ez and Jewish influence from the pre-Christian period. Theologically they believed in the one, divine nature of Christ; they had many local rites; and they owned churches and monasteries. The king held a special place in the church. One of his titles was the Lion of Judah, a title which continued to be used until the last emperor, Haile Selassie. It is said that only in the Church of Ethiopia are the Psalms still sung and recited as they used to be in ancient Israel. In the twelfth century were built the strangest buildings in Ethiopian church history. King Lalibala had twenty chapels hewn out of the rock near Laska; their roofs are at ground level. The general and church history of Ethiopia from 650 to 1270 is unclear. There were certainly confrontations with the Muslims from the north. The Muslims also sent missions to the south. The whole Christian kingdom of Aksum moved over a period towards the south to the inaccessible plateaux – the roof of Africa – which still form the heart of Ethiopia. In 1270 Yekuno-Amlak took power. He claimed direct descent from Solomon and the Queen of Sheba. Amlak fought the Muslims successfully and under his reign literature in Ge'ez began to flourish. Translations were made from Coptic and Arabic, but original works were also written, including extensive historical accounts. This blooming of national literature continued until the eighteenth century.

Around 1300 Amharic became the language of the people and in the fourteenth century there began two hundred years of Arab attacks. When the Arabs obtained fire-arms, the situation became critical.

King Leban-Dengel sent various delegations to Portugal asking for help. The story of the Christian kingdom of King John, surrounded by Muslim countries in the middle of Africa, became known all over Europe. At the last moment, the Portuguese came to help 'King John's kingdom'. One year after Leban-Dengel's death in 1541, Christopher da Gama arrived in Ethiopia at the head of 400 armed Portuguese. In 1542 he conquered the Muslims.

Christian Ethiopia survives with a significant Muslim minority, and a unique form of Orthodoxy with great pilgrimages for the many saints, and a thirteen-month calendar: twelve months with 30 days, and one with five or six days. It is remarkable that the Ethiopians did not take the gospel further to the south. Did they perhaps have their hands full with repelling Muslim attacks from the North? Or did they consider the 'slaves' from the south unworthy of the gospel?

It remains a fact that the Ethiopians of today, whether rich or poor, developed or illiterate, feel themselves superior to Africans from the south, Europeans from the north or Muslim Hamites. They are proud of their Nilotic descent, but still more of being (as they claim) members of the oldest church in the world, with a liturgy and a Bible in their own language.

5

Two Responses to the Arab Invasion

The Pax Romana, the peace and order of the Roman Empire, greatly favoured the spread of Christianity. In a few centuries its frontiers stretched from Britannia to the Sahara and from Spain to Persia. During and after the fall of the Roman Imperium, the 'people of the Way' went further, to the Germanii in central Europe, to India and to the Nubians and Ethiopians in Africa.

In the seventh century Islam came to the Holy Land, Egypt and North Africa. The Muslims cut off the remains of Christianity in Africa from Christian Europe. By around 1200, all that people in Europe knew was the strange story that behind the 'Moorish' lands, somewhere in Africa, there was said to be a Christian kingdom, with a king called John.

A few centuries before Christ there was intensive traffic between North and West Africa, and between Egypt, Nubia and Lake Chad via the Sahara. The Sahara was much greener then, it had much more water and it could be crossed by horses. About the beginning of the Christian era, the Sahara began to dry out and this influenced human communication. The horse had to be replaced by the camel. Green areas became rarer and this process has continued to the present day. Towns which, in the early middle ages, were still surrounded by trees are now in the desert. The many roads through the Sahara were limited to two on the east, between Egypt and Lake Chad, and three on the west.

Between the rain forests of West and Central Africa on the one hand and the Sahara on the other, there flourished from 300 to 1500 kingdoms such as Ghana, Mali, Songhai, Kanem and Bornu. They provided in the 'caravan ports' of Ghana and Tombouctou, gold-dust, cola nuts, peppers and slaves, destined for North Africa on the other side of the Sahara. In the same 'ports' could be bought copper and materials, horses, weapons, and cowries for use as money. The traders were North Africans, and from the seventh century more and more Arabs. The inhabitants of the Sahara themselves worked as guides, tax collectors, suppliers, and even brigands. The Sahara was not a barrier but a means of communication. The participation of Europeans in this trade, as buyers and sellers, was intensive; only not in Africa itself, but in the sea-ports of North Africa.

The Arab and North African traders brought Islam in the ninth century to the kingdoms of West Africa and in the eleventh century round Lake Chad.

In 1033, two Berbers from Mauretania made a pilgrimage to Mecca. Their names were Yayia-ben-Ibrahim and Abdallah-ibn-Yacine. On their return, they founded on the coast a monastery organized on military lines. This was the birthplace of a religio-military movement which, a generation later, resulted in the founding of the Muslim Berber kingdom of the Almoravides, which stretched from Senegal to Spain. Their 'Holy War' aimed at the spread of Islam; in time, it made 'Moorish' Spain the most highly developed country in Europe. Cordoba, the city with the greatest Moorish mosque in Europe, had in the tenth century a million inhabitants. Moorish expansion was based on faithfulness to Allah and on the refusal to be subject to caliphs in Damascus, Baghad or Cairo. The Moors were finally halted near Poitiers in France and only long afterwards they were driven out of Spain and Portugal. In Africa, the end result was that a limited number of peoples went over to Islam, while in the kingdoms of Mali, Goa, Kanem and Bornu only the elite upper class were Islamized. Around Lake Chad, the peoples of Baguirmi, Quadai and Darfour-Kardofan, that is the 'port area' of the eastern caravan routes, became Muslim.

Islam brought a new, non-commercial motive for communication across the Sahara. Africans went on pilgrimage to Mecca and learned Muslims came to Ghana, Mali, etc., in order to study African cultures but above all as teachers. After 1300 Tombouctou grew into one of the most important centres of scholarship and study in the entire Muslim world.

The *lingua franca* for trade and learning around the Sahara was Arabic. This whole development really began with the Berbers: a few centuries after they had belatedly come into contact with Christianity, they were bringing Islam to West Africa.

Diaspora Jews, who lived all over North Africa, also made their contribution. The most celebrated of them was the theologian and philosopher Maimonides, who was born in 1135 in Cordoba, in Spain, and died in 1204 in Cairo. His theological and philosophical work built a bridge between Islam and Jewish thought, Christian Platonic philosophy, and especially Aristotle. His writings, translated into Latin, had a great influence on such Christian theologians as Thomas Aquinas.

Through the spread of Islam, the number of Arabic speakers steadily increased so that Christians living under Arab rule felt the need of Arabic translations of the Bible. This led to the remarkable phenomenon that, at the height of the period of the caliphate between the ninth and the thirteenth centuries, a whole series of Arabic translations were made of both New and Old Testaments. Nestorians and Melchites from Syria and Palestine played a great part in this work, as did the Sinai Monastery and at a later stage the Copts in Egypt.

From manuscripts, many kept in the Vatican Library, the following Arabic translations may be identified:

- Vatican Arabic no. 13; the oldest extant translation of the Gospels, probably from Greek, from the ninth century.
- Isaac, the son of Velasquez of Cordoba, translated the Gospels in 949 for Christians in Spain and Marocco, probably from the Latin Vulgate. This translation was also known to Muslims, since Ibn Hazm of Cordoba (994–1064) quotes it in his anti-Christian polemic.
- Sinai Arabic no. 151; the oldest extant translation of the New Testament epistles.
- Vatican Arabic no. 95, with the Gospels probably translated from Old Syriac.
- The Gospels translated with an allegorical commentary by Ibn-al-Tayyib (died 1045), a monk, medical doctor and theologian, who counted the Caliph of Baghdad among his patients.
- The so-called Coptic Vulgate (Vatican Coptic No. 9); a manuscript in Coptic and Arabic, with an introduction dated 1205 which among other things states that the manuscript was copied by the monks of the Monastery of St Antony in the desert between Bibi-Sweyf and the Red Sea. Many copies of this manuscript must have been made. This translation seems to have been for centuries the only Arabic version used in Egypt.
- Finally one must mention the Coptic biblical scholar Hibat Allah Ibn al-Assal (1252). This man collected in the thirteenth century twelve manuscripts of various Arabic translations of the New Testament from Greek Orthodox, Syrian Orthodox and Coptic Orthodox churches. He worked out a system of symbols and references, presenting a unified text with notes giving variations in the other manuscripts. This work, of which a number of copies were made, is one of the greatest scholarly works on the Bible text from the middle ages.

The oldest parts of the Old Testament in Arabic date from the eight century. The Psalms were the first to be translated. Famous, and long used in the Coptic church, is the translation of the Psalms by the Melchite deacon Abdu'l-Fath Abdallah ibn Al-Fadl. The Copts were given the Pentateuch in an Arabic translation made by a great medieval Jewish scholar, Said ibn Yusuf al-Fayiumi, known as Gaon

Saadia. The rest was translated, mostly from the Syriac and the Septuagint, between 892 and 942. But there is no complete manuscript of the whole Bible in Arabic.

When in 1615 the publisher Erpinus printed in Leiden in Holland a complete Arabic New Testament, he used various manuscripts, and after De Propaganda Fide in Rome decided in 1622 to publish a complete Bible, many years' study were needed to compile a single Bible from parts found in various manuscripts. (See also chapters 14, 22, 26 and 38).

So while, in the area dominated by Arab Muslims, Christians were trying to make Arabic translations of the Bible, Christian contact between Europe and Africa remained from 800 to 1400 fragmentary. It goes without saying that the Crusades did not improve Muslims' image of Christians or vice versa. In the eleventh century, the rulers of North Africa agreed to the request of a few Christian enclaves in Draa and Bugia in Mauretania to have a priest go to Rome to be consecrated bishop. Some time later, another pope sent priests to give pastoral care to Christian mercenaries in the armies of some North African rulers. In Morocco, it was possible to do something now and then for a few communities of Christian refugees from Spain. This service to foreigners in a Muslim world was all. Preaching the gospel to the North Africans themselves was forbidden.

The new monastic orders of Dominicans and Franciscans wanted to bring the gospel to Muslims also. Francis of Assisi himself visited Egypt during the Fourth Crusade, and was authorized to preach before the Sultan. That was in 1219. In the same year, Franciscan missionaries in Tunis began to attack Islam so fiercely that the only way the Christian traders there could rescue them was to put them on the first boat to Europe. From 1222 onwards, Dominicans arrived, and seem to have had more success, since they were more diplomatic and less aggressive than the Franciscans. They worked among Christian soldiers and Christian slaves, and tried cautiously to speak to a Muslim now and then. Their interest in study made them the first to realize that missionary work in the non-Christian world required special training. This included learning the language and finding the right method of presenting the gospel to non-Christians. In the thirteenth century, Raymond of Penafort founded a language school in Tunis. As for the method, Thomas Aquinas developed a kind of missiology entitled *Summa Catholicae Fidei contra Gentiles*, the first Christian theological approach to Islam. In the second half of the thirteenth century, a time when the attitude of Muslims in North Africa was very hostile because of the Crusades, the Spanish scholar Raymond Lull spent his whole working life trying to reach them with the gospel. He studied Christianity and Islam, and in 1290 translated his book *The Art of Finding Truth* into Arabic, in which, in order not to meet the Muslims head-on, arguments about the Trinity were omitted. In 1292 he travelled to Tunis. After discussion with the Muslims he was arrested, condemned and deported. In 1307, 75 years old, he landed in Bugia where he met resistance to his claim that the law of the Christians was holy and the sect of the Moors false and corrupt. Thanks to the support of traders he was allowed to remain for six months and in 1314 he made his last journey to Tunis and Bugia. He seems to have had success in Tunis, but in Bugia he was stoned.

Efforts to reintroduce Christianity into North Africa proved vain.

The traders of Venice and Genoa who did business in the ports of North Africa with caravans from the Sahara came to the conclusion that the Arab and North African caravan traders were earning too much. They wanted to reach West Africa themselves, but failed to do so by land, because the lines of communication were too firmly in African hands. So they founded geographical societies in order to look for other solutions. These societies surrounded their search for information with as much secrecy as space research in our own times. Portugal also took a share. The idea arose of trying to go by sea 'behind' the Moors with the aims of trading, exploring and spreading Christianity. The story of this mysterious Christian kingdom of Prester John played as large a part in all this as rumours about the kingdoms of 'the Indies'. In this period of transition from the middle ages to the Renaissance all these motives were inseparable. A Portuguese prince, Henry the Navigator, became the great stimulator. This brother of the king was a specialist in geography who saw voyages of exploration as a Christian calling.

It began with the discovery of the Canary Islands and the Cape Verde Islands. In 1482 Portuguese ships reached the River Congo and in 1487 Bartholomew Diaz became the first European to land on the Cape of Good Hope, the most southerly point in Africa. The attempt to get 'behind' the Moors was beginning to succeed.

Meanwhile, Spaniards arrived in the Americas. The pope, as world ruler, divided the newly discovered territories between the Portuguese and the Spaniards so that by far the largest part of Africa fell to the Portuguese. As spiritual ruler, the pope challenged the Portuguese to Christianize the new territories, giving them the task of 'destroying the Moors and the enemies of Christ and proclaiming the Christian faith'.

In 1482 the fort of Elmina on the Gold Coast was built with bricks brought from Portugal. Today the Gold Coast has taken the name of the old Mali kingdom Ghana. This first European settlement in West Africa began with a Christian celebration. The Portuguese flag was tied to a tree, a mass was celebrated, and prayer was offered for the conversion of the 'natives'.

In 1497 Vasco da Gama sailed round the Cape to reach Mozambique and the Arab towns of Mombasa and Malindi in what is now Kenya. From there he made the crossing to India, becoming the first European to do so.

The limited geographical knowledge of those days and the state of shipbuilding and navigation made this an almost unbelievable undertaking. The Africans found the ships very large, but they would seem very small to us. For Africa all this meant the beginning of a period of blood, sweat and tears lasting at least until 1850. In 1490 neither Africans nor Portuguese could foresee this. For Christianity it was an ambivalent period as we shall see for example in Zaïre and Angola, in Mozambique and in Fort Elmina in Ghana, and also in the kingdom of Prester John, Ethiopia.

6

'The City of the Saviour'

It began simply. In the spirit of the commission given by the pope, Franciscan friars settled in 1402 in the Canary and Cape Verde Islands. In 1514 a bishopric was founded there.

On the coast of Africa the Portuguese tried to make contact with the African rulers and vice versa. For both parties the reasons for this were political and commercial. Before any agreement could be concluded, the Portuguese required the rulers to be converted to Christianity and monogamy. Some of them in Sene-gambia, Sierra Leone and even Benin in Nigeria allowed themselves to be baptized. They were impressed by Portuguese might, looked for allies and wanted to establish trading relations. They did not think it ridiculous that the white foreigners should link this with a religion, for religion and life were also bound together for them and the Muslims had followed the same practice. The religious consequences of this kind of agreement, however, were little in evidence once the Portuguese delegation had left.

In 1848 the Portuguese Diego Cao visited the Kikongo kingdom, which stretched from the River Congo over parts of what is now Congo, Zaïre and Angola. At first he did not go as far as the capital, Mbanza-Kongo, but found a chief in a coastal town who was sincerely interested in the culture of the Portuguese and especially in their religion.

Diego Cao took a few Kikongo with him to Lisbon so that they could learn more about the Portuguese and Christianity. When he brought these Kikongo back to their homes in 1485, he was received by the Mani-Kongo, the king. The reports of the returning Kikongo and the personal impression made by Diego Cao led the Mani-Kongo to ask for priests to be sent to the Kikongo kingdom. Diego Cao must have been a remarkable man, because respectful stories about him were still told on the River Congo in the nineteenth century.

The first missionaries came in 1491. The king, Mani-Kongo Mbemba Nazinga Nkuwu, the queen, and the crown prince were baptized. They took Christian names from members of the Portuguese

royal family: Joaõ, Eleonora and Affonso. Mbanza-Kongo, the capital, was baptized as Saõ Salvador, 'the city of the Saviour'. A large
church was built there, but polygamy and the gods of the ancestors
remained strong, even at the court. After the death of King Joaõ,
there were difficulties about the succession, and intrigues in which the
Portuguese took an active part. Finally Nzinga Mbemba became king,
taking the name of Affonso I. He reigned until 1547, and proved to be
a good Christian and a good European king. In 1512 the king of
Portugal sent Captain Sima de Silva with five ships to the 'City of the
Redeemer' to build a house several stories high for the king, 'so that
he may keep his court in a Christian manner'.

Many people took Portuguese names; an (unsuccessful) attempt was
made to set up a kind of European administration and some Kikongo
were sent to Portugal for their education.

It is remarkable that in this period there was a kind of relationship of
equals between Portugal and the Kikongo kingdom. Things changed
when Portuguese farmers started plantations on the island of Sa Tomé,
opposite the Guinea coast, and asked for slaves to work there. King
Affonso wrote in 1526 to the king of Portugal:

> 'Sire, in our kingdom there is a great problem which in no way serves God.
> Many of our people are greedy for the things from your kingdom, which
> your people bring here. In order to satisfy their greed, they capture many
> of our people, whether born free or freed, and often kidnap even nobles
> and sons of nobles, and take them away to sell them to the whites who are
> in our kingdom. And as soon as the whites have them in their hands, they
> brand them with iron and fire. That is why we appeal to Your Highness to
> help and support us in this matter, by ordering your traders not to send any
> buyers or goods here, for it is our will that in these kingdoms there should
> be no trade in slaves at all.'

One of Affonso's sons travelled to Lisbon to be ordained priest. In
1518, this man, Henriques, was consecrated by the pope as titular
bishop of Utica and apostolic vicar of the Congo. We do not know
whether he ever worked in the Kikongo kingdom. Affonso II (1547–
1614) followed the Portuguese Christian way. One of his marquises
travelled as a special ambassador to Rome. The facts are not entirely
clear, but Christianity does not seem to have been more than a kind of
varnish under which the old Kikongo traditions continued to flourish.
In the middle of the sixteenth century the Jesuits came. They baptized
five thousand people in three months. A generation later, a Jesuit
baptized another 1500 people at the king's request. He visited a
number of Christian villages. The Franciscans and the Capuchins also
sent missionaries to the Congo. The largest single contingent comprised 45 men.

In 1560, Jesuits accompanied an expedition to the kingdom of
Angola, which was subordinate to Congo. The Ngola or king of

Mbundu was baptized in 1574, and twenty years later, the Portuguese settled in his kingdom, because there were silver mines. On the coast, they founded the town of Luanda. The centre of Portuguese and Catholic influence moved to Angola. Churches and even monasteries were built.

It is estimated that between 1645 and 1700, 600,000 people were baptized in the Congo and Angola, and for some time afterwards, about 12,000 a year. Religious instruction was minimal. In 1650 the missionaries asked Rome whether stupid and backward people could be baptized without instruction. Rome answered that this might be done *in fide ecclesiae*, that is, with the Church's faith as a guarantee. Latin was used in the mass. Fr. Carodozo made in 1624 the first catechism in a Congolese language and a prayer book in Kimbundu, a language spoken in Angola. A few more booklets were printed, but there was no teaching, no regular instruction in the language of the people and no Bible translation. Rulers were the first to be baptized. The people indeed followed them, but without even learning what baptism really meant. The missionaries were all men, so that no real contact with the women was established.

For the rest, the most interesting export product was not ivory or even silver, but slaves. They could scarcely be captured while maintaining relations of Christian equality. The monastery of Luanda came to own 12,000 slaves and when, in order to supply the new plantations on the other side of the Atlantic, the great slave trade between Angola and Brazil began, a stone seat was set up on the quayside at Luanda for the bishop to sit on while he gave his blessing to the departing slaves. Between 1536 and 1836, an average of 5000 slaves a year passed through Luanda harbour.

Now and then, the Dutch fought the Portuguese for the best markets. The Dutch were Calvinists so that a bishop in Angola complained to the pope in 1619 about the heretical books which the Dutch traders from Fort Padro-de-Pinda were distributing among the heathen. In 1640 the Dutch, under the leadership of Maurits van Nassau, conquered a large part of north-east Brazil. In order to gain control of the supply of slaves, they drove the Portuguese in 1640–48 from the coast of Angola. In this they collaborated with Anne Zingha, the queen of the inland Mbundu.

This woman, who lived from 1582 to 1661, spent her whole life opposing the Portuguese on the coast. For her religion was strictly a political means to this end. As a girl she followed the religious instruction of the Catholic fathers and when in 1657 she concluded a relatively honourable peace treaty with the Portuguese, she became a Catholic at the end of her life.

The story of Donna Beatrice in the Congo is quite different. The Kingdom of the Kikongo had to struggle not only with the constantly increasing Portuguese demands for slaves, but also with problems of succession and internal divisions. In 1678 Saõ Salvador was destroyed and in 1694 Pedro IV became king. All parties appear to have recognized him, but he did not dare to establish himself in the city of Saõ Salvador to rebuild it and be a real king again. Then a movement began under the leadership of a Congolese girl called Kimpa Vita, who was baptized as Donna Beatrice. She aimed to re-establish the king's power in the name of Mary and Saint Antony. She called on the people to purify itself by burning all fetishes and all Christian crosses. Was that because even Christian crosses had become fetishes? Donna Beatrice proclaimed a black Christ, born in Saõ Salvador, with black disciples. In other words, Donna Beatrice wanted a Christ identified, not with the powerful Portuguese, but with the ill-treated Africans. She came to see in the restoration of the Kikongo kingdom a kind of return to a paradise of wellbeing. This African Joan of Arc was put to death in 1706 at the insistence of the Portuguese priests. For Donna Beatrice with her Antonians, the Christian faith was an African way of solidarity which would give back to the Kikongo their own identity as a purified and therefore prosperous nation.

The Portuguese remained on the Angolan coast, but when in 1854 David Livingstone came to Luanda in the course of his journey across Africa one of the cathedrals had been turned into a carpenter's workshop and the other into a cowshed.

In Massangano he found the ruins of two churches and a hospital. The crucifixes and pictures of saints survived as chiefs' and sorcerers' fetishes. Funeral ceremonies still had a vaguely Christian colouring.

The first Christianity in the Congo disappeared because the Word was not effectively communicated and because there was no follow-up to the mass baptisms. It also failed because of the Portuguese traders' unchristian way of life and because of the slave trade. European Christians had done the very opposite of feeding the hungry and setting the prisoners free, as the gospel says. The 'City of the Redeemer' is now an overgrown ruin.

7

Te deum laudamus

The people who lived on the east coast of Africa had known for a long time foreigners who came to trade in ivory, slaves and gold. They were Persians and people from India, even Chinese, and especially Arabs. The Arabs were originally shepherds from the Saudi Arabian desert, but the Persians had taught them how to sail along the coast in their *dhows*, wooden ships with one mast and one sail. Since 650, Arabs and Persians had settled on the coasts of Africa, or rather on small islands off the coast, which they had obtained from the African chiefs in exchange for materials and other goods.

The Arabs and the Persians were Muslims and spoke Arabic. They often married African women; sometimes Africans went to live and work in their city states. It is here that Swahili, the great trade language of East Africa, was created from a mixture of African structures and Arabic elements.

Now and then, there was rivalry between the sultans of the various city states. The one who governed Sofala (in what is now Mozambique) was important, because this was the port which handled the gold trade from Mashonaland. Naturally, a mosque was built in each sultanate, but the Arabs and Persians came mainly for trade and not as missionaries.

In Europe meat was salted in summer so that it would last through the winter. Rich people wanted spices to make that meat more tasty. The Portuguese travelled by sea to India to find these spices. They knew about them from traders who brought them overland from India. But the land route had been cut off by the Ottoman kingdom of the Turks, so now they tried the sea route. In 1487 Bartholomew Diaz reached the Cape of Good Hope, but did not dare to go any further because of the strong wind. Ten years later, in 1498, the Swahili in Mozambique saw foreign ships coming with wonderful sails and unknown people. They were Christians from Portugal and their leader was called Vasco da Gama.

The inhabitants of the Mozambique coast knew that the caliphs had fought for a long time against the Christians, so they drove the

Portuguese off. But Vasco da Gama needed fresh water and green vegetables and also a guide to show him the way to India. He was amazed to see the stone houses of Kilwa and Mombasa. He discovered that the sultan of Malindi was on bad terms with the other rulers. He struck up a friendship with Malindi, thus obtaining the help he needed to make the crossing.

India seemed to be a very rich place for trading. But the sultans on the east coast of Africa were not inclined to co-operate with Portuguese trade by supplying water and vegetables. They wanted to keep their monopoly of trade and as Muslims they would have nothing to do with Christians. The Portuguese therefore decided to conquer the coastal towns. They had the military capacity to do this, because they had better cannons. The Portuguese also still remembered and resented the occupation of their own country by the Muslim Moors. Between 1502 and 1507, they took possession of the towns. In some, such as Fort Jesus in Mombasa, Portuguese castles were built. All sultans, with the exception of the sultan of Malindi, were forced to pay tribute. Thus in 1505 the Portuguese took possession of the town of Kilwa. A cross was erected there. Franciscans sang the 'Te Deum' and then Kilwa was declared open for plundering.

When in 1509 the Portuguese won a sea battle against the Arabs, they became for a hundred years the masters of the sea off the east coast of Africa. The conquered sultans were forced to believe in the God of the Portuguese and to become Christians. They readily agreed to do this, but without conviction. The importance of East Africa for the Portuguese was not primarily in trade, but in supplying water and food to ships on their way to India. Administratively and also ecclesiastically, East Africa came under Goa, the Portuguese centre on the coast of India. And naturally in the wake of the Portuguese there came also missionaries: first Franciscans and later Jesuits.

When the Portuguese heard of enormous deposits of gold in Mashonaland, they became interested. Since, in those days, church and state were solidly linked to the glory of God, the Portuguese first sent priests to the interior to test the temperature in what was called Zimbabwe, the kingdom of the Monomopata. Father Concalo Da Silveira was warmly received by the young king Nogoma Mapunzagatu, who gave him presents. He showed the king a picture of Mary and the king was so impressed by this that he allowed himself to be baptized.

The Arabs were furious: now the Portuguese were going to interfere in African trade as well! They told the king that Da Silveira used dangerous magic. The missionary was strangled in his sleep, thus becoming the first martyr in southern Africa. In 1577 the Dominicans made a second attempt at missionary work. They began with Mozambique, in Sofala, Sena and Tete. Father Dos Santos baptized 1700 people there. Around 1626, the Portuguese helped a Monomopata influenced by Christianity to gain the throne. He was baptized with the name of Philippe. His successor was not a Christian, but accepted baptism in 1652. When this news reached Europe, services of thanksgiving were held in churches in Lisbon and Rome.

By the end of the seventeenth century the influence of the Portuguese on the Monomopata had greatly diminished. This also implied the end of missionary work. Had the mission become too much involved in political and commercial aims? There is a story about one Brother Manuel Sardinha, who managed to raise an army of 20,000 men for the war with the Monomopata. Under this kind of pressure Portugal's political power collapsed and Christianity declined with it. The fathers confined their efforts henceforth to the Portuguese in the forts with a Dominican monastery in Mozambique as their base.

8

The Minister of Elmina

In March 1593 the trader-captain Bernhard Erecksoon returned to the Netherlands. Three years before he had sailed for Brazil, but his ship had been driven off its course and he had landed on the West African coast, where the Portuguese were in control. Erecksoon and his crew were the first Dutchmen to land on the Guinea coast. The crew perished in the Portuguese prisons on the island of Saõ Tomé, but Erecksoon managed to escape. He reported that there was gold in West Africa, and that it could be bartered for such trifles as mirrors, beads and cloth. Since the Dutch were still waging an expensive war of independence against Spain, this gold aroused great interest. Erecksoon himself managed to open the coast for Dutch trade, and fifteen years later about twenty Dutch ships a year were visiting the west coast of Africa.

In 1612, the Dutch built their first fortress, Fort Nassau, three and a half hours' walk from the large Portuguese fort at Elmina on the Gold Coast.

In 1621 the Dutch West Indies Company was founded. This was a pseudo-private enterprise which had a trade monopoly on the tropical coasts of West Africa and America and a twofold military task: to undermine Portuguese and Spanish sovereignty in the area assigned to them and to obtain as much gold as possible to support the costs of the war in the Netherlands. An important factor in this was that from 1590 to 1640 Spain and Portugal had the same king so that Portugal automatically became as much an enemy as Spain to the Netherlands freedom fighters.

In the West Indies and Brazil, the Dutch drove the Portuguese out of many of their settlements. Dutch plantations were set up and these needed labour. Africans seemed suitable for this work. So there began for the Dutch a very lucrative three-cornered trade which went on for a long time. Ships came from the Netherlands with products for West Africa, which were used there to buy slaves. The slaves were transported to the Americas and then the products of the American plantations were brought to the Netherlands.

The small African kingdoms on the Gold Coast were affected by this slave trade. They held a balance of power among themselves, but because the Dutch provided various rulers with modern weapons, muskets and other fire-arms, in exchange for prisoners of war who were transported as slaves, the old African balance of power was disturbed.

The Dutch won a foothold on the Gold Coast, not by building more fortresses themselves, but usually by driving out the Portuguese. In 1625 Piet Heyn failed to occupy Elmina, the most important Portuguese fort, but in 1637 Maurits van Nassau, the first and only Dutch governor of Brazil, succeeded in capturing Elmina by land after a siege lasting four days. In 1640 the Dutch took St Anthony near Axim and when in 1643 the Portuguese were also driven out of St Sebastian, the Dutch became masters of the coast. This situation did not last long, because the British soon began to penetrate, and the Swedes, the Danes and the Brandenburgers followed.

The history of the forts was one of war and treachery; some of them changed hands several times. After 1660, the Dutch lost their dominant position, but in 1665, Admiral Michiel de Ruyter with a fleet of warships tried to kill or expel all the enemies of the Dutch. A map of 1760 shows on this part of the coast eleven Dutch forts, thirteen British, one Danish and one Brandenburgish (i.e. German). The Dutch remained at Fort Elmina until 1872.

Elmina is now a museum. It is the oldest brick building on the west coast of Africa. It was build by 600 Portuguese of prefabricated materials, that is, of doors and window-frames sawn in Portugal and bricks baked in Portugal. The Dutch enlarged and rebuilt it several times. It is now 80 metres long, 40 metres wide, and has cool passages through its thick walls. There are Dutch drawbridges and a cemetery with the tombs of a number of Dutchmen, most of whom died young. Reasons for this included their use of warm 17th and 18th century European clothing and their doctors' ignorance of tropical diseases.

On the battlements stand cannons of 'Maurits the Brazilian', and in the harbour there is a memorial to the conquest of Java by the Dutch. Inside, there are graceful Dutch step gables. Below are the cages for slaves, and a large room in which the slaves were 'stored'; the merchants could examine them from above through spy-holes. One can still see the big tunnel leading from the bottom of the fort to the sea, along which the human herds were taken to the ships. It is estimated that in more than two hundred years between two and three million slaves went through that tunnel. Half of them reached the Americas alive.

The Dutch remained good Calvinists in Fort Elmina. The rooms were decorated with texts from the Heidelberg Catechism and pious verses by a minister from Vere, in Zealand. Captain Willem Bosman wrote in his *New and Accurate Description of the Coast of Guinea*:

'We are very religious; anyone who fails to attend the daily church services must pay a fine of 25 pence. I suppose you will object that this is forcing people to worship God and that people will not always go to church with the right intention. It must be admitted that the situation is not so good: if this rule did not exist, some people would go to other places than church.'

In Elmina the Ghanaian guide tells visitors that many Dutch bachelors in the fort would choose on Saturday evenings a pretty girl from the slave cage. If the girl became pregnant, both mother and baby were set free, and the mother could choose a Dutch name for her child. After all, the father was a Christian! That is why, still today, one can meet on the coast of Ghana and in Accra Ghanaians with Dutch names like Van Luyn, Van der Pui or Van der Lek.

In the eighteenth century, Aarnout Steenhart, the captain of a merchant ship, bought an African boy on the Gold Coast. The captain gave the boy to Jacobus van Goch, a Dutch merchant, who named him Capitein after his first owner; this name was later extended to Jacobus Elisa Johannes Capitein. When the boy was eleven, his master took him back to the Netherlands. In 1737, when he was about twenty, he was admitted to the University of Leiden, where after five years' study he made an oration in Latin defending the thesis that slavery did not conflict with Christian truth. The oration went into four printings.

Jacobus Capitein was ordained a minister of the Netherlands Reformed Church, thus becoming the first African Protestant Minister.

The Amsterdam church council appointed him chaplain of Fort Elmina. Once there, he did not want only to serve the Dutch, but he also translated the 'Twelve Articles of Faith' into Fanti, one of the languages of the Gold Coast. This was printed in 1744.

He wanted to marry an African woman, but the Amsterdam church council did not sanction this, because the woman was not baptized. Then he married a Dutch woman and became unhappy. In Elmina, the African minister Jacobus Capitein was not really accepted by the Europeans and he was completely rejected by the Africans. The first African minister died at about thirty years old — perhaps of loneliness?

9

The Christian kingdom of Prester John

In the fourteenth century it was discovered in Europe that the Christian kingdom of Prester John, behind the Muslim countries of Africa, was Ethiopia. In 1487, the Portuguese King Joaõ II sent Pedro de Covilham there by land. He reached Ethiopia but was not allowed to return. In 1520, an ambassador sent from India to Ethiopia met de Covilham. Francisco Alvarez, accompanying the ambassador as his confessor, wrote an account of his impressions of Ethiopia, being the first European eye-witness to do so. It is a mild, for those times tolerant, account by a man amazed and impressed by what he had seen. After six years, the party returned to Lisbon, taking with them an Ethiopian and leaving in exchange as a hostage a Portuguese called Bermudez. Later this Bermudez travelled to Europe to ask for help against a great Muslim invasion which was threatening to engulf Ethiopia.

Christopher da Gama came with 300 men in 1541, just in time to save the kingdom. Thanks to their superior weapons, the Portuguese won. Meanwhile, Bermudez made an unsuccessful attempt to get himself appointed *aboena*, patriarch of the Orthodox Church.

It is said that Ignatius Loyola, the founder of the Jesuit order, himself tried to go to Ethiopia, but that the pope would not allow it. In 1557 Andreo de Oviedo reached the country with a group of priests. As a monophysite, the king was not inclined to recognize the authority of Rome and did not wish to become too closely linked politically with Rome. The *aboena* also remembered what Bermudez had tried to do.

In 1589 Pedro Paez set out for Ethiopia. He was imprisoned by pirates and worked for seven years as a galley slave. His order eventually managed to buy his freedom and in 1603 he reached Ethiopia. He settled in the Fremona monastery near Aksum, where within a year he learned to read, write and speak the church language, Ge'ez, fluently. He also became competent in Amharic, the language of the people. Paez became a respected teacher and preacher. He was also a capable architect; but he was best loved for his patience and discretion. He was able to convince King Susenyos by his teaching and in 1622 the king made a public confession of his Roman Catholic faith. It even seemed that the Jesuits would succeed in bringing the Ethiopian Orthodox Church back under the authority of Rome. Then Pedro Paez died and the king asked Rome for a new patriarch. The pope appointed Alphonse Mendez, a Spanish Jesuit who seems to have been the exact opposite of Paez. He ordered all priests to be reordained, churches to be reconsecrated, Christians to be rebaptized, and the whole liturgy to be changed. The king was forced to swear loyalty to him and Roman pictures were put in the churches.

The king saw only one way out. He refused to accept any of Mendez's reforms, broke with Roman Catholic belief and restored the religion of the ancestors. Then he abdicated, a disappointed man, handing the throne over to his son Fasiladas. The Jesuits were driven from the country.

Jerome Lobo, a Jesuit who accompanied Mendez, wrote a book on the church of Ethiopia. He acknowledges that Ethiopian Christians, despite their break with Rome, have maintained the devotion of the first, primitive Christians. He criticizes their traditions, but praises the piety with which they celebrate the great mysteries of the faith: the passion of the Lord and the cross. They have great devotion for the Virgin Mary, angels and saints. They celebrate many festivals and respect Sunday. They are very strict in their fasts. But Lobo had difficulties with the noise in their services. He writes:

'No country in the world has so many churches, monasteries, priests and monks as Ethiopia: you cannot sing in one church without being heard in the next. They sing the Psalms of David, of which, as of the whole Bible, they have a very accurate translation in their own language. They sing and dance to the rhythm of little drums which they hang round their necks so as to beat them with both hands. They begin by quietly tapping on the ground with their feet; but when they have worked themselves up, they begin to jump, dance, and clap their hands; and meanwhile they sing more and more loudly until eventually, all melody disappears. They justify this form of worship by appealing to the Psalm of David which says: 'Clap your hands, O nations.' In this way they pervert Holy Scripture in order to defend practices which ill accord with others of which I have spoken above.'

Later Rome tried again to enter Ethiopia, this time with a few Capuchins. Two of them survived, but the rest were killed. Then King Fasiladas arranged with the Muslim Turks, who controlled the Red Sea, that they would let no more priests through alive. The Turks took good care of this.

The attempt to give the oldest church in Africa a place within Roman Catholicism failed because Rome held its own traditions to be the only true ones and because it considered the western form of European Christianity superior to others. After Mendez's expulsion,

Christian Ethiopia shut the door on western Christianity until the twentieth century.

On the roof of Africa there was and remains the only church which, in its faith and its translation of the Bible, was truly African. The Ethiopian Orthodox believers consider themselves a chosen people because of the link between their Queen of Sheba and King Solomon.

10

Founded on the Book

Between 1792 and 1830, missionary societies were formed everywhere in Protestant Europe and in the United States. They are one of the fruits of pietism and revival, in which personal conversion and personal witness are central. They are independent as organizations, but 'related' to the Anglican, Baptist, Lutheran, Reformed and Methodist churches. Their creation marks the beginning of a new age for Christianity in Africa. The Moravians of Herrnhut were the precursors of this new surge of missionary activity. In 1738 they sent a man called Georg Schmidt to South Africa to proclaim to Hottentots and Bushmen the gospel of redemption in Jesus. After ten years' constant harassment by the Dutch Boers' church councils the good man went away.

In 1765, a British Christian society concerned with the spiritual care of Anglicans in the West Indies and America sent out an African called Philip Quaque, ordained as an Anglican in England, as 'missionary, teacher and catechist for the negroes of the Gold Coast'. Quaque worked there for the rest of his life with great devotion and faithfulness and, to the consternation of his British society, finally earned his living as a trader.

The British missionary societies were in this early period the largest and most important. Board members of these missions were also leading men in the struggle against slavery in parliament and society. The British pietists inspired in their turn ministers and lay people in the United States and in continental Europe to found missionary societies.

Forty years after the Protestants, Catholics joined the movement, when, after the difficult Napoleonic period, the Roman Catholic Church in Europe took on new life. Missions were reorganized and new ones founded. The French played a leading part in this. In the person of Cardinal Lavigerie Rome found a missionary who also became a fighter against slavery.

The new missionary societies had world-wide ambitions. In particular, they were interested in India and other countries of the Far East. They also were very concerned for the slave communities in the New World.

In 1710 Carl Hildebrand, Baron Von Canstein, founded a Bible Institute in Germany. His aim was simply to produce cheap Bibles for his own subjects. The baron had technical talents. In order to print Bibles, which have a large number of pages, he improved the technique of typesetting. A.H. Francke, the founder of the Halle orphanage, continued the baron's work after his death. A hundred years later, 'Canstein' had distributed three million cheap Bibles and New Testaments in German, Czech and Polish in Germany, America and Russia.

About 1800, at the time of the Napoleonic threat, a wave of religious feeling flowed through Britain resulting in the setting up of hospitals and benevolent societies, the founding of missionary societies and the start of anti-slavery campaigns. Demand also arose for Bibles for everyone at a price they could afford. The few existing institutions for distributing Bibles and Christian literature were considered inadequate.

Then one morning in Wales, a working class girl called Mary Jones knocked on the door at the manse of the Rev. Thomas Charles in Bala. She had walked for hours and saved for years. She wanted a Bible in Welsh. The only way Thomas Charles could help her was by giving her a copy which he had reserved for a friend, who however could read English. Later, Charles visited London and laid before a few friends the problem of the severe shortage of Bibles in Welsh. One of them had just been in Paris (France and Britain were at peace at that time), and he reported that in that entire 'City of Light', not a single 'Light', that is not a single Bible, could be obtained. Then a Baptist pastor, the Rev. Joseph Hughes, said: 'If for Wales, why not for England? If for England, why not for the world?'

These gentlemen made contact with the same people who had founded missionary societies and who formed the anti-slavery pressure group in parliament. On 7 March 1804, the urgent need for Bibles in England, Wales, France and Germany was laid before a meeting in London attended by 300 people from all the churches in England. These 300 people founded the British and Foreign Bible Society (BFBS). Its board was made up of lay people: fifteen Anglicans, fifteen free church representatives and six foreigners living in London. The new society had three secretaries: one Anglican, one Baptist and one German Lutheran. The society's aim was to be the distribution of the Holy Scriptures without note or comment to everyone in the world in a language they could understand and at a price they could afford. The Bible Society rapidly became the institution in which all Christians could work together.

London headquarters of the BFBS, 1868–1985.

By 1817 the Bible Society had local committees throughout Great Britain. These committees did two things: they collected money and they distributed Bibles in their area. Monthly contributions from as many people as possible, varying from five pence to a shilling, partly for Bibles for the poor and partly for Bible production and distribution elsewhere: that became the system. In this way the Bible Society, founded by rich and pious people in the City of London, became a concern of all Christian people in Britain. Even if the churches, led by men, found this strange at first, women's auxiliary committees were a great success. Once Napoleon's continental adventure was over, Bible societies were set up before 1818 in west, north and eastern Europe through visits by representatives of the BFBS. In the United States, a hundred local Bible societies formed from 1808 constituted together in 1816 the American Bible Society.

The idea of a Bible society became very popular for two reasons: one for the churches and one for the outside world. Most Bibles at that time were published with notes produced by denominational agencies in order to propagate in the notes the views of the churches in question. These separate editions of the Bible made for small printings and high prices. The idea of Bibles without note or comment opened the way for broad practical co-operation and for large, much cheaper editions.

The outside world was living through the Age of Enlightenment in which also the ideas of the French Revolution were disseminated in pamphlets and books. The revival movements among an elite which had given birth to missions, benevolent societies and also the Bible societies, wanted a Christian answer to modern thinking. What better answer than the Bible itself at an affordable price and in a language people could read?

Distribution of the Bible 'without note or comment' under the auspices of a non-denominational organization also led this organization to be extremely cautious about any revision of the Bible text. In Britain, and to a lesser extent in the United States, the Bible societies were always very prudent in the area of revision or amendment of the text of the English King James Bible in order not to create fresh divisions. This had two consequences. Christians in Africa, insofar as they learned English, were brought up on the classical King James version, while in England and in America, notably in the twentieth century, a large part of English Bible production 'without note or comment' in revised versions was in the hands of commercial publishers.

In the first decades of the Bible society movement, there was much dispute about the Apocrypha or deuterocanonical books. Lutherans, some Anglicans and the Russian and Greek Orthodox included them in their Bibles, as did the ancient eastern churches, such as the Copts and Ethiopian Orthodox in Africa. Since active Bible societies were soon formed everywhere in continental Europe, even as far away as Russia, they went into areas where 'their' Christians and churches started to ask for Bibles including the deuterocanonical books. In Africa the missions seeking a revival within the ancient Christian churches of Egypt and Ethiopia were also wanting such editions.

The BFBS committee, which supported many of these Bible societies in their work, was thus confronted with the question whether or not to publish Bibles with the Apocrypha or deuterocanonical books. At first, from 1812, it decided to allow co-operating societies to do so and issued some such editions itself. This led to major controversy and the decision was reversed in 1826. Scottish societies nevertheless broke off their connection with the BFBS and in 1861 joined together to form the National Bible Society of Scotland, which was also to be active in the spread of the Bible in Africa. In continental Europe, the decision not to include the Apocrypha led to the withdrawal of support from London for those European Bible societies which published Bibles with the Apocrypha. London even opened its own offices alongside such national societies, for example in Germany, the Netherlands and France.

The pious men who had founded the British and Foreign Bible Society wanted to enlist the help of all Christians in distributing the Bible to the ends of the earth. They were devoted Christians, but had also a touch of imperialism in line with British thinking in those days. The situation changed wherever national Bible societies wanted to be more than auxiliary committees of London. The Apocrypha question induced the BFBS to begin separate British work in countries which already had their own Bible societies. When, in 1854, the BFBS celebrated its golden jubilee in London, scarcely a single overseas society was invited! The path chosen so consistently by the BFBS had led for too long to Bible societies working alongside each other in a number of places.

Yet the BFBS was, and long remained, the largest society with the greatest international experience. In its early years, there was even here and there Roman Catholic co-operation, until in 1825 an encyclical of Pope Leo XII warned against dangers which Bible societies presented. Roman Catholic canon law prescribes that the Bible may only be read with notes approved by the church; at that time, Rome thought it extremely dangerous to put the Bible into the hands of every lay person. The 'without note or commment' clause was thus a hindrance to co-operation. In addition, Rome continued to insist that the Bible must contain the deuterocanonicals.

In 1806, two years after the foundation of the BFBS, the first Bibles went to Africa. They were English and Dutch Bibles, sent to Cape Town in South Africa by the BFBS and the Netherlands Bible Society.

The first auxiliary committees in or near Africa were set up in 1812 in Mauritius, in 1813 on St. Helena and in 1817 in Malta. In continental Africa, Freetown became the first in 1816, followed by Cape Town in 1820. Everywhere these auxiliaries were founded by governors, naval officers, businessmen and ambassadors. For example, in 1818, officials of the (British) African Company sent gold dust worth £100 from Gold Coast to help the good cause.

In Africa, as everywhere else, money was collected and the Bible was distributed. In 1808 the first Bibles went to Sierra Leone and to Goree in Senegal and in 1811 the first Bibles were shipped to Malta.

In 1816, the BFBS printed a gospel in Bullom, a language of the West African coast spoken in Sierra Leone. The three ports of entry for Bible distribution in Africa became Malta, Freetown in Sierra Leone, and Cape Town.

Bible Society operations in Africa were a British affair, except for Egypt where British and Americans soon agreed to divide the work. In addition, here and there national Bible Societies started to help missions of their fellow countrymen. For example, the American Bible Society assisted in the Zulu edition in South Africa and in the first publications for Gabon. From 1882 to 1889, the mayor of Monrovia was the first honorary ABS agent in Africa. The Scots went to help their missionaries in Nigeria in publishing the Efik edition and in various language editions in Nyasaland. Occasional help was also given by the German Bible Societies and by the French and Netherlands Bible Societies.

11

African People of the Book

From 1791 freed slaves from America and the West Indies started to return to their homelands in Africa. Liberia was founded for them in 1822. The British brought their freed slaves to the new city, appropriately named Freetown, in Sierra Leone. Among the slaves freed on the far side of the Atlantic were Anglicans, Methodists, Calvinists and Baptists, who set up their churches in Freetown, mainly with lay preachers.

In addition, slaves freed from ships intercepted off the African coast also were brought to Freetown. In this way people who originally came from Dahomey, Nigeria, Cameroon or Congo came under the influence of the gospel in Freetown. When they returned to their homelands, they took with them the Good News which they had found in Freetown. They were helped by the new missions from Europe, but also by missionary movements among former slaves in the West Indies.

In 1827, the first European secondary school in Africa was founded in Freetown. An important task of this school, Fourah Bay College, was to prepare men for missionary work. In order to train African Bible translators even Hebrew and Greek were on the curriculum. One of the best known Fourah Bay pupils was Samuel Crowther, who later became the first and only nineteenth-century African Anglican bishop in West Africa (see also chapter 12). This was a time of great enterprises, in which not only missions and the Bible Society, but also the British government and business firms, co-operated.

In this way the Niger Expedition of 1841, a large scale effort to start agriculture and evangelism in Nigeria along the Niger, set out under the motto: 'The Bible and the plough must do it'. It proved a fiasco. Dozens of European members died on the way unable to cope with the climate and the tropical diseases. The humid and hot west coast proved extremely unhealthy for Europeans. The rainy season was oppressive and people had no idea how to combat tropical diseases.

West Africa became a missionaries' graveyard. After 1850, the missions sent out a minimum of new European workers and scarcely dared to extend their work. The first condition for going out to Africa was a completely fit and healthy body. Highly educated missionaries went to Asia because the leadership of the missionary societies judged that the great religions made higher intellectual demands than the 'black superstition of the heathen in Africa'. Thus the great pioneers in Africa were the mechanic Alfred Saker in Cameroon and the gardener Robert Moffat in southern Africa (see also chapters 13 and 18).

The key figures, however, in West Africa are not missionary workers from Europe, but Africans, especially Africans from the West Indies: the former slave Crowther in Nigeria, the half-caste Thomas Birch Freeman, Joseph Merrick in Cameroon, and other Jamaicans in Calabar, Eastern Nigeria, to name but a few. Freed slaves from the West Indies wanted to proclaim the gospel in their fatherlands and slaves freed off the African coast joined them.

Around 1850, English and Africans were active on the Gold Coast, in Dahomey and in Nigeria. Jamaicans and Scots were working in Eastern Nigeria, Germans and Swiss in Togo and on the Gold Coast. In 1870 the British Baptists began work in the Congo. For Roman Catholics the dates were 1843 in Senegal and 1866 in Angola and the Congo. Preaching the gospel, translating the Bible and basic education were almost everywhere accompanied by development work. This was done in an effort to replace declining income from the slave trade by co-operating, freely or of necessity, in agriculture, trade and industry. In this way Alfred Saker tought the Duala on the coast of Cameroon to bake bricks and the Basel Mission set up trading houses, for example on the Gold Coast and in Cameroon.

Notably on the Gold Coast and in Dahomey, Nigeria and Cameroon, missionaries were regularly caught up in wars between African chiefs, if only because their houses were in the front line between competing villages. Chiefs were also constantly stirred up against the missionaries by priests and sorcerers of African traditional religions who feared competition.

Almost all European missionary societies dreamed of preaching the gospel one day to a 'pure' tribe in the interior, which would not yet have been 'corrupted' by the European slave trade, European liquor and weapons and also European venereal diseases.

Christians, that is Protestants and Anglicans, became the People of the Book.

Between 1808 and 1816, 804 Bibles and 2027 New Testaments were sent to Sierra Leone and to Goree in Senegal.

In 1816, a Bible Society auxiliary committee was set up in Freetown, the first on the African continent. In the same year the first Gospel in a West African language, Bullom, spoken in Liberia, was printed by the

Bible Society. The translator, Dr. G.J. Nylander, believed that
Bullom was an important language, but later it became clear that it
was spoken only by a small coastal people. No more of the Bible ever
appeared in Bullom.

Muslims, especially Muslim traders from the interior, showed
interest in the ports for Bibles in Arabic. But was Arabic an important
language in West Africa? When the Basel Mission began work in 1827
on the Gold Coast, the BFBS sent English, French and Arabic Bibles.
The 1841 Niger Expedition took with it Arabic and even Hebrew
Bibles. The British and Jamaican Baptists, when they started on the
island of Fernando Po, also took Arabic Bibles. As late as 1872 the
first Baptist missionaries started with Bibles in English and Arabic in
the Congo.

Slowly but surely it appeared that among the vast majority of
Muslims knowledge of Arabic was limited to Qur'an texts learned by
heart, most of which they did not understand (see also chapter 37).

Everywhere on the coast, African evangelists trained in Sierra
Leone, African preachers who had come over from the West Indies,
and European and American missionaries, began by preaching the
gospel and at the same time by translating the Bible.

There were several reasons for this: to send evangelists as quickly as
possible to the next village with the Good News literally in their hands;
because the missionaries knew that many of them would die young and
that they must therefore strive to produce something permanent, that
is a translation of the Bible; and to strip the sorcerer of his weapons by
giving people God's own story to read for themselves. The missionaries also built small printing factories in Sierra Leone, Eastern Nigeria,
Cameroon, Gabon and elsewhere.

The BFBS sent paper, or printed or published Scriptures. The ABS
printed for American missionaries in Gabon and the North German
Bible Society did the same for German missionaries among the Ewe in
Togo. The National Bible Society of Scotland helped the Scots in
Eastern Nigeria.

The results were impressive:

Gospels by 1850

1816	Bullom	Sierra Leone
1837	Mandinka	Gambia
1838	Grebo	Liberia
1843	Ga	Gold Coast
1844	Bassa	Liberia
1846	Isubu	Cameroon
1848	Duala	Cameroon
1849	Fernando Po (Bube)	Fernando Po

New Testaments by 1880

1859	Ga	Gold Coast
1861	Duala	Cameroon
1862	Yoruba	Nigeria
1862	Efik	Nigeria
1863	Twi	Gold Coast
1868	Temne	Sierra Leone
1869	Omyene	Gabon
1877	Ewe	Togo/Gold Coast
1880	Hausa	Nigeria

Bibles by 1885

1866	Ga	Gold Coast
1868	Efik	Nigeria
1871	Twi	Gold Coast
1872	Duala	Cameroon
1884	Yoruba	Nigeria

No one knew how many languages were spoken. No one knew how many people spoke a given language. In five of the eight languages in which a Gospel had appeared by 1850, nothing more was translated because the number of speakers proved too small. Slowly the 'big' languages were identified and by 1885 there were complete Bibles in the first five larger languages: Ga and Twi on the Gold Coast, Efik and Yoruba in Nigeria, and Duala in Cameroon.

Africans, some trained at Fourah Bay College in Sierra Leone, played a great part in this translation work. On the Gold Coast there was the Rev. Augustus W. Hanson; in Sierra Leone the Rev. Henry Johnson (Mende); in Nigeria Samuel Crowther and Thomas King (Yoruba); in Dahomey an African committee (Gu or Popo); in Cameroon the West Indian Joseph Merrick (Isubu).

The story of the Efik in Calabar, Eastern Nigeria, is typical. At the request of Jamaican Christians the Scot Hope M. Wadell began missionary work in 1846. He received further support from Jamaica. So the Rev. H. Goldie, the Rev. H.B. Newhall and a Mr Hamilton also came to work in Calabar. Goldie was the translator. He prepared a dictionary, school books, a grammar and a hymn book in Efik. The NBSS printed 'his' New Testament in 1862. It was its first publication for Africa. The first convert, Esien Esien Ukpabio, sent a personal letter of thanks to Edinburgh. After the New Testament, the Book of Genesis was published at the expense of a church in Jamaica. In 1866 the Rev. Alexander Robb completed the Old Testament, which the Scots printed in 1868. And in 1887, the Efik king, Eyo VII, sent a gift of £10 to Scotland for a missionary campaign.

Jacob F. Schön, a German missionary of a British Anglican mission, the Church Missionary Society, developed into the first West African linguist. He translated into Mende, Hausa, Ibo, Nupe and other languages.

By 1846 Americans in Gabon had already printed eighteen thousand books and booklets in a trade language called Mpongwe. It later appeared that Fang was the most important language in Gabon.

It is striking that in many languages, after one or more Gospels, the next parts of the Bible to be translated were Genesis, the Psalms, Proverbs and a number of Old Testament stories. Only then was the New Testament completed.

Bible distribution was done through missions and schools. Following Sierra Leone, a Bible Society auxiliary committee was set up in Gambia in 1858, and in 1864 in Lagos, Nigeria, after the British had driven out the local king who was causing trouble. In 1896, the Methodist missionary C.K. Johnson became a Bible Society agent for West Africa. From Lagos in Nigeria he visited all missions along the coast from the Gambia to the Congo. That meant travelling long distances by ship and often also on foot. He spoke with translators, established relations with the translation department in London and founded depots. In Accra on the Gold Coast an auxiliary was started and the Basel Mission was given a depot. In Dahomey, the African minister and Bible translator T.J. Marshall set up an auxiliary, but then died at the age of 34. Like many European People of the Book he too succumbed to the West African climate. Europeans, together with Africans from Africa and from the other side of the Atlantic, ensured that by 1885, from Senegal to Angola, Bibles and books of the Bible had been translated, printed and distributed in a long list of languages.

12

Samuel Adjai Crowther the African

In June 1822, the British warship HMS Myrmidon intercepted off the Nigerian coast, a day's voyage from Lagos, a Portuguese ship called *Happy Hope* with 187 slaves on board. Among them was a 12-year-old Yoruba boy who had been captured in a Fulani slave raid with his mother and two sisters at Ochopegenu in Nigeria. He had been resold four times and now, with 186 others on the *Happy Hope*, he was on his way to America. The Myrmidon freed the slaves and put them off at Freetown in Sierra Leone. This 'town of freedom' had been founded by the British as a reception centre for freed slaves. On 11 December 1825, the Yoruba boy Adjai was baptized in Sierra Leone as Samuel Adjai Crowther. In 1827 he became the first pupil in the first secondary school in Africa, Fourah Bay College in Freetown. When he had completed his schooling there, he remained in the college as a teacher.

One of the leaders of the anti-slavery movement in England, Thomas Fowell Buxton, founded in 1839 the Society for the Extinction of the Slave Trade and the Civilization of Africa. He started from the principle that Africa's freedom could only be achieved by calling on Africa's own resources. 'The Bible and the plough must do it'.

In the spring of 1841, three ships sailed to Africa with the purposes of beginning, somewhere on the Niger, a model project combining agriculture, medical care, teaching and mission. In Sierra Leone they took on African volunteers. Two missionaries were appointed for the Niger Expedition: the German linguist Schön and the African teacher Samuel Adjai Crowther.

The Niger Expedition was defeated by the Niger mosquitoes. Of the 145 Europeans who took part forty died on the way and only fifteen got no malaria. The African members were seen to stand the climate much better than the Europeans, This first attempt to establish a settlement in the West African interior failed, despite enthusiastic preparation by individuals, government and mission in Britain and Sierra Leone. Crowther's diary of this journey was published and made a great impression. He was invited to come to England and early in 1843 was ordained priest in the Church of England. He was welcomed back in Freetown with great enthusiasm at the end of 1843 as the first African Anglican minister. Two weeks after arriving he preached to freed slaves in Yoruba, his mother tongue.

Even before the Niger Expedition, the mission in Sierra Leone had planned to begin work in the interior. One of the reaons why Fourah Bay College had been founded was to train pioneers for new work. Crowther had learned Greek and Hebrew in the college so that translating the Bible could form part of the pioneer work.

Among the freed slaves who came to Freetown was a whole group of Yoruba. Some of them went into trade and when one of these traders, visiting Lagos on business, recognized it as the place from which he had once been shipped as a slave, the Yoruba freed slaves realized that their homeland was in the hinterland of Lagos, in what is now Nigeria. They organized a movement for repatriation from Freetown to Lagos. Around 1841, about 500 Yoruba had returned to their fatherland.

Most of them settled in a town called Abeokuta. They sent to Freetown to ask permission to start mission work in their home area. The king of Abeokuta was ready to welcome the missionaries. The Anglicans seized the opportunity. The Englishman Townsend, the German Gollmer and the Yoruba Samuel Adjai Crowther were appointed as pioneers. In January 1845 they arrived in Yorubaland. They were not, however, allowed to enter, because meanwhile the friendly king had died and his successor wanted to have nothing to do with Christianity. Only 18 months later were they able to begin. Their approach was modern: evangelism, teaching, medical care, but also improvement of the economic situation. The missionaries introduced palm oil production and cotton planting.

Things went well. In 1852 the Yoruba chief stated that never, since the end of the slave trade, had his country known such prosperity. Spiritual and material progress took place under very difficult circumstances. Lagos, the port, wanted to continue the lucrative slave trade. The king of Porto-Novo saw the missionaries' activities as a threat. The Fulani from the north made incursions into Yorubaland. Civil war broke out from time to time among the Yoruba themselves. Crowther and Townsend had their hands full preventing and resolving political conflicts. They even prevented one battle with the Adu by simply pitching their tent between the two parties.

There were also opponents in Abeokuta itself: the priests and sorcerers who saw the missionaries as competitors. Meanwhile, new missionary workers kept arriving as regular as clockwork. Most of them were either buried within five years or had returned home. In this whole work the tireless labourer Samuel Crowther was the key figure. For him, preaching the gospel was central. While preaching one of his first sermons in Abeokuta, he recognized in the congregation his own mother and sisters, 25 years after he had embarked for America. In 1848 he baptized his first Yoruba Christians, his mother among them. For her, he translated the Anglican baptismal service into Yoruba. In the same year, Crowther made a first Yoruba reader. He took great pains to find the best way of writing down the high and low tones of the language.

Samuel Crowther was later accused of having become too much of an Englishman in his way of thinking. However that may be, it is a fact that when he started to translate the Bible into Yoruba, he began with Paul's abstract Letter to the Romans, being convinced that it plainly stated the heart of the Christian message. And that was an un-African choice. The BFBS supported publication of Romans. In 1850 Crowther prepared a Yoruba selection from the Anglican Book of Common Prayer. In 1851 there followed the Gospel of Luke and after that a concrete African choice, the Book of Genesis. The Yoruba evangelist Thomas King translated Matthew. Crowther revised and corrected his work. In 1854 came the Book of Exodus.

Samuel Adjai Crowther paid another visit to England. He received an honorary doctorate of Divinity. In 1864 he was consecrated in Canterbury as the first African Anglican bishop. But he did not become Bishop of Yorubaland. The mission wanted a fresh start along the Niger in Eastern Nigeria. The intention was to set up a completely African mission. Crowther was to be the leader of this team and that was why he, a Yoruba, was consecrated Bishop of the Niger, that is the Bishop of Iboland. His colleagues were recruited from among old pupils of Fourah Bay.

When in 1865 the Yoruba New Testament came from the press, Crowther was thus working on the Niger, far from his own Yoruba people. He was no longer young when he went to the Ibo. He did not learn Ibo. Had this African bishop really become too English? Even on the Niger he remained a devoted worker who built up the work from nothing.

In 1880 a Yoruba committee in Abeokuta completed its translation of the whole Bible. In 1889 Samuel Adjai Crowther died. For the next fifty years all his successors were Europeans. However hard he worked as bishop, Crowther could not meet the efficiency standards of his British mission. The basic principles of the CMS, self-support, self-government and self-propagation, went into cold storage, because Samuel Adjai Crowther, the Yoruba slave boy, could not do everything and because modern colonialism, with its 'superior' Europeans, had begun.

Samuel Adjai Crowther was one of the first Africans who translated the Bible himself for his own people.

13

The Englishman Alfred Saker

The British Baptist Missionary Society (BMS) began its work in 1813 among black slaves in Jamaica. In 1839 converts in Jamaica sent an urgent request to the BMS Committee in London for missionary work to be started in their African fatherland. The London committee was not really interested, but did not dare to reject the call from Jamaica. After an exploratory journey, it was decided to begin in the Gulf of Guinea with the island of Fernando Po as a base. Fernando Po belonged to the British West Africa Company.

A mixed group of Jamaicans and British travelled to Clarence on Fernando Po with the aim of beginning missionary work among the inhabitants, including villages of freed slaves.

In addition, it was planned to make missionary journeys to the very unhealthy continental area opposite Fernando Po in what is now Cameroon.

The Jamaican minister Joseph Merrick, accompanied by a Fernando Po convert called Thomas Horton Johnson, paid a first visit of two months to the continent. They spoke with the chiefs, they preached, they gave English lessons in the Duala and Bell villages on the River Wouri, and made exploratory journeys into the interior. The Portuguese called the Wouri, Rio-del-Camerones, the River of Shrimps. Early in 1844 Merrick settled with another Jamaican family, the Fullers, in an old slave depot in the village of Bimbia in Cameroon. Before being ordained, Merrick had worked in a printing factory in Jamaica, so one of the first things he did in Bimbia was to set up a small printing press. Merrick had a gift for languages. He prepared and printed a first Duala reader. He learned another coastal language, Isubu. In Bimbia he printed his translation of Matthew, John, Genesis and a selection from the rest of the Old Testament, all in Isubu.

So the mission to Cameroon was begun by Africans, Merrick and Fuller, at the request of Africans in Jamaica.

In 1845 Europeans came to strengthen the work in Bimbia. Within two years, they were all either dead or invalided home. In 1848 Joseph

Merrick left for England on leave, but died on the way home. Fuller remained at Bimbia until in 1858 he was transferred to Duala. Bimbia, the first mission station on the coast of Cameroon, was closed.

Then, on 16 February 1844, an Englishman arrived with his wife in Fernando Po. He was thirty years old, his name was Alfred Saker, and he had been sent out as a maintenance technician. Saker was not content to remain on the island; he wanted to cross over to the mainland. There Thomas Horton Johnson became his guide. After negotiations with the chiefs of Akwa and Deido, Alfred Saker settled in 1845 on the Wouri in Cameroon, halfway between Deido and Akwa, where the city of Duala now stands. He was to remain there for thirty years, with T.H. Johnson as his right hand man. Saker had to build his own house and grow his own food. At one place in his diaries he complains that for nine months they had not had any tea to drink, because too few ships called. That must have been a sore trial for an Englishman on the Wouri.

Saker had the greatest difficulty in surviving. In Duala, three degrees north of the equator, there were five metres of rain a year. It was a fearsomely damp and unhealthy place. Saker was regularly involved in tribal wars between the chiefs of the Duala. One or two battles were fought literally on Saker's doorstep. He severely criticized the European traders, who wanted, together with the Duala, to continue the very lucrative slave trade by importing alcohol and weapons.

Saker built a chapel, and as early as 1845 began a small school in Duala. Then this maintenance technician began to work hard at learning the Duala language. He wanted to talk to people about their Father in their mother tongue. He was also afraid that he would not be able to stay long in Duala because of the bad climate. He suspected that many more thousands of Duala speakers lived in the hinterland. He wanted as soon as possible to make something that would last, a Bible translation which would communicate the Good News even without missionaries. Saker's theological training was minimal, so he sent to England for all kinds of theological books. He also used Joseph Merrick's study notes. In 1848 Merrick printed in Bimbia a Gospel of Matthew in Duala translated by Saker. The New Testament was finished in 1862 and the whole Bible in 1872. The manuscript went to England, but by return post (a year later!), it came back to Duala because the BMS had no money to print it. Joseph Merrick's printing press had meanwhile been moved from Bimbia to Duala. There, in the humid heat by the Wouri River, the first 200 copies of the Duala Bible were printed. The Bible Society in London took care of later editions.

Meanwhile, many other things had happened.

In 1849 Alfred Saker baptized T.H. Johnson's first convert. The same evening, Saker drew up a church order and the Baptist Church of Duala was founded. A year later Saker went to England on leave.

In this small building in Duala, which no longer exists, Alfred Saker printed the first Duala Bibles in 1872.

In his absence, the entire leadership of the mission was African: the Jamaican J.J. Fuller at Bimbia, T.H. Johnson in Duala, and another convert, John Wilson, at Clarence on Fernando Po. Despite Saker's urgent pleas, the mission committee in London refused to send out fresh personnel: the death rate was too high. Saker himself was allowed to return. At the end of 1851 he baptized five of Johnson's converts, among them the Duala prince and ex-slave George Nkwe. Later this man was to become the first Cameroonian minister. In 1855, by which time the church had fifty members, T.J. Johnson was ordained and the Duala Baptist church became independent.

There followed a period of persecution for the small Christian community. The Christians' ethical standards inhibited the chiefs and sorcerers in the exercise of their power. Saker's response seemed at first sight strange. He founded a technical school; he taught the Duala to bake bricks of river clay, and to grow new crops. These activities gave the Duala new sources of income, which were urgently needed because intermediate trade between the interior and the Europeans on the coast was in the process of losing its most important product, slaves. The Duala, like many coastal peoples of West Africa, lived largely by this intermediate trade. Fuller played a great part in the brick-baking and the technical school, since he had earlier been a bricklayer in Jamaica.

In 1845 the island of Fernando Po became Spanish. At first, the Catholic Spaniards tolerated the Protestant mission, but in 1858 the Baptists were expelled. *Cuius regio, eius religio* was the rule even in Africa. Alfred Saker contrived to get compensation from the Spaniards and founded for the ninety Baptist refugees a town on the west side of Mount Cameroon, which he named Victoria after his British queen.

Meanwhile, in 1854, the Baptist mission had sent new workers to Cameroon from England and Jamaica. This made it possible to open new stations in the interior. At first, the Duala were strongly opposed to this. They wanted to keep Christianity, with its church and school and clinic, for themselves. Later, they provided evangelists, teachers and nurses for the interior.

From 1865 to 1874, no new missionary workers came out. The missionaries complained that Alfred Saker was too concerned with 'the work of civilization' and that he had lost his spiritual vocation. They also saw him as an individualist who did not take sufficient account of his colleagues' points of view. A certain Mr. Innes, who had worked for a short time in 1859 as a missionary in Duala, even published on his own account in London a kind of 'black book' on the 'atrocities' committed by Alfred Saker in West Africa. Saker's reply, in one of his letters to the BMS in London, ran roughly as follows:

> There are people who think that a missionary is someone who goes and sits under a tree with a Bible in his hand to tell the natives about Jesus. But this is meaningless if the poor wretches are not also freed from sickness and hunger and do not get a decent roof over their heads. Finally the secretary of the mission, Underhill, came from London to Duala to investigate the 'Saker case'. Underhill found Saker innocent and later wrote a kind of saint's life of him.

In 1876 Alfred Saker returned to England for good. He had buried four of his children in Duala. He had been a wilful, possessed man who did not make life easy for his colleagues. He had built churches, schools and a technical school and founded a Baptist church in which he had ordained a Jamaican and a Cameroonian. He had translated the whole Bible into Duala. He had fought abuses by the whites and by the Duala chiefs. In all this, he had given the Duala a fresh vision of the future, both here below and 'beyond the stars'. And the Duala had understood him and his message. When they want to express their belief that spiritual and material things are not and must not be separated, they still say in their Duala language: 'Let's do it in Saker's way'.

14

The ancient churches

The new missionary societies and the Bible Society were very interested in the ancient churches of Africa: in the Copts in Egypt and in unknown Christian Ethiopia. As early as 1818, efforts began to start a revival among these Christians.

Since the seventeenth century, Catholic missions had tried to work in Egypt. First there were Capuchins and Franciscans; then in 1879 the Jesuits returned, especially to open schools. In 1862 Pope Pius IX founded the Congregatio Pro Nepotiis Ritus Orientalis, which opened seminaries for the Eastern Rite in Rome with the aim of giving the eastern churches with their own liturgies a place in the Roman Catholic Church. The competition between the Roman Catholics, who had reopened work in Egypt in 1830, and the Protestants also took on political colouring. French and Italian missions were at work in the same country in which the Frenchman Ferdinand de Lesseps was building the Suez Canal. British and American Protestant missions were active in Egypt, which the British occupied. Politics was important too in Ethiopia. There the rulers began by seeking to make contact with Germans working for British Protestant missions. Then they tried to establish links with the home country of French Roman Catholic missionaries; and finally the Italians, who had also begun missionary work, occupied Eritrea. In 1888 the Orthodox Church of Ethiopia tried to unite with the Russian Orthodox Church. This was intended to keep out British, French and Italian political influence and spiritual pressure from the Egyptian Copts. Eventually Ethiopia managed to defend itself against both the missions and the threat of colonial domination.

As early as 1811 a Bible depot was set up on the island of Malta in the Mediterranean.

In 1815 the BFBS printed the Psalms in Ge'ez, the Ethiopian church language, and in 1817 the first 1439 Bibles in Arabic were published. In the same year the CMS sent the Rev. William Jowett to Malta to stimulate a revival in the ancient eastern churches: the Greek Orthodox Church; the Maronite church in what is now called

Lebanon; the Syrian Orthodox; the Coptic Orthodox Church in Egypt; and the Ethiopian Orthodox Church. This work was to be supported by publishing Bibles and Christian books and by the building of schools. To this end Jowett was to install a printing press and collect manuscripts. As early as 1819 Jowett visited Egypt. In the 1820s the Malta press was working with an international team of British, German and American missionaries, all busy translating, revising, typesetting and printing manuscripts. Missionary societies co-operated with the Bible Society in this effort. For years the Malta press produced on average twelve thousand Bibles and portions a year. Apart from theological problems (the ancient Orthodox churches in Africa were monophysite, that is they believed that Jesus had only one, divine, nature), they had to work with churches which had always used for the liturgy a kind of sacred language which the common people did not understand. Jowett and his colleagues tried to take account of this situation, working both in the language of the liturgy and in that of the people.

In Egypt the church language was Bohairic Coptic. In 1716 the New Testament appeared in this dialect of Coptic. In co-operation with the patriarch, the four gospels were published in 1829 on the basis of that text with Arabic in another column. Around 1840 parts of the Old Testament, including the Psalms, were printed.

We do not know whether Mohammed was familiar with the Bible in Arabic. Since the twelfth century, the whole Bible had been available in that language, though not in a single complete manuscript (see also chapter 5). Beginning in 1546, new translations were printed. In Leiden, in the Netherlands, T. Erpenius published a New Testament in 1616 and in 1662 the Pentateuch. The text was based on Melkite, Nestorian, Syrian, Maronite, Coptic and perhaps even Spanish sources. De Propaganda Fide, the mission department set up by the pope in Rome, issued in 1671, after 46 years of revision work, a complete Arabic Bible with the Latin Vulgate in a parallel column.

In 1725 and 1727 there came the first editions of the Psalms and the New Testament prepared by a non-Roman Catholic organization, the SPCK, in London. Initially the BFBS distributed other translations, but when the Arab Christians were found to reject the SPCK version, the BFBS published the Roman Catholic text. In 1820 the New Testament appeared and in 1822 the Old. The style of the translation was rather poor and difficult to read. A famour scholar, Farius al-Shidyak from Lebanon, made a new version in co-operation with British translators. This whole Bible came out in 1857, but was soon overshadowed by the Van Dyck translation.

In 1850, the American missionary Eli Smith, assisted by Butros al-Bustani and Naseef al-Yaziji, began work on a new translation. After Smith's death his place was taken by another American, Cornelius

Van Dyck, who engaged Jusif al-Husayni as a stylist. Van Dyck's motivation for appointing a Muslim stylist is striking: he found it an advantage that this follower of Islam knew not a single Arabic translation of the Bible. He was forbidden to look at other translations and told to refer exclusively to the Arabic. From 1866 this Van Dyck version became for more than a century the Bible of Christian Arabs; it was not only outstandingly translated, but also excellently printed. Eli Smith had discovered that European typesetting gave a bad reproduction of Arabic letters, so he himself prepared his own excellent Arabic font. The Bible was printed in Beirut in this much better type. A copy of the type was sent to the BFBS in London and the ABS in New York: the first example of technical co-operation between Bible Societies. In 1876–80, in Beirut, the Jesuits published a translation of the Bible which was a kind of Roman Catholic answer to Van Dyck (see also chapter 37).

The Van Dyck version was in the official literary Arabic of the Qur'an, as used in teaching. In the Maghreb, where Bible distribution had developed slowly from 1832, attempts were made to make translations in the language of the people who did not know and could not understand the official language. Muslims often did not want or dare to co-operate in this work, because the spoken language, 'colloquial Arabic', had no status. It was an offence to God to speak to him in the vulgar language of ordinary people. In 1830, a big 'new' language, Kabyle, was discovered in the Atlas Mountains. W.B. Hodgson, an ex-American consul in Algiers, translated the four gospels and Genesis with the help of mountain Kabyles. The Bible Society bought the manuscript for £150 and published in 1833 the Gospel of Luke. The next gospel was printed half a century later, for Kabyle, the language of the Berbers was also considered by the Muslims unworthy to be a literary language alongside Arabic.

Bible translation, improved printing techniques and teaching initiated by the missions also played a part in the start of a new literary movement in Arabic. It was called al-Nahda, the Renaissance, and Christian writers from Syria and Lebanon contributed significantly to it. There also appeared in Arabic a number of newspapers, often owned by Christians. Later, after 1910, these papers greatly helped to develop modern political consciousness in the Arab world.

But the team in Malta wanted to go further than North Africa and Egypt.

Since 1846 there had been Roman Catholics working in the Sudan, supported by the Austrian emperor. After the Mahdi's insurrection in 1881 they were expelled. In 1865, a missionary called Christian Frederic Spittler began Protestant work in Khartoum. But there was also a desire to take the Bible into ancient, unknown Christian Ethiopia. There the church had its own language, Ge'ez. As early as

1513 the Psalms had been printed in this language in Rome, followed in 1548 by a New Testament. In 1701 Job Ludolph, a German orientalist from Thuringia, published the Psalms. Through the mediation of Salt, the British consul general in Egypt, Ludolph's Psalms were reprinted by the BFBS in 1815. The Ethiopians were amazed to find that all copies were the same. Thomas Pell Platt collected and revised manuscripts and in 1826 the four gospels were published, printed with fonts left by Ludolph. In 1830 the New Testament appeared, but the whole Bible did not follow until 1918.

In 1820 Jowett obtained in Cairo a manuscript of the New Testament in Amharic, the common language of Ethiopia. It comprised 9539 hand-written pages and was revised for ten years by the French consul in Cairo, Asselin de Cherville, with the help of the Ethiopian monk Abu Rumi. When the New Testament was ready for printing, Abu Rumi went on pilgrimage to Jerusalem in order, as he said himself, to die in the Holy Land. And so it happened.

In 1823 the four gospels were printed in Malta, followed by the New Testament in 1829 and the whole Bible in 1840. Much later, in 1878, Ludwig Krapf and three Ethiopians undertook a revision at St. Chrischona in Switzerland. In 1878 the Bible Society also published a diglot edition of the Psalms and the New Testament in Amharic and Ge'ez.

In 1819 Jowett met in Egypt an extraordinary adventurer called Nathaniel Pearce. He had been in Russia and China; he had worked as a so-called Muslim in Arabia and had served for fourteen years in the Ethiopian army. He knew another Ethiopian language, Tigre. Pearce translated Mark and John into this language, but for some reason his translation was never published. In 1831 the missionaries C. Kugler and C.W. Isenberg made a fresh start. Ludwig Krapf made the first translation in the Ethiopic Oromo language, spoken by the Galla. The Gospels were printed in 1841 and the first New Testament in 1875.

In 1885 there even appeared a Gospel in Kara, the language of Ethiopian Jews, who are now called Falasha.

All these editions for the ancient churches were distributed by the missionaries.

In 1825 the CMS sent five German missionaries to Egypt. They began to distribute the Bible and also founded a boarding school, which later developed into the Coptic Evangelical Seminary and a Christian university (see also chapter 16).

American Presbyterians came to work in the Nile Delta. They did not succeed in gaining an entry into the Coptic Orthodox Church, so they set up their own Coptic Evangelical Church, largely made up of Copts 'converted' by their good western schools. Ludwig Krapf and his fellow-Germans of the CMS tried to build an 'Apostles' Street' of twelve mission stations running from Cairo to Ethiopia. In addition to

Bibles and schools, they introduced a new element, handicrafts, in order to build mission stations and teach people various trades. Their greatest problem was the opposition of the Coptic and Ethiopian Orthodox clergy. In addition, the caravan trails through the Sudan and Ethiopia were long and unsafe and the political situation unstable. The rulers saw the missionaries primarily as pawns in their own struggle for power. The ancient churches have always been despised by the Muslims in Egypt and to the south. Especially in Egypt they had learned all kinds of ruses in order to survive. They were therefore suspicious even of European Christians wanting to bring renewal to their churches. Moreover, the language of the liturgy gave the priests a certain status and authority in their communities, so they were not interested in publishing the Bible in the language of the people. Throughout the Near East, western Christianity was generally linked with imperialism. The memories of the Crusades died hard.

In North Africa there was much opposition from the Muslims, but after France had occupied Algeria in 1830, new Protestant work began around 1850 through French colonists: the French Bible Society; a mission to North African Jews; and a seamen's mission in the port of Oran.

The Catholics were very active among French and Italian immigrants, but for the Archbishop of Algiers, later Cardinal Lavigerie (1825–1892), North Africa was first and foremost a mission field. This brought him into conflict with the anticlerical policy of the French Third Republic. He demanded from the government freedom to preach and in 1867 founded the White Fathers, a missionary order of priests clothed in African bubus. Their aim was to convert the whole continent, starting from North Africa.

From 1846 to 1860 Bible Society work in Malta was directed by Isaac Lowndes. Thereafter Malta, North Africa and Egypt were linked with the Italian agency. Work in Malta was made more and more difficult by opposition from Roman Catholics and eventually the agency was closed down. In 1870 Egypt became a division of the Constantinople (later Istanbul) agency in Turkey. Three years later there began in the Nile Delta sensible co-operation between the BFBS and the ABS, the latter managed in Egypt by American missionaries. In 1881 the Rev. J. Löwitz was put in charge of a new agency in Algiers for Morocco, Algeria, Tunisia and Libya. Attempts at colportage were made with the help of the NBSS and others.

The cutting of the Suez Canal increased Egypt's political importance for Europe. After the occupation of the country by the British, a new British agency was set up in 1883 and the ABS became responsible for the towns along the Nile between Cairo and Aswan. The Coptic Orthodox Church showed itself open to greater co-operation, perhaps as a psychological consequence of British occupation.

In 1886 Ethiopia was closed to all missionary work.

The year before a Bible depot had been opened at Port Said on the new Suez Canal. It was managed by a former petty officer from the Royal Navy called W.H. Taylor. Port Said grew into a supply centre for Egypt and the whole of East Africa as far as Mozambique.

15

Pioneers and Kings

One of the missionaries who worked to bring about revival among the ancient churches of Ethiopia was Johann Ludwig Krapf. When the way through Egypt proved impassable, he tried to reach Ethiopia from the south. In 1844 he arrived in Mombasa in East Africa where there was also a movement for the liberation of the slaves, but Krapf refused to go and work among the freed slaves in Zanzibar. He settled on the mainland, in what is now Kenya. Krapf was very interested in Bible translation, and had great vision. He worked out a plan for a chain of mission stations from east to west, from Kenya to Nigeria, from Krapf to Crowther, straight across Africa.

Only two of these were built in a period of forty years (see also chapter 16).

The high death rate among missionaries and the intrigues of the Arab sultans who wanted to have nothing to do with the missionaries or their ideas limited Christian mission work for the first twenty years to the two centres on the coast.

After 1863 a fresh start was made on the island of Zanzibar among freed slaves. The slave trade by sea had been forbidden and the British were freeing slaves from ships of all nationalities. A problem arose because no one knew where in the interior the Arab slave traders had obtained these people. The best solution was thus to settle them in new villages on the coast. The British government offered missions a modest grant for building and managing these villages. In these fortified coastal villages there sprang up the first Christian communities of East Africa among uprooted former slaves. These Christians became the African pioneers of the missions who early in the twentieth century would spread the gospel among the peoples of East Africa.

The main language spoken in these new villages was Swahili, the coastal language of East Africa, a mixture of African languages with Arabic and Persian. Krapf set about learning it and in 1844 translated the Book of Genesis. Johann Rebmann came to help him. In 1848 he finished the translation of a Gospel in KiNyika and in 1850 the translation of a Gospel in Kamba, a coastal language was printed.

Stanley's meeting with Livingstone.

Krapf left, but Rebmann remained. Many years later in 1874 the Rev. John Steere, who had been working in Zanzibar since 1868, found the now half-blind Rebmann with a few Christians. In honour of Rebmann his Gospel of Luke in KiNyika was published in 1877, but proved not to be in good Swahili.

Steere, who had been Anglican Bishop of Zanzibar since 1874, built on the old slave market place a cathedral for a congregation of freed slaves. Schools and a printing press were started. In 1878 a Gospel was printed in better Swahili than Rebmann's, followed in 1880 by the New Testament and soon after by Genesis. Archdeacon Hodgson continued to work on the Old Testament and in 1892 the complete Bible was printed in Zanzibar on paper supplied by the Bible Society. It was discovered that this mixed Swahili was the trade language of millions of people in East Africa, living in areas which now form parts of Kenya, Tanzania, Uganda and Zaire. Swahili varies from one region to another and it took a long time before all Swahili speakers had a 'union' version of the Bible. In any case Swahili proved to be a big language of East Africa. And to discover a big language was the ideal of all pioneer missionaries.

Henry Morton Stanley, the journalist who had found David Livingstone, the missionary explorer, hated Africa because of the discomforts and dangers of travel. Yet he returned to the continent to continue Livingstone's explorations. In 1874 he came to the court of King Mtesa in Uganda. The oustandingly well-organized Nilotic kingdom of the Buganda had existed since the fifteenth century. Stanley showed the king the Gospel of Matthew in Swahili which had just been printed by Steere on Zanzibar. With the help of an African, Robert Feruzi, he read parts of it to the king. From an English Bible they even translated the ten commandments, which the king's secretary, Idi, carefully noted down. Until that time, the king had honoured the gods and powers of his fathers, but he had also heard the teaching about Allah from Arab traders. He was inclined to choose Stanley's Christianity, because he was impressed by the white men's technical knowledge and inventions and because the whites did not practise slavery. He decided to become a Christian and had a first small church built.

Back in England in 1875, Stanley published in a newspaper his famous call for missionaries for Uganda. The CMA responded, encouraged by the enthusiastic reaction of British Christians. Six months after Stanley's call, a group of missionaries sailed for Zanzibar. In summer 1877 they arrived at the court of Mtesa who welcomed them with open arms.

In 1879 the Roman Catholic White Fathers came to Uganda and there arose competition between Muslims, Anglicans and Catholics for the king's favour. Mtesa began to waver. For him this was a choice between the Arabs, the English and the French and he began to fear European imperialism. Since, in African thinking, worship, politics, power and daily life are inseparable, a choice of religion also had political implications and vice versa.

In 1880 the brilliant Scottish engineer Alexander Mackay had reduced to writing Luganda, the language of Mtesa and his Buganda. He began to print leaflets with reading lessons, using wooden type which he made himself. He translated the ten commandments, a few Psalms and the beginning of Matthew. Then Mtesa died and his 18-year-old son Mwanda succeeded him. This young man had received instruction in both Anglican and Catholic Christianity, but his Buganda advisers and the Arab traders were able to convince him of the Europeans' bad intentions. In 1885 a persecution of Christians broke out with the murder of Bishop James Hannington and his fellow-believers. Mackay had just printed the first 350 copies of a number of pages of Matthew. Within ten years from first hearing the gospel, 45 Ugandan Christians had died as martyrs for their Catholic or Anglican faith.

Even before the Arabs began to sail the coasts of Africa in their *dhows*, people from Malacca or Indonesia crossed the ocean and settled on the almost uninhabited high plateaux of the 'Great Island', Madagascar. They brought their rice-growing culture, complete with terracing, and organized a form of society which, by its strong family structure, reminds one of the *marga* of the Bataks in Sumatra, Indonesia. The large family graves in Madagascar also resemble those by Lake Toba in Sumatra. Their language, Malagasy, is a Malay language.

Down on the coasts of Madagascar, there settled here and there groups from other peoples from the African continent.

In the sixteenth century the Portuguese visited the island and in the seventeenth there was a French attempt at colonization and mission work. In 1672 the French colonists and the Carmelite Fathers left the 'Great Island'.

Madagascar has its own, non-African, culture and history. In the highlands, hard to reach from the coast, the Merina kingdom flourished under the royal family and the nobility, the Adriana class, followed by the large group of Hova, the free citizens, and under them the slaves, the Andevo. The highlands also gave natural protection against Arab and Portuguese slave raids.

At the beginning of the nineteenth century the British, in the course of their fight against slavery, concluded an agreement with King Ramada I. Just like King Mtesa of Buganda later, this King Ramada sensed that the world was changing. He wished to strengthen his position by obtaining the powerful knowledge of the Europeans. The Tananarive court therefore asked the British for missionaries. The London Mission Society (LMS, now the Council for World Mission) began in 1818 by sending David Jones and David Griffiths. Before the end of the year both their wives, their children, and Bevan himself had died of malaria. Jones went to the island of Mauritius, further out in the Indian Ocean, and returned in 1820. He became friendly with the king who was happy to learn and adopt things from the western world.

All ancient practices, including child sacrifice, were abolished. Ten Malagasy youths were sent to England for education and the king wanted young people at his court to acquire European knowledge.

Jones reduced Malagasy to writing and began to translate the Bible. In 1816 the BFBS sent 150 reams of paper on which to print the New Testament. This New Testament was to be printed on a press which had to be carried with endless difficulties from the coast to the highlands. In 1828 the first Gospel, that of Luke, was published, followed by the New Testament in 1830. The entire Bible appeared in parts and was completed in 1835. The whole project was an unbelievable achievement in both translation and printing technique – all the more so since the translation proved to be of exceptional quality. The appearance of these books made a great impression. People besieged the press in Tananarive to ask what they contained. On 29 May 1831 the first twenty Christians in Madagascar were baptized. The LMS missionaries meanwhile had opened a hundred schools on the high plateaux of the 'Great Island'. They used the New Testament as a manual and a reader. Especially among the élite great interest in Christianity was aroused.

In 1828 Ramada I was succeeded by one of his wives, Ranavalona. She was against (too) rapid changes. She broke off relations with Britain and in 1836 prohibited the Christianity of the British missionaries. The old practices were restored and the missionaries fled to Mauritius. The Christian schools were closed and Christian books confiscated. A few hundred copies of the Bible had just been produced. In 1837 a woman called Rafaravavy became the first martyr; others followed. About ten thousand people were condemned because of the new teaching, many of them to long periods of forced labour. The persecutions went on until the queen died. Then it became clear that the underground church had grown tremendously. Thousands had secretly become Christians. The New Testaments and the three hundred Bibles had been read in secret by individuals and groups. Some of the Bibles had been taken apart so that their pages could go from hand to hand as a message of faith and hope.

In 1861 Queen Ranavalona I died. Her son King Ramada II was not a Christian, but he was interested in Christianity. The persecutions ended. In 1868 Queen Ranavalona II succeeded and she was baptized together with her husband, the prime minister. The images of the old gods were burnt and under the leadership of the royal family a great movement to Christianity began. The LMS sent more missionaries, the Catholics were allowed entry and in 1866 the Norwegian Lutherans began missionary work, mainly in the south. Around 1880, the LMS alone had more than a thousand churches, with almost 250,000 members, while the Catholics counted 80,000 baptisms.

All this was not just a question of Christian belief. Missionaries helped the queen to make Christian laws and to organize the administration in a Christian spirit. A Greek-style law court was built in Tananarive. Life-style and even clothing at the court became European. Even today houses on the Madagascar plateau remind one of miners' dwellings in Wales where many of the missionaries were born. People called for European teaching and medical care and the queen aspired to take her place beside the rulers of European countries.

In all this the Bible played a central role. The spirit of English pietism impressed the court and the nobility. People of high birth thought it an honour to be ordained.

In 1864 the ambassador of Madagascar to London attended the annual meeting of the BFBS. In 1866, a revised Bible was printed in London and in 1872 a committee of all non-Catholic churches on the island began a fresh revision of the translation. Up to 1885, the BFBS printed 351,311 Bibles, New Testaments, and portions.

In this greatest success story of the Bible in Africa from 1800 to 1885, the Bible of the martyrs of Madagascar, the island of Mauritius has been mentioned several times.

This little island in the Indian Ocean between Africa and the route to India had played a part in the period of European expansion in the seventeenth and eighteenth centuries because of its location. It was named after Maurits van Nassau of the Netherlands and became French in the eighteenth century. Roman Catholic missions came to work there. After the Napoleonic Wars, the island became British, but French culture maintained great influence. After the freeing of the slaves in 1830, the British brought in thousands of coolies from India for the sugar plantations. They even became the majority on this densely populated island. As early as 1812 Governor-General Wade set up a Bible Society auxiliary on Mauritius. In 1817 868 Bibles and 2295 New Testaments were received and distributed. After the liberation of the slaves, they were given Bibles from the BFBS's 'slave fund'. But the slaves were not able to read.

In the 1860s Mauritius suffered greatly from disasters and epidemics. In 1882 Bibles and portions were distributed on this plantation island in seventy languages, including Hindi, Bengali, Uriya, Hindustani, Tamil, Telugu, Marathi and Chinese from Asia, Malagasy from Africa, and French and English from Europe. The island had become a melting-pot of peoples and religions.

In 1884 there appeared a Gospel in Mauritian Creole, the mixed language which had developed on the island.

Pioneers, of whom many died young, such as Krapf's colleagues, Jones's family, and MacKay; the travels of Stanley and Livingstone, front-page news in Europe; the activities of the king of the Buganda and the persecution in Madagascar: all these were significant for East Africa during this period.

Here too the abolition of slavery was the milestone which marked the end of much suffering. The Bible became the book of hope for the rootless in the villages of freed slaves in Kenya and among the mixed population of Mauritius.

The kings of the Buganda and the rulers of the 'Great Island' sensed that a new world was coming. They tried to find their place in it by asking the Europeans for weapons and also for the Bible, for techniques and also for the white men's schools. Their thinking was not very different from that of the British 'Saints' who founded missions and the Bible Society, but who also fought against slavery.

16

Johann Ludwig Krapf the German

In 1837 Johann Ludwig Krapf was sent out to Ethiopia by the evangelical Anglican Church Missionary Society (CMS). Krapf came from Württemberg in Germany. As a young man he had decided to be a missionary, but he completed his regular theological studies. Once ordained, he made himself unbearable in his first parish by the frankness of his preaching in which he did not deal cautiously enough with local relationships and sensitivities. Thus Krapf became one of the many Germans working for the CMS.

From the beginning it had been one of the ideals of the CMS to start a revival movement in the ancient Christian churches of Africa. Did not the Psalmist speak of Ethiopia stretching out its hands to God? The CMS had been working to this end in Ethiopia since 1818 and had sent a group of German missionaries to work among the Copts in Egypt. When Krapf went out, two of these missionaries had been expelled from Ethiopia, but three others were still working there. Krapf began with six months in Cairo to learn Arabic. Then he travelled to Ethiopia with a load of Bibles and New Testaments. In December 1837 he landed at the Ethiopian port of Massawa. With some difficulty he reached his CMS compatriots, C.W. Isenberg and C.H. Blumhardt, in Adowa.

At that time Ethiopia was a divided, dangerous and unstable country. The emperor, the *negus negusta*, was the nominal ruler, but in fact a number of regional princes ran the show. The most important of these was Shoa who ruled in Tigre and Asmara. The Galla, a non-Christian people who had been making incursions from the south since the sixteenth century, were becoming more and more brutal. The only binding force was the Orthodox Church, but it had no power. Here and there in the church, there was openness to the motives of the missionaries; but the rulers saw Europeans as people who could supply weapons and new techniques for the coming battle for the hegemony of the whole of Ethiopia. Three months after Krapf arrived in Adowa, the ruler of Tigre expelled him and his colleagues from the country. The reason was that Roman Catholics had arrived. They too wanted to

'Christianize' the Ethiopian church. The ruler saw more to be gained politically by their presence than by that of the representatives of the British CMS.

Ludwig Krapf wanted to win back Ethiopia for the Lord. While his colleagues were still hesitating, he decided to go to the territory of one of the other rulers, Sahela Selassie of Shoa. Isenberg went with him, but soon had to return to Europe to have books printed. The working method of these pioneers consisted in translating the Bible into Ethiopian languages, teaching Hebrew to young Ethiopians and setting up small schools to enable Ethiopians to study the Scriptures in order to come to a more Bible-based form of Christianity. As early as 1824, the BFBS had managed to publish a New Testament in Amharic, the language of a large part of the Ethiopian people. Then it was also printed in Ge'ez (Ethiopic), the church language which only the clergy understood. Krapf and his colleagues used these editions together with the Arabic Bible. Isenberg worked on a translation of Luke into the Tigre language and on an Amharic dictionary and grammar. The Ethiopians were very interested in these editions of the Bible.

Krapf succeeded in reaching Ankobar, the capital of the Shoa. Ankobar lies in the centre of present-day Ethiopia. Krapf was warmly welcomed by King Sahela Selassie. The king would have preferred European craftsmen and doctors rather than missionaries, but he gave Krapf permission to open a small school.

The Orthodox priests came every day to ask for Bibles, but they also did everything they could to prevent members of their flock from going to Krapf's school. With great difficulty he gathered five pupils.

Ludwig Krapf was very interested in the Galla. Could they be the great non-Christian people who lived in a still unknown part of Africa to the south of Ethiopia? If so, could the Galla with their Oromo language be the key which would open the door to this vast area to the south? In Ankobar there lived Shoa as well as Galla. Krapf began a little school for them also, perhaps mainly in order to learn the language himself. In 1839 he published what, in a long Latin title, he called a *tentamen imbecillum*, a 'stupid' draft translation, of John's Gospel into Galla. On the title page he also gave full credit to a Galla helper named Birkius. Krapf was a well trained man, but he knew his limitations and that of this first published effort in translation. He also knew that a missionary never does his translation work alone, but depends heavily on mother-tongue auxiliary translators. After John, Krapf translated Luke, Matthew, Mark and the Acts of the Apostles, and also Genesis into Oromo, the language of the Galla.

A British trading delegation came to talk with the Shoa king. Krapf acted as interpreter and adviser to Sahela Selassie and was given a silver sword in payment. At the end of 1841, Krapf decided to make a journey to Cairo. He wanted to visit Gondar to see what could be done with the new *aboena* or head of the Ethiopian churc; and also

Adowa to explore the possibility of making a new start among the Tigre people. He wanted to get Bibles in Malta and what is more he wanted to get married. Laden with presents from King Sahela Selassie, he set out on his travels in March 1842. Months later he reached the coast, having been robbed of all he had with him. Back in Cairo he married the Swiss Rosina Dietrich. Together they returned to Ethiopia with a consignment of Bibles and New Testaments. At the port of Seila they heard that they were forbidden to return to Ankobar. Orthodox priests had worked on King Sahela Selassie to make him forbid entry to the missionaries, because their pupils, basing themselves on the Bible, were criticizing the priests too sharply. Moreover the king saw greater political advantage to be gained from the French than from this German from Britain. Ludwig Krapf then proposed to take a rest from Ethiopia and to turn missionary efforts towards the Galla through whom both Ethiopia and the unknown south could be penetrated. The CMS refused. It was decided to try work among the Tigre among whom at least he could distribute his Bibles and New Testaments. He managed to bring the Bibles to the Tigre. He also managed to recover a number of old Amharic and Ge'ez manuscripts which he had left in Adowa. But he did not succeed in establishing a permanent mission in Adowa. Once again on his way to the coast he encountered bands of robbers. On the way, somewhere in the bush, Rosina's first child was born prematurely. Krapf baptized her Eneba, which means 'Tear'. The baby died a few hours later. Ludwig and Rosina buried their Tear under a pile of stones.

In 1842 Ludwig Krapf was given an honorary doctorate from the University of Tübingen in Germany for his research into the ancient Ethiopic manuscripts he had collected. He travelled to Aden in an attempt to reach Galla from the south. Much later he was to be once more connected with work in and for Ethiopia.

Two months later, in a leaky Arab ship, the Krapfs came to Zanzibar, the headquarters of Said Said, the Arab Sultan of Muscat. On the way they had been able to see in various ports how the slave trade, though officially abolished, was still flourishing in secret. They also gathered much information about the unknown peoples in the interior.

The British and American consuls of Zanzibar pressed Krapf to begin work on the island among freed slaves. But Krapf wanted to go to the mainland, to the Galla. The sultan agreed and even wrote a letter of recommendation stating:

'This letter comes from Sultan Said Said with greetings to all our subjects, friends and governors. This letter is written to commend Dr Krapf . . . a good man who wishes to convert the world to God. Receive him well and render him every assistance.'

Krapf went to Pemba, and settled a few months later in Mombasa on the coast of what is now Kenya. He began with great energy to study Swahili without however realizing that this was the trade language of many millions of people. He also learned the coastal language, Nyika. Arab sheikhs and Wanyika chiefs helped him. But Ludwig and Rosina, who was pregnant again, caught malaria. On 5 July 1844 Rosina died. Krapf was too ill to attend her funeral. Ten days later the baby died. Krapf himself recovered. Was hard work his remedy for sorrow? By October 1844 he had completed not only a Swahili grammar and dictionary, but also the New Testament and Genesis. In 1850 these books were printed in Tübingen.

Meanwhile Krapf had made fresh and ambitious plans. He had given up the Galla project; now he wanted a 'chain' of mission stations right across Africa. Mombasa on the east coast had to be linked with Crowther's work on the west coast. In this way the heart of Africa could be reached with the gospel and the advance of Islam halted. Fourah Bay College in Sierra Leone, together with Europe, would supply the manpower.

Missionary circles in Europe reacted enthusiastically and in 1846 the first link in the chain was forged. Johannes Rebmann, a new colleague from Württemberg, settled 40 km from the coast at Rabai-Mpya among the Wanyika. Krapf, together with Rebmann, set to work once more with African languages. Rebmann revised Krapf's Swahili translations, while Krapf translated John, Luke, Romans and Ephesians into Nyika, the language of the Wanyika. Luke, the Heidelberg Catechism and a reading book in Nyika were printed in Bombay in 1848. Krapf and Rebmann travelled alternately into the interior to prepare the 'chain' of mission stations. They came in contact with 'republican' peoples who chose their own chiefs and 'monarchical' peoples with hereditary kings.

They were the first Europeans to see the snow-capped peaks of Mount Kilimanjaro and Mount Kenya. European experts refused to believe their reports. There could not be everlasting snow so near to the equator. As if men from southern Germany were unable to recognize snow when they saw it!

An attempt in 1850 to set up a station in Kambaland, as the second link in the chain, was a fiasco. Krapf lost his porters, his money and his goods, had to travel by night and hide by day and reached the coast more dead than alive. Powerless chiefs, tyrannical kings and scheming Arab slave traders made further stations in the interior impossible. Moreover, the new men whom the CMS sent out either died in a few months, returned home ill or did not dare to travel. Krapf himself had to return to Europe for reasons of health, returning to East Africa at the end of 1854. He wanted to build another 'chain' of mission stations in Egypt, Sudan and Ethiopia: the Apostles' Road, a series of twelve mission stations running from Cairo to Gondar in Abyssinia and staffed by craftsmen. A Galla girl played a part in developing these plans. She had been taken back to Europe by a German nobleman and baptized as Pauline Fatme. She came in contact with Christian Friedrich Spittler, one of the founders of the Basel Mission. On her deathbed, at the age of twenty, she vowed that the gospel should be brought to the Galla.

In Gondar Krapf saw that Ethiopia was changing from a divided to a united kingdom. One of the regional princes had conquered almost the whole country. This emperor, Theodorus, approved of Krapf's crafts-men on condition that they included a gunsmith and an architect. But Krapf could not go far south, because the emperor was still at war with the Galla. Krapf's return journey down the Nile was difficult and dangerous and in 1855 he returned ill to Germany. He went to live at Kornthal in Württemberg, optimistic about the 'chain' which he still hoped would be established between East and West Africa; optimistic too about the Apostles Road from north to south. Four stations were built on the Apostles' Road. Craftsmen went out to help Emperor Theodorus to build roads, bridges and houses. Three shipments of Bibles and New Testaments reached Ethiopia. Krapf helped to train technicians in Basel. He began work once more on a Galla New Testament, since Ethiopia was open again. Yet everything went wrong. Emperor Theodorus became a complete tyrant; in the end he arrested all Europeans. A British expeditionary force from India came to free them. In 1868 the emperor committed suicide.

As for Kenya, in 1874 British missionaries found Rebmann half-blind in Rabai-Mpya. He had remained there for twenty-nine years without leave and still the next station in the 'chain' to West Africa had not been built. Finally, Rebmann also settled in Kornthal.

Until his death Krapf remained active. In 1866 he helped the Ethiopian Debtera Matteos prepare the four Gospels in Tigre for the press. He worked on editions of the Bible in Amharic and Ge'ez. In 1870 he prepared a Galla Luke with the help of a Galla called Roof and an Ethiopian called Debtera Sanab. In 1872 Genesis was pub-lished in Galla.

Later the work of Krapf and Rebmann in Swahili proved not to be usable, because it was the Swahili of the Arabs and not that of the Africans.

Dr Johann Ludwig Krapf was one of the first linguists and mission-ary strategists in Africa. He was also a devoted Swabian from Württemberg with weak health but immense endurance.

17

Buffers on the Frontier

During the Napoleonic era, the establishment of the Dutch United East India Company on the southern point of Africa passed into British hands.

The Calvinist farmers over there admitted their house servants and slaves to their family prayers. Some of the mixed population which had arisen from the meeting of Dutch, negroes, Javanese and Hottentots became members of the Boer churches. But the British went further. Their missionary societies came to the Cape to bring the gospel to Hottentots and Bushmen and also to the Bantu peoples who were advancing steadily to the south. British colonists came to settle in large numbers, especially in Natal. They founded the town of Durban there in 1824. Many Germans also came to the colony. In contrast with the British, they joined the Dutch Boer community and later assimilated to them.

But the Dutch Boers were fundamentally opposed to the liberal attitude of the British administrators and missionaries towards the African population. In the end, they loaded their ox-wagons and founded to the north their own Boer republics of Transvaal and the Orange Free State (see also chapter 34).

In this situation mission meant, geographically speaking, working in the area between the northward-moving European Boers and colonists from the Cape on the one hand, and the Bantu kingdoms expanding to the south on the other. The missionaries regularly became the buffer between these groups, while African leaders tried to use them as support against the invading Boers (see also chapter 18).

Dr Johannes Theodorus Van der Kemp, the Dutch secretary of the London Missionary Society, married in Cape Town a slave woman from Madagascar. Following his example a great number of single missionaries married local women so that their own lives could build a bridge between the races.

At the end of the nineteenth century English, Scottish, American, Finnish and French missionaries were at work from the Cape to

Northern and Southern Rhodesia. One of the Scots from South
Africa, David Livingstone, was the great explorer of Africa. He was
the first to travel right across the continent. Back in Scotland he
persuaded his Presbyterian church to start work in Nyasaland in order
to set up a Christian barrier against the Arab slave trade. When, at the
end of the nineteenth century, Nyasaland became British, a Scottish
cathedral was already standing in a town named Blantyre, after
Livingstone's birthplace.

Livingstone had maintained that the Christianity brought to Africa
must be a message of salvation and liberation, but linked with
commerce as an independent source of income for Africans. In
accordance with these principles, the Scottish mission in Nyasaland
both preached the gospel and set up a commercial development
company. In 1882, a South African church in Spelonken, which had
grown out of a French-Swiss mission, sent a missionary to the Tsonga
in Mozambique. He was Yosefa Mhalamhala, himself a Tsonga
refugee, who had come to know the gospel in the Transvaal. Thus
there arose in the south a purely African church which later became to
a certain extent Europeanized when Swiss missionaries came to help
it. Yet the gospel had a great impact; in 1886, in Rikatla, later an
important centre of the Presbyterian church, there was a great revival
movement.

The Catholic mission in South Africa began in 1851.

When, in the 1870s, diamonds and later gold were discovered,
European adventurers flooded in and new conflicts of interests caused
acute conflict both between Boers and British and also between black
and white. At the end of this period Cecil Rhodes was active with the
Africa Company in Rhodesia. The mission there translated the first
gospels in Ndebele, the language of the Matabele warriors of Rhodesia.

In 1812 an auxiliary committee of the BFBS was set up on the island
of St Helena. This committee gave a New Testament to the exiled
Napoleon Bonaparte.

As early as 1806, the first English New Testaments were sent to the
British garrison in Cape Town. Following an appeal in 1809 by the
missionary C.I. Latrobe to both the BFBS and the Netherlands Bible
Society, in 1810 Dutch Bibles and New Testaments were sent to the
Cape for the Dutch-speaking Hottentot Moravian churches. At first
the supply was hopelessly inadequate. From 1812 attention was paid to
the urgent need of Dutch Bibles for the colonists. In 1813 a British
missionary set up a 'Bible and School Committee' to combine
education for the poor with Bible distribution. This committee
obtained Bibles from the BFBS. In 1818, under the influence of the
Boer minister C. Fleck, the South African Bible Union was founded to
distribute Bibles among whites living in remote areas. It worked both
with the Netherlands Bible Society and with the BFBS. The first

shipment of Bibles was sent from Amsterdam in a ship called *The Three Brothers*, which was smashed on the rocks of Tafelbaai. Between 1818 and 1868 this Society distributed 52,000 Bibles and New Testaments among whites, coloureds and Hottentots. The Dutch Reformed Church publishing house grew out of this South African Bible Union. When in 1820 an auxiliary committee of the BFBS was set up in Cape Town, the South African Bible Union continued to exist for three reasons:

- Some saw no need for a Bible Society auxiliary committee.
- The South African Bible Union distributed Bibles with notes, as in the margin of the Dutch States-General Version; the BFBS did not.
- The South African Bible Union distributed Christian literature as well as the Bible; the BFBS did not.

Naval officers such as Sir Jahleen Brenton, and missionaries such as Dr John Philip, Van der Kemp's successor at the LMS, played an important part in the establishment of the South African auxiliary committee. From 1823 the British tried to involve Boer ministers in the Bible Society. In the 1840s, the chairman of the South African Bible Union was also a member of the auxiliary committee.

The Boers urgently needed Bibles for themselves and their house servants, but they did not think it necessary to distribute scriptures more widely to Hottentots and 'Bantu peoples'; and the slave-owners opposed Bible distribution among Africans.

The Cape was also affected by the struggle against slavery in Britain. In 1834, slaves in the Cape Colony were set free. There was a campaign to give each of them a Bible. They were given Dutch Bibles, but many proved unable to read them, so Bible distribution in schools was stressed. In 1836 Dr Philip took an African Christian and a Hottentot Christian to London. Their witness produced a deep impression.

In 1846 T.J. Bourne was sent out to South Africa as the BFBS agent. He took with him 20,000 Bibles and New Testaments in English and Dutch. He set up an organization and made long journeys on horseback. By 1868 there were eighteen branches. Bourne discussed with the Boers the use of indigenous languages. The Boers were basically against education of the 'natives', but their interest in the Bible Society slowly grew. By 1877 there was an official Bible Society committee in the Dutch Reformed Church of the Orange Free State. In the same year Dr Charles Hole took over as agent.

When the diamond rush began, Bible Society colporteurs went too with the Word. Translations were made in African languages and Gospels were brought from India for the coolies in Natal. In 1882 the cheap shilling Bible also appeared in Dutch. By 1880 the Bible Society had 47 branches and many auxiliary committees. A quarter of a million books had been distributed and £46,000 raised locally.

The BFBS and the National Bible Society of Scotland (NBSS) made great efforts to distribute Bibles among British soldiers fighting in the so-called Kaffir Wars.

The translations in southern Africa were made by British and German Protestant missionaries serving British and later also German missions. The French were busy in Basutoland and the Americans amongst the Zulu. In Nyasaland Scottish translators worked and later Finnish Lutherans came to South-West Africa. Missions sought help for printing their translations from the Bible societies in their own countries with which they already had relations.

Up to 1885 the picture was as follows:

Setswana:
Language of the Bechuana in the western Transvaal, the northern Cape Province and Bechuanaland.

1830	First Gospel.
1834	BFBS gives £50 sterling for printing Luke and in 1835 250 reams of paper for the New Testament, published in 1840.
1840	Bunyan's Pilgrim's Progress translated and printed.
1857	Bible printed at the Kuruman mission station. The BFBS helps with paper and binding materials.
1863–64	Revised New Testament. Great demand.
1869	An interchurch working group makes a revised translation of the Bible.

Nama:

1815	Rev. C. Albrecht begins work on Matthew.
1825	J.H. Schmelin of the CMS translates the four Gospels; they are printed in Cape Town in 1832 with BFBS support.
1863	G. Krönlein of the Rhenish Mission completes New Testament; published in 1866.
1881	The complete Bible is translated, but not published because the Namaqua despise their own language and do not want to read.
1882	Psalms reprinted.

Xhosa:
The Rev. William B. Boyce reduces the language to writing and prepares a grammar. From 1833 Wesleyan missionaries translate the Gospels and a few Old Testament books.

1846	New Testament printed. BFBS contributes 50 reams of paper.
1853	New Testament revised.
1859	First translation of the Old Testament published with BFBS help.

1866   Translation of the New Testament by Rev. J.W. Appleyard published. The Appleyard version is so widely criticized that the American Presbyterian missionaries, together with those of the Free Church of Scotland and the LMS, decide at a conference at Lovedale to ask the NBSS to make a better translation. The Scots consult the BFBS and after much pressure and argument London agrees to support a revision made by members of six missions working in Xhosa. Among them is the Xhosa minister, the Rev. Tiyo Soga. Typically for the picture at home even Bible Societies' publications often refer to the Xhosa language as kaffir, an Arab pejorative term for heathen.

1872   The revision committee begins its work.

Sesotho:

Missionaries of the Paris Missionary Society begin evangelism and translation.

1837   Th. Arbousset and E. Casalis send Matthew and other parts of the New Testament to Paris. They are published in 1839.

1840   The French and Foreign Bible Society prints a selection. 50 chapters of the New and Old Testaments, translated by Arbousset, printed in Moriah, Basutoland.

1848   Psalms.

1849   Four Gospels.

1855   New Testament.

1878   Bible printed in Moriah. Tremendous interest.

Zulu:

First grammar made by a Norwegian, the Rev. H.P.S. Schroeder; first attempts at translation by British naval officers.

1846   Selections from Genesis and the Gospels published by the American Newton Adams.

1865   New Testament prepared by German missionaries.

1883   Bible published by the American Bible Society. Great demand.

Herero:

1737   Pioneer work by George Schmidt. Baptizes a woman named Helen, who gives him a Dutch New Testament published in 1694.

1875   Rhenish missionaries publish Psalms.

1879   New Testament printed in Germany.

Between 1830 and 1885, translation work was already begun in Setswana; in Ndebele, the language of the Matabele of Rhodesia; in Yao for Nyasaland and Mozambique, and in one dialect of Chinyanja, also in Nyasaland. In Nyasaland translations, the NBSS helped at the request of Scottish missionaries.

18

Robert Moffat the Scot

Robert Moffat was born in 1795. He went to evening school and worked as a gardener. He was converted in a Methodist revival meeting; the Letter to the Romans had much to do with this. As a converted evangelical, Moffat remained a Scottish Presbyterian. Then he went in Warrington to a meeting of the (Congregational) London Missionary Society (LMS) and from that night he knew he had to be a missionary. He had the good fortune to be taken on as a gardener by an LMS missionary named Roby. Despite his limited education he was finally accepted as a missionary worker. After very modest training he sailed for South Africa. In 1817 he arrived at Cape Town, aged 23.

In 1795, during the Napoleonic wars, the British had conquered the Dutch Cape.

The Boers, Dutch by descent, mingled with French Huguenots and later Germans, had in the eighteenth century at first allowed the Moravians to undertake a mission to the African population, but later they made it impossible for them to continue.

Since the arrival of the Dutch in Cape Province, the Hottentots and Bushmen, the original inhabitants of the area, had been driven back. They had also become familiar with a few doubtful symbols of western civilization, such as alcohol, firearms, prostitution and venereal diseases; they were powerless against them. In the eyes of the whites they had become inferior and troublesome neighbours. The Boers had brought Malaysian and African slaves to the Cape as house servants and workers.

Despite their Calvinistic principles, the Boers, enthusiastically seconded by the seamen, had produced a pretty large group of halfbloods, or coloureds. In church councils it had been long discussed whether negro slaves could become Christians; for baptized people were supposed to be set free and that could not be allowed to happen. The Boers found the Hottentots and Bushmen unreliable. You had to keep them at a distance; it did not pay to preach the gospel to them.

The Bantu peoples from the north began in this period to press further and further south. This had to do with the establishment, in what is now Zimbabwe, of expanding African kingdoms. On the other side, more and more European emigrants came to the Cape and the land hunger of the Boers drove them northwards. Missionary work among the African population thus meant working in the area where Europeans and Africans were in collision, with the Bushmen and Hottentots as already defeated groups between them.

After Napoleon the Cape remained British. The British authorities took a more positive line both on the Hottentots and Bushmen and also on the 'Kaffirs', as the Bantus were called. The Moravians returned and the directors of the London Missionary Society won particular influence. The first director of the LMS in South Africa, the Dutch medical doctor J.Th. Van der Kemp, who came to Cape Town in 1799, made his intentions very clear by marrying a Malagasy woman. His successor, Dr John Philip, also strove for open, close and friendly relationships with Hottentots, Bushmen and 'Kaffirs' alike.

Dr Philip appointed Robert Moffat to mission work among the Naquama, a Hottentot people who lived to the north and south of the Orange River. The British governor refused to let Moffat travel there because he thought the area was unsafe. So the young missionary used his waiting time in Cape Town to learn Dutch, the colony's main language. In 1818 he was able to leave with his ox-wagon and after a difficult journey came to the kraal of Jager Afrikaner on the far side of the Orange River. Jager Afrikaner, a coloured man, was the head of the Naquama. He was feared throughout the Cape for his terrible raiding expeditions on the farms of the Boers. A few years earlier he had authorized a missionary called J.L.H. Ebner to evangelize the Naquama. The reason was not Jager Afrikaner's desire to save his own soul. It was rather that, under constant threat from the Bantu peoples in the north, he saw the presence of a European missionary as a shield at his back. Ebner had baptized Jager Afrikaner and two of his sons.

Robert Moffat took over the work and through his direct Scottish approach he soon won Jager Afrikaner's trust. Afrikaner's political choice of Christianity grew into sincere Christian conviction.

When in 1819 Moffat went to Cape Town to meet his Scottish bride, Jager Afrikaner went with him. The former robber of the Europeans found in the gospel the courage to speak with his former enemies. His task was to ask for help from the British so that his Naquama would not in the near future be crushed in the coming collision between Europeans and Africans. Jager Afrikaner's arrival in Cape Town was a sensation. He was received in the British governor's palace where the governor gave him a handsome *ossewa*.

When Moffat had first gone to Africa, the parents of his fiancée Mary Smith had not allowed her to go with him. Now he was meeting her off the boat to be married in Cape Town. The LMS officers decided not to allow Moffat to return to the Naquama, but to send him to the Bechuana. Jager Afrikaner went back to his kraal alone taking the handsome *ossewa* with him.

The Bechuana were a people who lived in a poor, barren area in the middle of southern Africa. Their country is now called Botswana. Robert and Mary Moffat were to spend their next 46 years living and working with and for these Bechuana. Once more the governor, fearing political implications in the frontier territory, refused to issue a travel permit. They were able to leave only in 1820. Their destination was New Lattakoo, an LMS mission station founded a couple of years earlier. Their first years there were dreadful. The mission station was badly sited and even Robert Moffat the gardener saw little chance of setting up an irrigation system and thereby obtaining land on which something would grow. The Bechuana stole everything in and around the mission house and the chief did nothing to stop them. They were not in the least interested in the gospel.

While on a journey, Moffat heard that the Mantatee were preparing to attack the Bechuana. Much further north, the great Zulu King Chaka had attacked Umsiligazi's Matabele. The Matabele were fleeing to the south before Chaka when they encountered the southern Bechuana and a large group of refugees called the Mantatee were occupying land in between. Moffat went straight back to Lattakoo to warn the chief. He convinced him that the Bechuana could not repel the Mantatee without help. Moffat himself went to get help from the Hottentots in Griquatown. Later, when both sides were preparing for battle, Moffat risked his life in an attempt to prevent fighting. He failed. The Bechuana and the Hottentots won. Afterwards, when Moffat saw how 'his' Bechuana finished off all the enemy wounded, women and children, he went back to Mary at Lattakoo, filled with loathing.

The part Moffat had played in this conflict earned him the trust of the chiefs and the goodwill of the Bechuana people. He convinced the local chief to move the kraal nearer to the River Kuruman. There, not only did Moffat's mission station become a flourishing garden, but he also taught the Bechuana how to enlarge and improve their farm land by setting up an irrigation system. Yet still they did not receive the gospel. Then, one morning, Mary said: 'How will you reach people with the gospel without speaking the language of the Bechuana?' With the Hottentots in Jager Afrikaner's kraal Moffat had spoken Dutch and the Naquama understood it. But the Bechuana scarcely understood the language of the Boers.

So Moffat started to learn Sechuana, the language of the Bechuana. He travelled all over the countryside for two months collecting information about the language.

By 1825 Moffat was able to preach in Sechuana. In the same year he completed a reading book. A school was opened and he began to translate Christian hymns into Sechuana.

The turning-point came in 1829. All at once a revival movement began and the first Bechuana were baptized. A church was built and by 1834 there were about 350 churchgoers. Meanwhile Moffat had begun to translate the Bible into Sechuana. In 1830 he sent his manuscript of Luke to Cape Town. It was printed by the state press on paper given by the BFBS. But the typesetters had problems with the strange Sechuana language. Moffat went to help them. The problems were solved and in addition Moffat learned about printing. He obtained a press from the mission and carried it on his own ox-wagon to Kuruman. From then on he translated, wrote and printed there himself. In 1833 appeared the first Bible selections 'printed in Kuruman'.

As he worked Moffat discovered how little he knew. He learned German and Greek. He sent for Bible commentaries from England. He realized how little Sechuana he knew. His spelling of the language was not good and he had underestimated its grammatical difficulties. Moffat studied hard and though self-taught became an excellent Bible translator. His methods were very modern: he issued each book he finished in Kuruman in a trial edition. By 1840 the whole New Testament had been completed and issued in trial editions.

His printing press in Kuruman was not able to bind such a thick book, so Moffat went to Cape Town to have the New Testament printed there. But even the state press could not do the job, so Moffat took the boat for England with his manuscript. The Bible Society helped and in 1842 the first 500 copies of the New Testament and Psalms were despatched. A new missionary took the parcels in his luggage. This was David Livingstone who later became Moffat's son-in-law. In 1843 Moffat himself returned to Kuruman with another 2000 copies. The book made a great impression and the first printings were soon exhausted. Moffat next translated and printed Bunyan's *Pilgrim's Progress*, followed by the books of the Old Testament. Each book, once more, was issued in a trial edition in Kuruman, after which the text was revised again.

Moffat translated the Old Testament in the midst of all kinds of other work. Work in the gardens for himself and in the Bechuanas' gardens, but also tasks arising from a few long journeys he made to the Matabele in the north. The LMS was beginning new work there and Moffat's authority was invoked to persuade the Matabele chiefs to allow missionaries to come among them. The Bechuana themselves lived in a very quiet political situation because their land was too barren for the white Boers and for any African invaders; but Moffat nevertheless played his part in this difficult frontier area between black and white.

This all meant delay in his Bible translation work. It was not until 1857 that he completed the first manuscript of the complete Bible. Years more passed in revision and correction before the Old Testament was first printed separately. In 1872 the Bible Society printed the first one-volume edition of the Sechuana Bible.

Two years earlier Robert and Mary Moffat had returned to England. In biographies of Moffat, some of which are sheer hagiography, one may nevertheless read between the lines that he had lived and worked for 46 years among the Bechuana as a pure Scottish Calvinistic evangelical. He never went deeply into the Bechuana's way of thinking. He preached a straight gospel of sin and grace, not as a fellow human being standing alongside the Bechuana, but rather as a good father who knew what was best for his children. He never became a Greek to the Greeks, that is, a Bechuana to the Bechuana. His Bible translation had great influence on the life of the Bechuana and in their church. For this ex-gardener made one of the best translations of the Bible ever produced in Africa. He knew what he was working for and 'his' Bechuana called the *Bible Molowe ao Jehova*, 'the Mouth of God'.

19

Strategy before 1885

In this period the main feature of Protestant missions was pietism, the gospel of Jesus as redeemer from sin and death. This message was brought by loving fathers from Europe and America to ignorant children. Their purpose was to redeem heathen idolaters living in darkness.

In southern Africa, Ethiopia, Uganda and Madagascar, Christianity was introduced through the action of African rulers. Sometimes this meant that the church grew rapidly with the people following the ruler's example. Often Protestant and Catholic missionaries also had to play a part in the rulers' political games.

In West Africa the key figures in pioneer evangelism were freed American and African slaves.

In East Africa the missions first obtained a response when they offered a new life to slaves in coastal villages who could not find their way back to their people in the interior.

Except for South Africa, Ethiopia, Uganda and Madagascar, missionary work began among coastal peoples whom the slave traders had misused for centuries as go-betweens between the inland 'slave reservoir' and the slave-ships on the coast. They had adopted all the bad things from Europe: firearms, liquor, venereal diseases and cheating. The first converts often included people who for some reason were not duly recognized in their own societies. The renewing power of the gospel proved so great that these 'dregs of society' produced the first evangelists for the interior. Missionaries often died young, so as soon as possible they began to give basic training to local people who could take the gospel further. The missionaries had an almost romantic nostalgia for the interior: behind the coastal peoples, they thought, there must live purely natural peoples uncontaminated by Europeans. Among these pure peoples (the philosopher Rousseau's 'noble savages'), it must be possible to re-establish a pure church, such as no longer existed in Europe. In any case up to the present day the simple village evangelists have been the people who brought the gospel to the ends of the gigantic African continent.

In all this the Bible was basic. The missionaries knew that disease and the climate could make their time short so they wanted to leave something permanent behind them, the Word of God. They therefore worked hard at learning African languages and reducing them to writing. They began by translating the Gospels, followed as soon as possible by the Psalms and the narrative books of the Old Testament, for Africans were found to be great story-tellers themselves. With the exception of some Germans, the missionaries were in general badly trained. However, some of them studying by themselves achieved impressive results in language study and Bible translation. Perhaps because of their limited education or else because the Enlightenment had given them a feeling of superiority, the missionaries had very little interest in African thinking. It is remarkable how little African religions were studied. They were seen as products of heathen blindness.

Modern colonialism with the resources it brought lay still in the future so the missionaries had to live like the Africans themselves. Since there was as yet no remedy for tropical diseases, the missionaries and their families died as easily as the Africans and at the same early age. The result of this was a deep human bond between the two groups. People in Africa still speak with great respect about these pioneers.

Living so close to Africans led the missionaries into strong social and political involvement. They were the first Europeans to show solidarity with the African population. They fought slavery and the crimes of white traders. They fought for peaceful co-existence between the white Boers and Africans in southern Africa. They fought against child sacrifices and against the tyranny of the traditional priests in Madagascar and Cameroon. They fought against the arbitrary misuse of power by some African rulers.

The following important strategic factors should be mentioned:

- The interest of European Christians in starting a revival among the ancient churches of Egypt and Ethiopia. The story of Prester John remained a challenge.
- The freed slaves in the Americas and on the west coast who themselves wanted to go and evangelize their home countries. Also the freed slaves on the east coast, as people needing to be evangelized.
- The conquest of the Cape by the British in the Napoleonic period directing the missionary impulse of the British evangelical revival to take the gospel beyond the Calvinism of the Boers to the indigenous population.
- The influence of great personalities and their stories on Christian public opinion in Europe:
  Pauline Fatme, the Galla girl in Switzerland (see chapter 16).

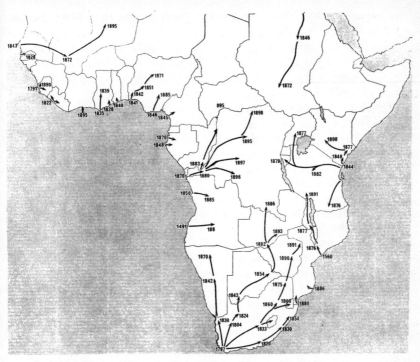

Missionary penetration in Africa before 1900.

Livingstone's report after his journey across Africa (see chapter 15).
The story Stanley told to the king of Uganda (see chapter 15).
Samuel Crowther's visit to England (see chapter 12).

- The effect of these stories was not only the setting up of missionary work, but also government intervention.
  Examples:
  (1) The British Niger Expedition – a government undertaking, publicized as widely as the first man in the moon in our generation (see chapter 11).
  (2) Campaigns against the slave trade, first in West and then in East Africa (see chapter 32).
  (3) The start of modern colonialism at the end of this period (see chapter 30).
- The constant link between mission and teaching on the one hand and improvement of agriculture and trade on the other.
  Examples:
  (1) In Ethiopia, the craftsmen of the Apostles' Road (see chapter 14).
  (2) In East Africa, the aim of total life improvement of the former slave villages, while the Scots in Nyasaland tried to raise the

people by coupling mission with economic activities (see chapters 14 and 17).

(3) In West Africa the motto of the Niger Expedition was 'the Bible and the Plough'. The Basel Mission also linked preaching with the stimulation of the economy through trade (see chapter 11).

(4) Alfred Saker in Cameroon both translated the Bible and founded the first craft school (see chapter 13).

• The fantastic plans of the pioneers, which seized the imagination of Europe.
  Examples:
  Building the Apostles' Road, with its twelve mission stations from Cairo to Gondar, as a channel of communication for revival and development in the ancient churches of Egypt, Sudan and Ethiopia (see chapter 14).
  Krapf's dream of founding a 'chain' of mission stations right across Africa from Kenya to Nigeria.

• The British missionary statesman Henry Venn's formulation of the aim of mission as the creation of self-governing, self-supporting and self-propagating churches. Venn's 'three selfs' were later adopted also by American missions. (In the colonial period, from about 1885, relations between Europeans and Africans changed with the result that the 'three selfs' were put on ice).

• Finally, it is striking how powerful was the appeal of the Bible in one's own language. In Europe, this idea bound together rich and poor, but also, and primarily, people from different churches, inspiring them to make great sacrifices together for Bible work. In Africa the idea of coming to know God for oneself in the Book and no longer depending on the traditional priest's knowledge and whims had a great impact.

20

Bible Translations first published by 1885

	First Book	First New Testament	First Bible
for the ancient churches:			
EGYPT			
Coptic (Bohairic)		1716	
Arabic	1516	1616	1671
ETHIOPIA			
Ge'ez	1513	1549	1918
Amharic	1824	1829	1840
modern languages:			
ETHIOPIA AND ERITREA			
Central Oromo (Galla)	1841		
Eastern Oromo	1870	1875	
Southern Oromo	1878		
Western Oromo		1893	1899
Tigrinya	1866	1909	1956
Bogos	1882		
Tigre	1889	1902	1988
Kara (Falasha)	1885		
EGYPT AND SUDAN			
Nubian (Fiadidja)	1860		
ALGERIA, MOROCCO AND TUNISIA			
Algerian Arabic	1872	1965	
Greater Kabyle	1885	1901	
Northern Shilha	1887		
Jewish Tunisian Arabic	1897		
West Africa:			
SIERRA LEONE			
Themne	1865	1868	
Mende	1867	1956	1959

Soso	1869	1885	

GAMBIA AND GUINEA-BISSAU

Mandinka	1837	1989	
Wolof: Gambia	1882		

SENEGAL

Wolof	1873	1988	

LIBERIA

Bullom	1816		
Grebo	1838	1989	
Bassa: Liberia	1844	1970	

GOLD COAST (GHANA)

Ga: Accra	1843	1859	1866
Twi-Akwapim	1859	1863	1871
Fante	1877	1896	1948

TOGO AND GOLD COAST (GHANA)

Ewe	1858	1877	1913

DAHOMEY (BENIN)

Gun	1886	1892	1923

NIGERIA

Yoruba	1850	1862	1884
Efik	1850	1862	1868
Hausa	1857	1880	1932
Igbo	1860	1900	1906
Nupe	1877	1915	1953

CAMEROON

Duala	1843	1861	1872
Subu	1848		

GABON

oMyene: Mpongwe	1850	1869	
Dikele (Kele)	1855		
Benga	1858	1871	

CONGO (including ZAIRE)

kiKongo: Fioti	1885	1891	1905
kiKongo: Cataract	1886		

SOUTH AFRICA, SOUTH-WEST AFRICA, BECHUANALAND (BOTSWANA), BASUTOLAND (LESOTHO)

seTswana (seTlhaping)	1830	1840	1857
Nama	1831	1866	1966
Xhosa	1833	1846	1966
seSotho (Southern Sotho)	1839	1855	1878
Zulu	1848	1865	1883

Herero	1875	1879	
seTswana: seRolong	1885	1894	

RHODESIA (ZIMBABWE, ZAMBIA)

Ndebele		1884	1978

NYASALAND (MALAWI)

chiNyanja: Western Nyanja	1884	1886	

MOZAMBIQUE

chiYao (Yao)	1880	1898	1920

East Africa:

KENYA

Duruma	1848		
kiKamba (Kamba)	1850	1920	1956
kiNyika Ribe (Nyika)	1878		

TANGANYIKA (TANZANIA)

chiKaguru (Kaguru)	1885		
chiGogo (Gogo)	1886	1899	1962

KENYA AND TANGANYIKA (TANZANIA)

Southern Swahili	1868	1879	1891
Central Swahili	1878	1909	1914

UGANDA

Luganda (Ganda)	1887	1893	1896

MADAGASCAR

Malagasy	1828	1830	1835

MAURITIUS

Mauritian Creole	1885		

21

European Africa

All the 1886 Berlin conference did formally was to recognize Leopold II's International Congo State, but the conference marked the start of the colonial carving-up of Africa.

Where there were well-organized states, there was resistance: among the Zulu in South Africa, the Matabele in Rhodesia and the Barotse in Basutoland; also among the Ashanti in the Gold Coast, Samory in what is now Mali, and by the King of Abomey in Dahomey. In the Sudan, before the British could set up a condominium to administer that huge country, they first had to kill the Mahdi, a kind of Muslim Messiah.

But there were also vulnerable peoples, which warmly welcomed the whites as their protectors. In some places completely artificial frontiers were drawn between colonies so that the same peoples found themselves living on both sides of a frontier. That happened, for example, to the Somali in Kenya, Somalia and Ethiopia and to the Moundang and the Massana in Cameroon and Chad. In other places there were risings at first because the colonists committed administrative blunders. This happened, for example, in German colonies such as Tanganyika and among the Bulu in South Cameroon; while the Germans crushed the Herero rising in South-West Africa with the only attempt at genocide, the destruction of an entire people, which Africa has ever known.

In certain places European countries bartered one territory for another: the Germans gave up their claims to Morocco in favour of the French, in exchange for a large area on the frontier between Cameroon and what is now the Central African Republic. On several occasions the British government was pressed by missionaries and by public opinion to take a territory under its protection. Such protectorates were set up in Uganda, Swaziland, Basutoland and Bechuanaland. For some years the British also recognized a so-called Charter Company, a firm with trading and administrative rights, as the coloniser. That happened in southern Nigeria, Kenya, Rhodesia and elsewhere. French occupation of Madagascar was a disaster because they came with their superior 'culture française', which left no room at all for respect for the Malagasy language, culture and state.

In southern Africa colonization meant the end of the struggle between the Bantu peoples pressing towards the south and the European colonists expanding towards the north. Opposition between the Boers in their own states of Transvaal and the Orange Free State and the British in the Cape, led to bloody conflict made worse by the discovery of gold and diamonds in the Transvaal. The Boer War (1899–1902) produced the first concentration camps in history: the British shut the Boer families up in them and treated them scandalously. The Boer War was especially bitter because it brought into conflict two nations, each of which was convinced that it had been given a special mission from God. The Boers lost the war and the British dominion of South Africa was the result.

Generally speaking, by about 1910 Africa had been divided up into colonies with the exception of Ethiopia (which much later, in 1939, was occupied by Mussolini's Italian Fascists) and Liberia (where the American Firestone Rubber Company formed a powerful state within a state).

This colonial situation had great consequences for Africa. Wars between the various African peoples were ended and further migrations prohibited. Where the colonist thought was in his interest he built up what Europe calls a modern infrastructure. He started by building ports, roads, and a number of railways; later also airfields. The telephone and the telegraph came to the large centres. This infrastructure made it possible for local petty officials and house servants and also for forced labourers, soldiers and traders to settle outside the area of their own people, for example where the colonist was setting up agriculture for export or mining. Ports such as Lagos grew into large cities; new centres such as Nairobi arose beside the railway lines, in mining areas such as Johannesburg, and later in the Copperbelt, around the Zambian copper mines and the mines of Katanga in Zaïre.

It is very significant that it was a new type of Europeans who appeared in Africa at this time. The African already knew the European slave traders and the Europeans who (especially on the west coast) sold alcoholic drink. He also knew the European missionaries. Now the European appeared as administrator, technician or expert; and the strange thing was that he was not just a European any more, but a Frenchman, an Englishman or a Belgian, a German or a Portuguese. In some territories, such as Algeria, Tunisia, Kenya, Rhodesia and the south, European immigrants also arrived. So French Equatorial Africa and British East Africa were created, but there was no concept of Africa as a whole, let alone practical links between the various colonies. Connections with the outside world always ran through the home country and Europe: Paris for the Senegalese,

London for the Nigerian, Brussels for the Congolese and Lisbon for the Mozambican.

The colonist of course imposed his own language as the official language. The various missions were asked to provide education according to curricula worked out by the colonist; these were often mere imitations of those in use at home. Whether the colonist tried to think in Christian terms or whether he was anti-clerical, the missions were mostly subsidized on pragmatic grounds to provide cheap education and training for the necessary lower grades of the administration. In the Belgian Congo and the Portuguese colonies, the Roman Catholic mission was even officially commissioned to set up the educational system. In those countries Protestant education was long subject to discrimination. In the British territories in East, Central and southern Africa both Protestant and Catholic missions were given land on condition that they used it for building educational institutions.

In the British colonies there was room for education in African languages, but the French prohibited this in their schools. It was allowed in church catechism classes. The Portuguese went one step further. In Angola they prohibited publication of Bibles or Bible portions in an African language; they allowed only diglot editions with the Portuguese text on one side and an African language text opposite. This rule applied in principle also in Mozambique, but less strictly.

It goes without saying that the colonial authorities were happiest with missions from their own country. Thus the British Baptists had to leave Cameroon when that country became German and the French in Madagascar tried to exclude all non-Catholic missions, since France was held to be a Catholic country. The Paris Missionary Society had to come to Madagascar to prove that there were also Protestants in France. Among the Portuguese, anti-Protestantism was fused with nationalism. The Belgians solved the problem by forcing all non-Belgian missionaries to apply for training in Belgium to teach them what Belgium was, how it was governed and what were the aims of Belgian colonial policy. In Germany there was even a great theological discussion about whether or not all missions in German colonies should be German; Gustav von Warneck was here the strongest critic of narrow nationalism. But the European national stamp on the various parts of Africa left the door open for missions from non-colonizing countries, such as Swedes and Norwegians, Danes and Finns, Swiss and especially Americans, also Dutch on the Catholic side, to work in Africa. The greatest 'supplier' of mission workers became the United States. At the peak of western missionary activity, 80% of all Protestant mission workers were Anglo-Saxons, and half were Americans. It goes without saying that the Anglo-American way of thinking and acting has set its mark on the whole Protestant missionary operation.

Among Roman Catholics, some missionary-minded popes in the nineteenth century organized or reorganized mission work in such a way that by about 1910 Catholicism had generally caught up with Protestantism in Africa. Together with the French, not only Belgians and Dutch, but also Canadians and Italians, made important contributions.

The new opportunities given in the colonial period for safe travel to new centres allowed Muslim traders to spread their faith further, but also allowed Methodist minor officials from Benin to go and work in Abidjan, taking their faith with them to Côte d'Ivoire. In the same way, miners working on the South African Rand who received Christianity there from Swiss missionaries took the gospel back home with them to Mozambique, where Swiss missionaries followed them.

There was a remarkable by-product in West Africa. Where once the slave-trading forts had formed centres on the coast, now, new ports sprang up around the houses and lands of the first missions. This happened, for example, in Abidjan, Kinshasa and Duala. Generally speaking, city churches were the places where Africans could meet one another and find community. There, far from home, they could sing and pray and talk with one another in their own language. In this way they took the pioneers' country churches with them into the new cities.

The opening of Africa by means of ports, roads and railways also made it easier for the missions to go and work in unevangelized areas. Among Protestants that happened mostly by means of missions born of the second great awakening, in 1857 in the United States. These were mostly faith missions; they went to work in areas further from the coast, behind the territories in which the missionary societies of the first wave were working. Interdenominational missionary work began in the Congo as early as 1878. The names of these missions spoke for themselves: Sudan Interior Mission, Sudan United Mission, Africa Inland Mission. Most of the pioneer missionaries had been individualists, but for the faith missions personal conversion was so central that their individualism was even more strongly marked. But in African society individual conversion is virtually impossible. There were many mass movements to Christianity and these caused great problems for the individualistic missionaries.

Moreover when missionaries went on leave and raised funds for their work, this was also done on an individual basis so that some mission stations were rich and others poor. The same thing happened in Catholic circles: some mission stations were well supplied because the priest in charge was an excellent fundraiser, while on other stations people lived very simply because their priests did not have that gift.

There was another side to Roman Catholic mission finance too. The orders gradually ceased to support their clergy so that they had to raise their own income. The result was that all missions developed industrial and agricultural activities through which they came to play not only a spiritual but also an important economic role in the country. In the Belgian Congo some Catholic missions even became large landowners through setting up what were called 'chapel farms'.

We have been using the expression 'mission station'. In West Africa the missionary's house was in most cases the place from which evangelism began; elsewhere the mission station was the centre of Christian work. For the sake of the health of the foreign missionaries, it was often built on a 'healthy hilltop'; ideally it consisted of a church, a school, a medical centre, a house for the missionary, and dwellings for the local evangelists, teachers and medical workers. In East Africa and the Belgian Congo some of these mission stations grew into whole villages because the first Christians there were people who had been made homeless by slavery or who for one reason or another had left their own villages to seek their salvation at the mission. In the Portuguese territories mission stations also developed into large centres, because, for example in Mozambique, Protestant education was allowed only on recognized mission stations.

The churches too recognized that they needed African leaders. Thus the first Protestant secondary schools were training colleges for teachers and also pastors. The Protestants generally moved forward step by step. That meant beginning with African evangelists, then choosing and training the best of these as pastors. Then came the ordained minister with theological school and later secondary school training. And finally, usually after the second world war, students were sent to pursue academic theological studies in Europe or the United States.

The Catholics did things differently. They too had village evangelists and teachers, but their priests had full training from the beginning in junior and senior seminaries. Many students dropped out during or at the end of junior seminary because of the requirement of celibacy. Few went on to the senior seminary and the development of African leadership was slower. But the priests who continued to the end had training at European level.

In the colonial period, however, the development of African church leadership was held back for a long time, since the missionaries adopted the colonists' view of Africans as inferiors, children not yet able to manage their own affairs. Although the missionaries lived closer to the Africans than did the colonists, the distance between missionaries and Africans was greater than in pre-colonial times. The missionary was able to live a more luxurious and comfortable European life than in the pioneering days. He also, just like the African, had to respect the rules of the colonial game. He no longer made his own rules; indeed he formed part of white power.

It is true, however, that missionaries often acted as the conscience of the colonial administration. They fought against domestic slavery and against the first imports of liquor by the Germans, British and Dutch, especially in West Africa. They defended the Africans' claims against European colonists. Since for Africans land is more than a place to build or grow crops on, but always also the place where the ancestors are buried and the spirits live, occupation of land by Europeans caused much ill feeling, which led much later to explosions such as the Mau Mau rising in Kenya.

Missionaries of all denominations also constantly opposed the practice of forced labour, first introduced by the Belgians, but later extended to Portuguese and French territories. A German colonial newspaper wrote that missions demoralized the blacks by having them sing and pray instead of working and by teaching them rights instead of duties. That is why the churches, and thus also the work of Bible translation and distribution, made enormous progress during these colonial years.

22

The European Way in North and East Africa

As early as 1886 there came from America a call for 'the evangelization of the whole world in this generation'. Under the influence of revival movements in the United States and Britain and the preaching of the well-known evangelist Dwight L. Moody, 760 students from twenty nations took up this cry in 1896 at a conference in Liverpool. At the first great international missionary conference held in Edinburgh in 1910 the mood was optimistic. 1200 representatives of missionary societies came together, including eighteen people from young churches. In view of the vastness of the task, Edinburgh advocated regional consultations. In Africa at that time the primary difference between missions was geographical and linguistic, since each new mission went further from the coast to work among another people. In 1879 74 societies were active in Africa and by 1914 there were 146. At Edinburgh 65 missions from Africa were represented: 22 British, 21 North American, 3 from South Africa and 19 from continental Europe (including 11 German). According to the regional reports before the conference, 4273 Protestant missionaries were at work on the African continent: the French territories and Mozambique were seriously under-staffed, while in Southern Rhodesia missions overlapped.

The Roman Catholics were divided between many orders and congregations, but they were held to a common policy by the leadership of De Propaganda Fide in Rome. By learning from the Protestants' mistakes, the Roman Catholic missions tried to catch up with their Protestant rivals. And they succeeded. There were two million Roman Catholics in Africa in 1900; five million in 1930; and 27 million in 1963. In 1924 the Conference of Catholic Missions in Africa was founded.

The great expansion of Catholic missions took place during a period in which the first medical answers were found to the great tropical diseases. The missionaries' life expectancy became higher than before and celibate Roman Catholic missionaries were able to live more cheaply then their Protestant colleagues. Everywhere the aim of Rome was to plant churches, while the Protestants went out to preach the gospel. 'We want to make Catholics; Christians will come later', ran a Roman Catholic slogan. The Roman Catholic Church also decided whether the Bible could be read and if so what parts of it; translating the church's catechism into African languages was more important than translating the Bible.

In contrast Protestants placed Christ, the Word become flesh, at the centre. Through the light of the Spirit the Word became clearly visible in him. That was why the Bible had to be translated and schools had to be built in which people could be taught to read the Bible. Hence the programme of Protestant educational work was more broadly based, trying to reach as many people as possible and underlining the importance of the African languages, while the Roman Catholics followed more closely the colonial educational requirements giving priority to a group educated in the colonial languages. Western education naturally appealed to all those Africans who wanted to climb the colonists' social ladder. Since many missions from many different churches went to work in Africa, this gave Protestantism a very varied appearance, while among the Roman Catholics there were great differences between the various missionary orders. Rome, however, kept tight organizational control over Africa by appointing right from the beginning apostolic vicars and later bishops. In 1912 Rome had in Africa 1508 missionary priests, 1218 brothers and 3251 sisters a total of 5977 missionaries. The Catholic missions were no longer dominated by the French; these had been joined by Italians and Belgians, Dutch and Germans, Americans and Canadians.

The Edinburgh Missionary Conference also pressed for regional co-operation. In 1921 on the global level a follow-up commission founded the International Missionary Council. In Africa regional co-operation with the Catholics was impossible. Even with high church Anglicans it was sometimes difficult, for example in Nyasaland, but missionary councils were nevertheless set up, for example, in Nyasaland, the Belgian Congo, South Africa, Eastern Nigeria, Tanganyika and Sierra Leone, while in Kenya the eight missions working among the Kikuyu went so far as to try to co-operate in founding a single church. In 1915 the Anglicans, at their Lambeth Conference, rejected this project. The Bible Societies which united Christians from many churches on the basis of the Bible without note or comment fitted in perfectly with this tendency towards co-operation in a great common task. The Rev. John H. Ritson, a General Secretary of the BFBS from 1899 to 1931, began at the London Bible House a kind of regular consultation with the secretaries of nineteen British missionary societies. This led to the foundation of the British Missionary Council. Since the Bible Society had to be careful about dogmatic differences, Ritson became ecumenically active in the British missionary world as a private person. But eleven BFBS staff members were on hand at the great Edinburgh Missionary Conference.

Yet when in 1919 the American Bible Society published a plan for setting up a world federation of Bible societies, Ritson wrote from the London Bible House a cool letter stating that 'the British & Foreign Bible Society does not come in the category of 'National' Bible Societies. From its very inception it has been a World Society . . . . The international character of our Society marks off its work from that of Societies which are limited to one country or a section of a country, and with which you are proposing we should federate.' The Americans went on trying to break through the British claims, but in vain: until the 1930s international relations between Bible Societies remained minimal.

In Africa the British and Foreign Bible Society (BFBS) naturally followed the lines of communication of the British Empire. At the beginning of the twentieth century its centres of activity were accordingly Port Said for Egypt and all the countries along the east coast served by the Suez Canal; Cape Town, and rapidly Johannesburg, in the south; and for West Africa Lagos which soon became much more important than Freetown in Sierra Leone.

Meanwhile the BFBS had developed a kind of organizational hierarchy among its agencies. This was typically British and therefore pragmatic but also a little colonial. At the bottom was the colporteur, a national, mostly with little education. His happiest experiences were recorded in London in the annual reports. Where there was a team of colporteurs, it was headed by a superintendent. The agency was directed by an agent, an Englishman in direct correspondence with the general secretaries in London. If part of his agency grew into a subagency, then there was a sub-agent responsible to the agent.

Through the El-Azaar Muslim study centre, through freedom of worship under British administration, but also through the Suez Canal, Egypt became a melting-pot for people from many parts of the world. The Bible Society agency was directed by the Rev. R.H. Weakley from 1884 to 1902 and afterwards by the Rev. A.A. Cooper. They also recruited fellow-workers and colporteurs, not only among Egyptian Christians, but also among Palestinians, Ethiopians and Armenians. When the American Bible Society also established itself in Cairo at the request of the American Presbyterian Mission, at first common discount agreements were arranged for editions of the Scriptures and later the work in the Nile Delta was divided. In distribution of Bibles and Bible portions, colporteurs and also Bible women played an important role. A separate operation was the growing colportage among seamen in Port Said. From 1885 a team worked there in many languages under the leadership of former naval petty officer W.H. Taylor. Between 1884 and 1904, 527,751 scriptures were distributed, including 222,066 by colporteurs. Almost thirty missions took 90,000 scriptures. The total included Bibles and other scriptures in 58 languages, but the proportion of Arabic scriptures grew during the twenty years from 34 to 64 per cent.

These seem large numbers, but the Egyptian agency in 1900 was serving Syria, Palestine, Cyprus, Malta, Arabia, the Sudan, Uganda, and the so-called East and Central African Subagency, with its office in Zanzibar. It is clear that in this whole area the function of Port Said was becoming more and more important. At the beginning of the twentieth century it was the largest coal bunker station in the world. In 1912 the headquarters of the Bible Society moved from Alexandria to a large five-storey Bible house in Port Said paid for from the BFBS Centenary Fund. On the upper floors were apartments which produced rent. Mr C.T. Hooper, an Englishman who spoke fluent Arabic, was agent from 1907 to 1925.

In Egypt itself Bible distribution remained low. The reasons for this were varied. At first the percentage of illiterates was very high. The Copts were not particularly co-operative: their priests confined themselves to their sacred church language. Some Muslims were interested in learning about Jesus, but to become Christian was not only a mortal sin, but it actually incurred the death penalty. It is not for nothing that the Presbyterians had the most success among Copts. Their church had 43,500 members by the end of the nineteenth century. They were almost all converted Copts. An important attraction of the American mission was its outstanding schools.

At the end of the nineteenth century, hostilities in the Sudan ceased and an Anglo-Egyptian administration was set up over a huge area. The north was occupied by Arabized Muslims and the south by followers of African traditional religions. In 1905 Hooper went on a long journey through the Sudan. Not until 1920, however, was a permanent worker appointed to Khartoum; three Egyptian colporteurs made regular distribution rounds. Translation work developed in southern Sudan only after the second world war.

Around the turn of the century efforts were made with varying success to enter Ethiopia from opposite Aden, where a sub-agency had been set up in 1886. Relations were successfully established with the aboena, the head of the Ethiopian Orthodox Church, and with Ras Makonnen, the father of the future Emperor Haile Selassie. New Testaments and Bible portions were supplied in Amharic and in Ge'ez, the church language. Meanwhile Swedes were working in Eritrea in Tigre and Tigrinya and with Onesimus Nesib's Bible translation in Northern Galla (Oromo), which he had printed himself. In 1913 Hooper made another long journey which took in Ethiopia and Eritrea. He obtained from the *aboena* of the Ethiopian Orthodox Church permission to set up a Bible depot in Addis Ababa and concluded agreements with the Swedish Mission in Eritrea for production and distribution in Tigre and Tigrinya.

An Armenian Christian called Athannasian travelled to Addis as Bible Society representative with a passport which he had made himself. He used donkeys to transport the Bibles for distribution in Ethiopia, and also Theresia thalers to pay for building a Bible house. He obtained customs exemption for the Bibles and a piece of land for a Bible house.

In Uganda the struggle for power between Muslims and Christians, Arabs and British, came to an end when first in 1890 the Arabs were defeated and then in 1894 the British made the country a protectorate. The CMS almost forced the British government to do this by raising £16,000 in ten days for a national fund to take Uganda into the British Empire. The British built a railway to the coast and also annexed the territory between Uganda and the coast. Thus Kenya was created. The persecutions of Christians in Uganda were long since past and the church grew at a tremendous pace. In 1896 there were 6905 baptisms and 50,000 'enquirers'. Remarkably the Buganda Christians appeared ready to carry the gospel to other peoples speaking other languages. The best-known evangelist was Apolo Kivebulaya. In 1898 the king of the Toro was baptized. Bishop A.R. Tucker, who worked in Uganda from 1893 to 1911, drew up in 1897 a plan for an autonomous Ugandan church in which Ugandans and missionaries would have to work together in spiritual equality. This was opposed by the mission workers who identified themselves more and more with the colonists and their British sense of superiority; Tucker's plan remained on ice for years.

In 1897 the Luganda Bible was completed. Ugandans had worked on it under Mackay's leadership: Henry Wright Duta, Sembera Mackay, Mika Semiotimba, together with Pilkington, a missionary and Greek scholar. In 1903 Uganda was given its own Bible committee, no longer under Egypt but working in direct relations with London. The number of Christians was increasing rapidly. In 1904 alone nine thousand people were baptized, including more than six thousand adults; the CMS paid great attention to Bible teaching. Between 1888 and 1913, 213,290 Scriptures were published in Luganda, including 16,000 Bibles and 6400 New Testaments. Translation work was begun in other Ugandan languages also. In order to facilitate Bible distribution, the CMS and the BFBS appointed a joint administrator in Kampala. As in many parts of Africa, Bibles and Scripture portions were supplied 'on missionary terms'. These obliged the mission in question to send to the Bible Society all the money it received in payment for Bibles and portions. Since only in Egypt and the Maghreb and in the new industrial centres of South Africa was it possible to work with colporteurs, and since also a very large part of the population of Africa south of the Sahara lived in small villages, the great majority of Bible distribution took place through mission stations and thus on missionary terms. This policy was related to the

BFBS principle that the Bible is a precious book for which a contribution must be made. Where there was no money payment in kind was requested. Bible Society publications contain many stories about the eggs, skins, fruit, animals and miscellaneous objects with which people paid for their Scriptures. African means of payment were also accepted, so the first shipments of 5300 Bibles to Uganda realized 6,800,000 cowries, that is, shells used as currency. In contrast with West Africa, where the first large churches sprang up on the coast, the first large Christian church in East Africa originated in the interior, beside the large lakes in Uganda. In the area between Uganda and the sea, in Kenya, where Nairobi now stands, the first Christians were baptized under a tree in 1908.

Since 1898 there had been a sub-agent of the Egyptian Bible house on the coast in Mombasa: the Rev. T.F. Shaw, who was followed by J.A. Bailey, based in Zanzibar, and then by E.M. Tinsley. Bailey is remembered for having raised Bible circulation in two years from 825 to 2400. One reason why the figures are so modest is that when a new edition of the Bible or portion appeared, it was usually sent en bloc to the mission working in the area where the language was spoken. Meanwhile translators in the field kept up regular correspondence with the translation department in London. This was complemented by personal contacts during furlough. In this setting, a Bible Society secretary was above all a collector of information about translations and new editions needed, a liaison officer between London and the field, and a coordinator of translation and distribution work. For example, it was discovered in London that two committees of two missions in Kenya were busy translating the Bible into Luo. The Bible Society brought them together.

In 1915 there was a reorganization which resulted in an East and Central African Agency separate from Egypt, including East Africa and Uganda. In 1916 the Rev. W.J.W. Roome became its secretary with his office theoretically in Kampala, though he spent little time there. He had worked as a missionary in Egypt and Sudan and he undertook long journeys throughout East Africa. In one of his books, he describes a 7000-mile journey, 2000 miles of it on a bicycle and 700 miles on foot, through Uganda, Kenya and Tanzania. He published all the information he gathered on the way and broke new ground by making a kind of linguistic survey of the whole area.

Madagascar and Mauritius, the large and the small island in the Indian Ocean, each has its own unique story.

In Madagascar the Bible in the national language played a great part in the steady growth of the churches. These, if they were Protestant, were of British and Norwegian origin, while the Catholic missionaries came from France. When France conquered this large island in 1896, the French colonial authorities were very 'lay', that is, anti-clerical, but they worked well with the Catholic missions. The Protestant Paris

Mission had to send missionaries to the island in order to make it clear
to the authorities that there were also Protestants in France and that
there should therefore be room in a French colony for Protestants
also. The Hova, who had been the leaders in the island and whose
kings had sought advice from the British missionaries on how to win
their place in the modern world, were pushed aside as a political
power; the consequences of this act extended well beyond the end of
the Second World War. By their commercial activities they maintained
their position as the most important group on the island. They also
played a large part in the Protestant churches and in further evangelism.

Bible distribution came under the responsibility of one Bible
committee in the north and another in the south, while in the capital,
Tananarive, the Hova set up their own Bible society, with the aim of
distributing and studying the Bible and collecting money for Bible
distribution.

As for little Mauritius, it was there that one of the first overseas
auxiliary committees of the BFBS had been established. Bible distribution continued to reflect the varied composition of the population. English and French scriptures were used, but also scriptures in
Indian languages and Chinese.

In North Africa, in the Maghreb, Mackintosh opened in 1884 an
agency in Tangier. He and his successor Summers distributed 114,000
Bibles and portions in twenty years. Löwitz worked in Algiers until
1893, when he was followed by J. May. Distribution was by colporteurs and Protestant missions. Attempts were made to reach even the
most remote oases. Then Morocco, Algeria and Tunisia were combined and even Spain was included. Madrid supervised North Africa
and there were small Bible shops in Tangier and Algiers.

Yet throughout the entire colonial period, Christianity in North
Africa remained a foreigners' religion. There were Catholic and
Protestant Christians among the many French and Italian immigrants.
Around 1900, a million French people were living in Algeria, and in
1930 there were 805,000 Roman Catholics there. The French state
consistently maintained that freedom of worship implied that the
Muslim must remain a Muslim. In the nineteenth century, Cardinal
Lavigerie had insisted on freedom of preaching, yet despite Roman
Catholic efforts to work in Arabic, the number of Catholic converts in
Algeria in 1930 remained no more than 700. The modest solidarity of
de Foucauld, who had gone to live as a hermit in the Sahara, and was
murdered there in 1916, aroused sympathy and a spiritual order was
successfully established, but no missionary results ensued. During the
colonial period, the indigenous population of the Maghreb so to speak
drew back into its traditional Islam. Protestant work by small faith
missions such as the North Africa Mission showed few results.
Attempts at Christian work among the large Jewish communities of
Morocco and Tunis were no more successful.

A special problem was the language. Protestant missionaries did admirable work in making translations and distributing Scriptures in the North African so-called colloquial Arabic dialects. But only the language of the Qur'an, classical Arabic, enjoyed the status of a written language; neither the indigenous Kabyle nor the regional low Arabic was accepted as a literary language. Insofar as the Bible was distributed, it was mainly in Arabic or French, and a real indigenous church did not emerge.

23

The European Way in West and South Africa

In studying the history of BFBS work in Africa during the first half of the twentieth century, one receives the impression that on the one hand staff in London regularly tried to set out strategic guidelines, but that on the other they were very dependent on the availability of qualified people. Qualified in BFBS terms meant English-speaking and British-thinking. But it was also necessary to have a grasp of other languages; to be prepared to travel great distances in primitive conditions; to have the diplomatic gifts required to get people on the field around one table; and finally to have business and organizational capacity. Missionaries of all denominations were often individualists, but Bible Society workers could work alone as much as they liked in their enormous areas.

In East Africa Roome was a fine example of this and in 1909 the BFBS found a French Methodist minister called J.A. Mesnard ready to go and work in West Africa for the Bible cause. Mesnard had been a missionary in Dahomey. He spoke English and Popo and quickly learned some Arabic. He became a sub-agent of the North African agency which had its main office in St Louis, Senegal. Plans were made for translation work in Bambara and he even visited Tombouctoo on the edge of the Sahara. But Mesnard could not stand the West African climate and returned to France in 1913. The Senegambia sub-agency was abandoned.

Between 1884 and 1904 portions of scripture were published in fourteen West African languages; they included two New Testaments and the whole Bible in Yoruba. The Fante New Testament was translated in the Gold Coast by an African minister called A.W. Parker. The Swede Westlind translated the Kongo-Fioti Bible for the Kikongo living in the French Congo, the Belgian Congo and Angola and this was printed in 1904; but for the rest, new Bible translations came out more slowly in the first half of the twentieth century than in the preceding pioneering period. The German missionaries completed the Ewe Bible for Togo in 1913. In Dahomey the Rev. O. Henry translated the Bible into Gun with a committee of African translators, including two generations of Marshalls; the work was completed in 1923. A complete Bible in Fante for the Gold Coast appeared only in 1948. In Angola during the 1930s only a few New Testaments were produced. In the Ivory Coast, the country in which Prophet Harris had summoned people to wait in empty churches until white men came to explain the holy Book to them, the New Testament in Baoul was published in 1953; but until then only Gospels, in about nine languages, were translated. (See also chapter 30.)

In the Igbo language of Eastern Nigeria, Crowther's translation of John's Gospel into the so-called Bonny-Igbo was a pioneer work, apart from a few Gospels which had previously appeared in the Isuma dialect. A third attempt at translation was made into Onitsha. Out of all this came, thanks to the work of T. Anyaegbunam, T.J. Dennis and others, one of the first successful so-called 'union versions'.

Bible translators and also the Bible Society discovered that in various parts of Africa important languages were spoken in several dialects. This applied to Igbo in Nigeria, but also for example Nyanja in Nyasaland, Shona in Rhodesia and Swahili in East Africa. The speakers of the various dialects could understand one another to a certain extent. The idea therefore arose of making a common 'union' literary language using as far as possible words and expressions common to the various dialects. The result was a literary language which had no precise counterpart in any spoken language. Where a so-called union version succeeded, such a Bible was able to make a significant contribution to the growth of a large indigenous (literary) language. The greatest union Bible was the Swahili, the language spoken in large areas of East Africa. Where a union version failed, it was often because of political and social conflicts between the groups speaking the various dialects, rather than because of linguistic problems. For example, a union version seemed possible for a whole group of languages in Southern Cameroon, Equatorial Guinea and Gabon, since Beti, Boulou, Ntumu and Fang all belong to the same family. Nevertheless when a Gabonese teacher and a French minister advanced this view in the 1960s in a church publication in Libreville, they were arrested because their idea was politically dangerous in view of the existing geographical frontiers. In 1905, at a translation conference in Asaba, Nigeria, the decision was taken to make a union version of the Bible in Igbo. This was done by T.J. Dennis of the CMS together with four European missionaries and six Igbo.

Because of interdenominational conflicts, the importance of Sierra Leone as a centre for mission activities declined, while Lagos in Nigeria became economically more important. Thus Lagos also became the base for the Rev. C.R. Johnson, the Bible Society secretary. The BFBS had in West Africa a handful of auxiliary committees on the coast and supported the printing and publishing of all kinds of translations. German Bible Societies helped first with Ewe. The Basel Bible Society printed a New Testament in Ga, the American Bible Society assisted American missionaries in Gabon and Southern Cameroon in publishing translations, and the National Bible Society of Scotland published the Efik Bible for Eastern Nigeria. In Cameroon the Bulu Bible first appeared in 1940 and the Fang Bible for Gabon followed only after the Second World War.

Johnson died of blackwater fever in 1899 while travelling in the Gold Coast. His successor Broome P. Smith had had an extremely varied career. He had been a lieutenant in the Zulu rising in South Africa, a trader in Madagascar and a faith missionary in the Belgian Congo. Unfortunately he could not support the climate of West Africa and had to return to England for health reasons in 1904. It was decided not to appoint a successor, but London supported missionary societies all along the coast in translation, printing and distribution.

It was also considered necessary to revise existing translations. The revision of the Yoruba Bible for Nigeria was completed as early as 1898. Even a cheap school Bible was published in that language. The CMS set up in Nigeria a chain of bookshops and the Bible Society agreed a special reduction, known as 'West African terms'. Slowly an attempt was made to introduce global reductions in the place of 'missionary terms', which in fact meant simply sending books to individual missionaries. It was curious that for all kinds of reasons translation work in some important languages, such as Mende and Temne in Sierra Leone and Hausa in Nigeria, notably stagnated.

Partly on the basis of missionaries' reports the cruel exploitation of the Congo basin by King Leopold II was ended in 1908. The Congo became Belgian. The government signed contracts of co-operation with the Catholics covering education and other matters. From 1914 the number of Christians grew by more than 30 per cent a year. This had to do with the need for stability in a country which had been disorganized on the east by the Arab slave trade, on the west by the cruel practices of Leopold II's rubber tappers, and later also by the rapid growth of industries in Katanga and plantations and the exploitation of minerals elsewhere. The Belgian Congo became an example of a territory in which the traditional religions had no answer to the changes which were affecting human lives. First separate Christian villages were set up and among the Catholics even whole agricultural companies on ground given by the colonial authorities, the so-called *fermes chapelles* or 'chapel farms', which threatened to develop into Christian ghettos headed by the white missionary. Then the American Presbyterian missionaries had the idea of sending evangelists with limited education out to other villages as was also done in Uganda. These were the great spreaders of the Good News. Indeed almost everywhere in Africa south of the Sahara the village evangelists with their modest income, their devotion, and their little churches used as schools in the mornings, for praying in the afternoons and for preaching in the evenings and on Sundays, became the indispensable workers at the grass roots. In 1898 Dan Crawford of the Plymouth Brethren came to Katanga. 22 years later, without ever having taken a furlough, he returned home and wrote a book entitled *Thinking Black*. Crawford pleaded for a Christian testimony which would become African to the Africans, as Paul became a Greek to the Greeks. By no means all missionaries were ready and able to think like Congolese. In this connection it is typical that in 1912, when the Protestant missions in the Belgian Congo decided to publish a news bulletin together, it was called *Congo Mission News* and appeared in English. It is true that in all kinds of conflict situations, the Protestant missionaries stood on the side of the Africans against the colonial authorities. Notably in the Belgian Congo they kept their distance from the colonial administration, since the great majority of Protestant mission workers were not Belgians, but mostly Americans or Scandinavians, and thus people from countries which had no colonies.

In 1916 a Canadian Mennonite, the Rev. R.A.W. Banfield, who since 1901 had played an important role in the translation of the New Testament into Nupe, was appointed Bible Society agent for West Africa. He was another great traveller. He managed to visit his whole area of work, which ran from Sierra Leone to Angola, and included British, French, Portuguese and Belgian colonies. His linguistic survey became a great help for London; he also, especially in the Belgian Congo, brought translation committees of different missions, who sometimes knew nothing of one another's activities, into contact with one another. Otherwise in the Belgian Congo it continued to be necessary to grant Bibles on mission terms until around 1920 in view of the large number of languages and the poor communications in that huge country.

In 1913 the British decided to federate northern and southern areas and to build up Lagos into a real capital city. Thus Nigeria was created, a large country with a population speaking many different languages. This opened the Muslim north, until then closed to mission by the British government. For the Bible Society it became essential to set up a permanent headquarters, a Bible house, in Lagos. Since the money from the Centenary Fund had been spent, an appeal was made for this special purpose to the auxiliary committees of the Canadian Bible Society which was looking for a more direct relation with the mission field. The Canadians paid for a Bible house in Lagos, opened in 1919. The BFBS had previously helped with the translation and publication of Bibles and portions in 54 West African languages, while on average 25,000 Bibles in those languages, plus 20,000 Bibles in English, were sent each year to West Africa.

In southern Africa the development of Bible Society work was strongly affected by political and economic developments. These were related not only to colonial interests, but also with colonists and European emigrants. The LMS missionary John Mackenzie succeeded in persuading the British to make Bechuanaland a protectorate, thus closing the door to Boers and British as colonists. The French succeeded in a similar move for Basutoland. That this was not superfluous is shown by the case of Matabeleland, where in 1888 the king signed an agreement with the whites, but was later cheated so that the English were able to establish Salisbury in the north of his country and to found their colony of (Southern) Rhodesia on the basis of a royal charter. In 1895 the Bible Society had depots in the new Rhodesia in Bulawayo, Victoria and Salisbury. From 1896 to 1903 the Rev. L. Nutall was secretary in the Cape. In 1896 the Bible Society had 188 local committees in southern Africa. President Kruger was the honorary president in the Transvaal and Steyn in the Orange Free State. They are one example of the frequent phenomenon that rulers and heads of government in many countries throughout the world stand behind the work of the Bible Society. An important factor in this was certainly the fact that all non-Catholic Christians used the services of the Bible Society.

The conflicts between the British and the Boers led to the Boer War of 1899–1902. The British Protestant missions sided with the British army in this war, while the Scandinavian, French and German Protestant missions had a better understanding of the Boers' point of view. The Bible Society helped both parties with Scripture distribution even in prisoner of war camps as far away as Ceylon. In 1908 the British made Cape Province, Natal, the Orange Free State and the Transvaal into the Dominion of South Africa, which was to become part of the British Commonwealth. A few Scottish ministers who had come to strengthen the ministry of the Dutch Reformed Church influenced the Boer churches in the direction of greater openness to pietism and revival; a great revival arose in a camp for Boer prisoners of war in Ceylon. This increased the interest in mission and for the Bible Society. Two Dutch Reformed ministers played a significant part in this development. They were the Rev. G.P. van de Merwe, secretary of the Bible Society in Cape Town from 1905 to 1914, and his successor the Rev. D.S.B. Joubert. The Bible Society was thus able to build a bridge between Boers and Britons. It was of course very important for the Calvinistic Boers that the Bible Society should publish and distribute Bibles without note or comment and also that it should reject the Apocrypha. Cape Town also was given a Bible house from the proceeds of the 1904 Centenary Fund. Economic and industrial growth in the belt around Johannesburg and migration to the area to the north of the city made a new agency necessary. In 1903 the Central South African Agency was set up in Johannesburg to serve the Transvaal, the Orange Free State, Swaziland, Bechuana-land, Basutoland and Rhodesia. Here too the Bible house was built with money from the Centenary Fund. The Rev. R. Lowe, a British Methodist missionary, became its secretary in 1904 and remained in office until 1925.

The Bible houses in Cape Town and Johannesburg tried to apply uniform rules on pricing and supply to the various missions. In 1906 the Rev. J.B. Rose, an English-speaking Baptist, became full-time secretary in Natal. In the area around Johannesburg there was growing up an extremely mixed urban population of industrial workers, while elsewhere missions had to deal with one people and one language. The Bible Society tried to help in both situations. The number of transla-tions and revisions completed in South Africa is impressive: Bibles in Xhosa, Tswana, Zulu (by the Americans) and Northern Sotho for South Africa, Sotho for Basutoland in a translation made by the French missionaries Louis Mabille and Eugene Casalis, first printed in parts locally in Morija, and then in one volume in Paris; the Scots made a union version in Nyanja for Nyasaland. The Tsonga Bible for Mozambique was translated by Swiss and published in 1907. Next there appeared translations in other languages, such as Bemba, Ndau and Shona for Northern and Southern Rhodesia and as early as 1915 the Bible Society called the various missions in Salisbury to co-operate in a union version for Shona. This was completed only in 1949. Nor was the Bible Society afraid to meet fresh challenges. It produced Bibles and other Scriptures in Indian languages for the Indian plantation workers in Natal. When the mines sent for 20,000 Chinese workers as an experiment, the Bible Society responded with Bible portions in Chinese. Johannesburg distributed in 1920 Bibles and other Scriptures in 50 languages.

Meanwhile the Boer population of Dutch, French and German descent had developed their own language on the basis of Dutch; the Boers called it Afrikaans. In 1917 the Bible Society decided to bring out a translation in Afrikaans. A translation committee was appointed and in 1919 the Synod of the Dutch Reformed Church adopted Afrikaans alongside Dutch as a pulpit language. The Bible in Afrik-aans appeared in 1933 and exercised a powerful influence in the emancipation and the national consciousness of the Afrikaans-speaking South African whites. It also became the Bible of the coloured people.

Around 1920 the Bible Societies had co-operated in the publication of Bibles and other Scriptures in 158 African languages, including complete Bibles in 23 and New Testaments in 36 other languages.

24

'Digest in their own way'

The evangelization of the world in this generation, of which the Edinburgh International Missionary Conference had dreamed, did not take place. For a generation the European himself, and thus also his God, were seen as superior, but when the Europeans went to war with one another that time came to an end. The whites from Christian Europe with their superiority complex ceased to be credible when they killed one another in millions in the First World War of 1914–1918. The hundreds of thousands of Africans who fought alongside them as soldiers or bearers, in Africa itself or in Europe, and who survived the conflict, told the whole story back in their villages. The average African began to think. In 1936 Italians trampled on Ethiopia, the one Christian country in Africa, which left a great impression – all the more so since European (Christian) nations scarcely did anything to resist this occupation. The moral authority of the Europeans suffered even more during the Second World War. There was fierce fighting in North Africa and de Gaulle formed in Africa his Free French Army, consisting for the most part of Africans. In the first instance the Germans simply beat the French; the British were also hard pressed. Because of the two world wars, the European fell from his superior throne and the African's own self-esteem correspondingly rose. He nevertheless played a full part as a soldier in the allied armies.

As far as the evangelization of Africa was concerned, Muslims proved much tougher than expected in their resistance to the Christian gospel. The same was true of Buddhists and Hindus in Asia. The great world religions withstood Christianity and the great flood of new Christians in Africa came from the world of the traditional religions.

Moreover there arose in Russia in 1917 for the first time in world history, after a bloody revolution, a major state in which there was no room for faith, the church or God. The Marxist-Leninist ideology of the class struggle claimed to explain religion scientifically as the opiate of the people.

The reaction to all this in the missionary-sending countries was that less stress was laid on the exclusiveness of Christianity: attempts were made to unite with believers of all other religions in the fight against atheism. This was the message of the great Jerusalem mission conference of 1928.

It is true that some of the (especially American) missions had no sympathy with this broad, almost syncretistic position. They preached the full gospel as the only way of salvation; they called for personal conversion. They were often Baptists or members of Pentecostal churches. Their interdenominational faith missions filled the blank spaces in the heart of Africa behind the 'ordinary' missions on the coast.

By 1938 the world looked very different. In Germany the pagan Nazis had come to power and war was threatening once more. A worldwide economic crisis was raging. At the great Tambaram mission conference for the first time there participated a large number of representatives from the so-called 'younger', mission-founded churches. Before this conference, the Dutchman Dr Hendrik Kraemer wrote a book which became famous, *The Christian Message in a Non-Christian World*, in which, with great comprehension and openness to other points of view, he confessed Christ as the way, the truth and the life. Despite a growing emphasis on Christian service, proclamation, as including service, was central at Tambaram. Each department of the church's activities must be directed towards evangelism. It was no longer a question of mission or Christianity, but of the whole church for the whole world. The representatives of the younger churches specially emphasized this call for total proclamation.

The late Jean Kotto of Cameroon once said: 'The African eats everything the white man puts before him, but he digests it in his own way.' The worldwide developments in mission and apostolate took on their own shape in Africa.

The Protestant and Catholic missions contributed during the colonial period to the westernizing of Africa. This happened in the faith missions through their strong emphasis on spiritual things. Within the New Testament, they were specially drawn to John's Gospel. Some of them made hymn books in African languages in which the word 'God' did not occur: everything was directed to Jesus, the redeemer from sin and death. The Greek separation between body and spirit, flesh and spirit, which is un-African, was carried through. The church-based ecumenical missions (including Roman Catholic missions) contributed to this westernizing process by paying great attention not only to vernacular education, but also to education using purely European curricula. For many to go to school meant to get a chance to become like the whites.

The churches grew, but African Christians digested all that in their own way. The reaction to this Greek, spiritual gospel was the emergence of independent African churches in which the total African experience of life was bound together with the Good News about Jesus; in them Africans had the feeling that they could believe in their own way. This movement was linked with the name Ethiopia where the church had always been African. It emerged first in South Africa, because there the European colonists behaved most clearly as superior beings. The African Methodist Episcopal Church in the United States acted for them as a kind of spiritual sponsor. In 1900 this American church made the Ethiopian Church in South Africa one of its districts and appointed bishops for it. The growth of these independent churches was gigantic. In 1913 there were 30 of them, in 1948 800, and in 1960 at least 2200.

Independent African churches arose also in such countries as Nigeria, Kenya and the Gold Coast. Brother Lawson, the leader of the Diving Healing Church in Accra, said that his church was founded because the Presbyterians' worship was too cold. Other independent churches arose because a mission refused to work in a particular language. That was the case, for example, among the Ngoumba in Southern Cameroon. In the Belgian Congo, stupid colonial policy led to the birth of the (now very large) Kimbanguist church. An evangelist called Simon Kimbangu was a prophet calling for renewal. The Belgians had no idea what to do with him and the Catholic mission gave tendentious and inappropriate advice. Kimbangu was arrested in 1921 and condemned for activities liable to endanger the state. He died in prison in 1951. The Kimbanguists are now a major church in Zaïre and the Congo Republic (see chapter 35.)

In East Africa, a revival movement began in the 1930s in Uganda and Rwanda which made Christian faith a matter of the moved heart rather than the cool understanding. One of its most striking effects was that in this movement the gulf which colonialism had created between Europeans and Africans was bridged by the discovery that all were brothers and sisters in the Lord.

The European education which all the missions offered had a quite different effect. Institutions of higher education multiplied and step by step Africans went to study in European universities. Coming from a life lived in community, in impersonal, cold Europe they visited one another and also sought together their own identity over against the whites and their dominant culture. They did not only talk about and study 'negritude', black existence (a subject in which, remarkably, the Belgian missionary Placide Tempels' book *Bantu Philosophy* was for a time their guide), they also became nationalists, wanting freedom for their fatherlands. The Bible which makes people free in combination with European education became the time bomb which, following the Second World War, was to explode and lead to the independence movement of the 1960s. It must be said that many missions anticipated this consciousness. In many African countries, churches were already autonomous and independent from the missionary societies before political independence came.

It is nevertheless remarkable that especially the Protestant missions and churches on the one hand contributed to westernization through their education furthering the knowledge of the European colonial languages, but on the other in their churches and their religious education used exclusively the African languages. They were also the first to print books in those languages: the Bible, hymn books, a catechism, other religious writings (including Bunyan's greatly loved *Pilgrim's Progress* in many African languages), but also ordinary stories, handbooks on hygiene and agriculture, and newspapers. All this material was produced locally on the mission's own printing presses. Learning to read was mostly promoted at the time of professing one's faith or on baptism, when the ability to read was required. Church and mission used, in preaching and in communion with the Lord and with one another, the language of the heart, which Africans had learned from their mothers, and in which they could be completely themselves. In education, however, church and mission co-operated in spreading the language of the coloniser which was necessary for wider contacts and for gathering western knowledge.

By its traditional role of supplying the Bible in a language which people could understand at a price which people could afford, the Bible Society played a significant part in this development. Both mission-founded churches, as pioneers in the interior, and also Christians in the independent African churches, needed the Bible in the languages of their people. In the western schools, too, the Bible Society provided cheap Bibles and New Testaments in the colonial school-languages. Even where the whites lost face in the eyes of the Africans during the two world wars, Bible Societies distributed Bibles and other Scriptures among the armies.

The Bible Society's translation policy in this period was sometimes to arrange a translation in a particular language or co-operation in translation between various missions and churches; but in general the Bible Society remained the handmaid of the church and thus dependent on the translation strategy of the various missions and churches. This meant that many more factors were involved than the facts concerning languages and numbers of speakers. Was the mission in question interested or not in literature work and were people available for the translation work? Were those responsible able and willing to make money available, since local contributions were necessary at the translation stage? Did the native speakers have a high opinion of their language? Moreover the existence and growth of Christian literature work was a stimulus for the translation of the Bible. For example, the American printing press in Beirut, Lebanon furthered Christian literature work throughout the whole Near East, including Egypt; the Presbyterian publishing house and printing press at Ebolowa in southern Cameroon served a wide area; the same was true for the joint literature work of the Protestant missions of the Belgian Congo in Léopoldville and for the large Morija printing press in Basutoland. In the wake of the British Christian literature organizations, there was naturally active work in the British territories of southern and East Africa, but also in the Gold Coast and Nigeria. In 1929 the International Christian Literature Committee for Africa was founded.

In translation strategy a remarkable shift took place. While the number of African languages in which parts of the Bible were translated rapidly increased beween 1915 and 1945, full Bibles in only 17 languages were completed (in the previous hundred years there had been 19); but in another 29 languages New Testaments were published. One gets the impression that the faith missions in particular were more interested in the NT than in the whole Bible. Indeed, instead of the concrete Gospels of Matthew or Luke, they preferred to begin with John, 'because it contains the full Gospel.' The nineteenth-century practice of beginning with Matthew or Mark, then all the Gospels, then Genesis and the Psalms, followed by the whole NT and finally the whole Bible, was replaced in many cases by the order: John, then the other Gospels, then the whole NT. This option, strongly directed to spiritual salvation, says more about the Protestant missionaries' conception of faith than it does about the Africans' thought-world.

The American Bible Society maintained its support to American missions in Egypt through its agency or direct from New York in the case of Zulu in South Africa and some editions for southern Cameroon.

The Scots continued to help in Calabar, Nigeria, in Nyasaland, and incidentally elsewhere. The Germans, because of the loss of their own colonies at the time of the First World War, then because of their economic problems at home, and later because of the Nazi régime, came to provide significantly fewer missionaries and Bible Society workers. That meant that especially during the Third Reich, from 1933 to 1945, the German churches stood outside the world church, and could not make their worldwide contribution. By far the most important contribution in translation, publishing and distribution of the Bible in Africa remained until after the Second World War that of the BFBS. Sometimes this was difficult, when people in England became less generous or because of economic decline less able to give, so that income fell. Yet the number of African languages in which at least part of the Bible had been published rose between 1919 and 1939 from 150 to 284.

From 1909 to 1932 the translation department in London was headed by R. Kilgour, an able man with wide practical knowledge, since before he came to the BFBS, he had worked in Bible translation in Nepal. However, despite great devotion and carefully collected information, it was impossible for the limited staff of the translation department to check and monitor each translation. They were thus heavily dependent on the ability of the translators in the field. The result was that translations of very uneven quality were published. Solutions regarding the orthography of distinctive sounds in an African language which do not correspond to anything in our Roman alphabet were also inconsistent, as was the translation of some abstract concepts in particular concrete African languages. But London did what it could, and even in 1940, during the Second World War, Kilgour's successor Dr Edwin Smith organized at Bible House another conference on African languages in which experts discussed the problems of translation work in Africa. The agenda included the consequences of increasing literacy, the need for more supervision at regional level, and the demand for more so-called union versions, together with questions concerning orthography and the most useful kind of concordances.

In Africa itself Port Said remained for many years the centre for Egypt and East Africa as far south as Zanzibar and beyond. This was also the Bible house in which people were trained for other agencies. In 1937 Egypt became the first so-called joint agency of the BFBS and the ABS in Africa. There were various arguments about how to divide the work in each of the many countries under the agency – a sign of how strong the various interests were. In Ethiopia, T. Bevan became agent in 1920 and remained there until the Italian occupation in 1937 forced him to withdraw. Bible distribution increased as the Ethiopian Orthodox Church gradually gave more importance to the Bible in Amharic, the present-day spoken language, alongside Ge'ez, the classical church language; the emperor also stimulated this development. The Italian occupying power insisted that Bible society work be tied to the agency in Rome and an Italian, the Rev. Manfredi Ronchi, came to Addis.

Meanwhile, Prince Albert Hamilton, a former professional soldier from British Guyana who had served in the British army in Palestine and elsewhere, worked from 1921 in Khartoum, Sudan. He made long colportage journeys and refurbished the Bible house. Money for the Bible house was collected locally; as he later smilingly remarked: 'In those years, it could happen that London forgot me for a few months.'

When the Italians took over Ethiopia, Hamilton organized in Sudan aid to the thousands of refugees; and in 1943, after the Italian occupation, he also reorganized Bible Society work in Ethiopia. This princely man retired only in 1966, after the Emperor Haile Selassie, who had honoured him with an order of knighthood, offered him land in Ethiopia in which to spend his declining years.

In North Africa the work was reorganized more than once until a permanent centre was set up in Algiers. The workers were the

Frenchman Charles Bonnet, later followed by the Swiss A.L. Jossi, then Mr H.W. Cummin as agent. The situation changed little: among the French and Italian population, there were many Catholics and a (French) Protestant minority; but in spite of efforts by the Roman Catholic and the various Protestant missionary societies, evangelism among the Arabic- and Berber-speaking peoples made little or no progress. Attempts to work in the popular Arabic dialects failed to make any impact because of the status of classical Arabic.

In Africa to the south of the Sahara, as already mentioned, the number of translations quickly grew. To quote a few more statistics: in Africa in 1919, there were Bibles in 22 languages, New Testaments in 36, and books of the Bible in another 92, giving a total of 150 languages. In 1939 there were 34 Bibles, 73 testaments and 177 portions in a total of 284 languages. In tropical Africa, the Protestant missions were responsible not only for translations but also for distribution, which was done mostly through their mission stations, schools and sometimes bookshops. The Rev. Banfield, who was responsible from Nigeria for the whole of West Africa from Senegal to Congo and Angola, attended in 1929 the great Léopoldville mission conference, which included 165 missionaries from the whole Congo basin. The following year he visited Angola and Northern Nigeria, then retired to Canada. Roome, the big traveller in East Africa, resigned in 1929. He had travelled 75,000 miles in East Africa for the Bible Society, 25,000 of them on a bicycle. In 1931, either because of lack of funds or lack of vision, the BFBS appointed W.J. Platt as successor to both Banfield and Roome with his headquarters in London! Platt had begun as a Methodist missionary in Dahomey. He had found in the Ivory Coast the followers of Harris waiting in their churches for the message. (See chapter 30.)

Platt made long journeys through tropical Africa, setting up Bible Society advisory committees in East Africa and Madagascar and trying everywhere he went to increase Bible distribution through the growing number of bookshops. On his return he pleaded, sometimes in impassioned terms, for the re-establishment of Bible Society secretaries on the field and he stressed the need to pay more attention to translation work. Dr Edwin Smith of the translation department, who had worked in Africa himself, entirely agreed with Platt, as he did with Platt's insistence on giving more attention to the translation of the Old Testament in order to help the development of an African monotheism. But years were to pass before the missions shared this insight.

The growth in the distribution of Bibles and Scripture portions in tropical Africa from 146,000 in 1930 to 250,000 in 1936 meant that the BFBS Africa committee did not see the need to appoint secretaries to work in Africa itself. Platt was first given a home office and in 1948 became one of the two BFBS general secretaries. W.J. Wiseman was appointed his successor for Equatorial Africa, but again with his office in London.

In the south the Rhodesia agency grew in importance; Bevan, driven out of Ethiopia, worked there until 1955. Salisbury served Northern and Southern Rhodesia, Nyasaland, Mozambique and for some time also Tanganyika and Madagascar. In South Africa, the Rev. M.J.M. van Coller greatly extended the work. The very mixed population in the industrial areas of Witwatersrand was asking for Bibles in many languages. It is striking that in this period not only was the complete Bible in a number of South African languages revised, but also new Bibles in languages of Mozambique and other areas bordering South Africa were completed or old translations revised. Van Coller managed to increase financial support from members of the white Calvinistic churches; he also built a new Bible House in Johannesburg.

As a consequence of the newly increasing self-confidence of the Europeans in South Africa, the work in the Cape, Natal, the Orange Free State and Transvaal, and also in the surrounding areas, was reorganized in such a way that in 1948 the South African Bible Society was created. The Rev. H.P.M. Steyn, who for 26 years had given the Bible Society excellent service as secretary, became its first General Secretary. Its most important centres were Cape Town, Johannesburg and Durban. In the industrial areas of Johannesburg, there was extensive colportage in many languages; in Durban the Indians were the target group, and elsewhere there was distribution through missions, churches and schools. Sales in the large African languages were enormous, while the Afrikaans translation for the Calvinistic churches of Europeans and coloured people was a huge success. Like the many different peoples of Africa, the white Boers with their Afrikaans translation were able to thank their heavenly Father for a Bible in their own language.

25

Their own way

After the Second World War, the colonial powers tried to carry on as before in Africa. The story is that Churchill, in the spirit of the Atlantic Charter, was an advocate of freedom, but only for whites and people not under British administration. However, Africa's growing educated élite wanted freedom and the returning soldiers understood that. The Africans held on to the promises made during the war and drew inspiration from Gandhi and developments in Asia. The new United Nations had to become a forum for all free nations. The ANC in South Africa was demanding rights on the basis of the Atlantic Charter; in 1943, the British colonies in West Africa requested dominion status; and the French territories invoked General de Gaulle's declaration at the 1944 Brazzaville Conference.

There arose clashes and conflicts. In 1947 a rising in Madagascar, where the French had gone much too far with the 'Frenchifying' of society, was crushed with much loss of life. Moreover in many countries leaders of newly established nationalist political parties were thrown into prison.

It is a remarkable fact that in the struggle for independence. The nationalist leaders obtained their ideologies from the capitalist West, and their weapons, if they needed or wanted them, from the communist East.

From 1957 when the Gold Coast became independent Ghana under the leadership of Kwame Nkrumah, the independence snowball began to roll across the African continent. The French tried to construct a transitional phase in their territories, at first by introducing a kind of French Commonwealth; but the new African leaders wanted their countries to become members of the UN directly rather than via a French representative, so the French territories rapidly became independent, beginning in 1960. In Cameroon there was a bitter struggle with the radical left UPC; while the birth of Zaïre, largely because of the lack of trained cadres and wrong taxation by the Belgians, took place amidst much blood and tears. In most countries where European colonists lived, decolonisation was a painful struggle. That was the case in Algeria, in the Kenya highlands (Mau-Mau) and in Zimbabwe. In the Portuguese colonies, independence was finally won, not by a long fight for freedom, but by a revolution in Portugal itself which overturned the fascist regime. Finally in 1990 the last colony in Africa, Namibia, became independent.

The new independent African countries not only took their place in the UN; they also made contacts with one another. Men like Nkrumah and Nasser dreamed their pan-African dreams of a United States of Africa. The Ethiopian emperor Haile Selassie used this situation to good effect by building in Addis Ababa a congress centre for the Organization of African Unity. Addis thus became the seat of the OAU and other international organizations. A kind of euphoria reigned both within and outside Africa. On the African continent it was believed states could now grow up which would avoid the mistakes and bad influences of both the western capitalist and the eastern socialist countries. African political leaders wrote blueprints for the society they wanted to build, and in the rich world the supply of money and people for development aid, later called co-operation in development, became a central concern. A kind of pervasive positivist optimism believed that if only Africa were supplied with enough money and know-how, new nations would be built up in a perfect state. (See chapter 38.)

Now we are more than 30 years further on; much has been achieved and much has failed. In many parts of Africa railways have been laid, roads and harbours built, and airports improved. In countries such as Gabon and Kenya, Niger and Nigeria, new industrial activities have developed. In Côte d'Ivoire, Cameroon and elsewhere, there have been great developments in agriculture. Capitals have been transformed from colonial administrative centres into centres of government, with ministries and embassies. In many countries, because of improved medical care, the population has more than doubled and numerous towns have become ten times as large. Education has grown by leaps and bounds; in many countries, universities have been established.

Yet things are not going well in independent Africa. In many countries the population has grown too quickly. Because of improved medical care, more children survive and people live longer; through the higher quality of education, they are being better trained, but the number of unemployed is growing each year. The raw materials which are Africa's most important export products are earning less on the world market, while the need to import technology has become greater. Africa's share of the world economy has diminished. Through the two oil crises and the subsequent fall in oil prices, both oil-producing and non-oil-producing countries have been hard hit. Too much money has been lent too easily to build up Africa, so that debt, especially to European governments and international institutions, has become much too high. It has become clear that the economic and technological power of the rich countries is too strong to leave African countries really to make their own choices. The African countries have followed the example of the rich North in buying far too many and far too dangerous weapons for their conflicts leading to bloody wars and many refugees. Almost everything that had been built up in the colonial period by way of regional economic co-operation within Africa has been dismantled by African leaders so that inter-African relations simply do not work economically or practically and are frustrated by closed frontiers and bureaucracy. The pan-African ideals have failed. Droughts and floods have caused great damage in the Sahel area from Senegal to Somalia and Sudan and recently also in eastern and southern Africa. Now Aids is spreading through many African countries as a deadly plague.

All that is true, but only as far as the macro-economic and world-political aspects of Africa's present problems are concerned. When you put on African spectacles, quite different features come into view.

Although the frontiers between African countries were artificially drawn by the colonial powers, they have been tenaciously maintained by African leaders. When Katanga tried to separate from Congo (now Zaïre) and Biafra from Nigeria; when the Somali, who live in four different countries, wanted to abolish the frontier between Ethiopia and Somalia; when the Christian and animist southern Chad came into conflict with the Muslim north, and southern Sudan wanted to free itself from the north, violent means were used to prevent it. The present-day holders of national power fear a state of complete chaos if each African people were to insist on its own independence. Great stress was therefore laid on nation-building within the old colonial frontiers. These frontiers are however artificial. In old Africa, it is true, there were kingdoms here and there, but there were also many peoples who had no conception of a state. Not only is the continent of Africa a European invention: so are the states within it; it was in Europe that the new élite discovered the existence of Africa. African nationalism can even be seen as a result of humiliation by and indignation against the European colonist. What has happened is that the inhabitants of Africa have signed a pact with the twentieth century, but on unequal terms. The result has been de-Africanization and alienation. The whole colonial period was too short for European structures to grow truly indigenous roots.

Not the discipline which capitalism demanded, but the greed which capitalism aroused, became the presupposition of social life. It was too easily supposed that socialism, which thought in structures, could be combined with an African collectivity based on personal relations and tradition. The word 'class' exists in no African language, so what is the meaning of a class struggle propagated by an élite? Class consciousness fades before ethnic consciousness, which is still strong everywhere.

De-Africanization and alienation: a teacher's wedding, Togo 1902

Africans forgot the work ethic through slavery and colonial exploitation; through the fact that the European colonizer preferred other people to work for him; and by too much education for white-collar jobs. To help one another was called parasitism. If you have to help your extended family, where does corruption start? When does love of one's country begin to conflict with looking after one's own family? It was all right to sabotage colonial authorities; but what about the authorities of your own nation? The preservation of law does not answer these questions. In traditional African law, the main task is that of compensating the victim, not punishing the criminal. Shame is more important for Africans than guilt. But now families no longer feel themselves responsible for putting right what the individual has done wrong. You get to the top, not through possessions, but through western training and the use of a western language. Urbanization, without the growth in productive capacity which is supposed to accompany it, leads to disinheritance and pauperization.

The result of all this is that production and efficiency decline; education is in decline and there is corruption even in the police. And today one of every two refugees in our world is an African.

Western systems of government do not work and neither do European ideologies. In a number of cases the multi-party state has collapsed in anarchy, and in others the one-party state has turned into tyranny. The freedom of the press has disappeared almost everywhere. The solution of a strong personality as president for life has had its day. The time of men like Jomo Kenyatta, Houphouet-Boigny and Bourguiba is past. But as in Europe and the United States, there are two forces in tension: on the one hand government interference, and on the other privatization. Bokassa was a leader who privatized the whole state, just like Mobutu Seke Seko. 'L'état, c'est moi.' It is not for nothing that the new élite in Zaïre (just as in Cameroon) were called 'the barons'. It has also happened that peoples without any experience of a state organization took power just to show that times had changed. That happened for the first time after independence in Madagascar; it happened in Uganda, where the Langa Obote became president, and not someone from the centuries-old Buganda kingdom. The worst example of a ruler from a people with no tradition of a state was Idi Amin.

Western civilization arose in Europe not because people had to grow food, but because they had to have houses and clothes in order to survive the winter. Africa does not have a winter in that sense, but it finds itself in a situation in which survival has become the challenge which Africans themselves have to face. At present the best answer is one of realism and moderation. A fundamental problem in this is the fact that Africa, because it had no winter, never needed to plan. An advantage is that the two world super-powers no longer seem interested in waging their cold war on the African continent. Although the whole world has become a single village, the future of Africa depends on the Africans themselves.

The history of the churches and of Christianity in Africa in this period is marked by parallels to the secular developments which we have just sketched, but also by differences.

Before political independence, many Protestant churches in Africa were already autonomous, while in the Roman Catholic Church the appointment of African bishops was in progress. The Africanization of Protestant mission work sometimes led to tensions between the so-called young churches and the mission organizations from which they had developed. Sometimes, far too European or American church structures were gratuitously transplanted with all the problems which that brought; while a number of faith missions had difficulty in setting up a viable church organization, because they were exclusively concerned with evangelism.

In 1948 the World Council of Churches was founded in Amsterdam; at that time, few African churches became members. That situation has quickly changed and the so-called young churches of Africa, Asia, Latin America and Oceania now form a majority in the WCC just as developing countries do in the UN. But there is more. The missions of the Protestant churches had met together since 1921 in the International Missionary Council. In 1962 the IMC became part of the World Council of Churches, so that mission was no longer a question of the Third World and evangelism the task in the old Christian west: people began to think and speak of mission in six continents. With this integration the IMC ceased to be an international platform for Protestant missions and the mission-founded churches met one another in the World Council. Missions ceased to be self-standing, internationally operating organizations, but became merely the mission departments of their own churches. Just as it went without saying for African countries that they should become members of the United Nations, so all churches wanted to be members of the World Council. This was true also for some churches who had come out of faith missions hostile to the World Council. At the African level there arose, just as the Organization of African Unity in politics, the All-Africa Conference of Churches, with its headquarters in Nairobi. Like the OAU, it has had difficulties with organization and finance, since for the churches too, 'Africa' scarcely existed; but its problems have now been largely overcome. The evangelicals set up their own African organization. The Roman Catholic missions bore a strongly French and Latin stamp, but 80 per cent of all Protestant mission work was Anglo-American. This had its counterpart in Africa in strongly Anglo-American-thinking and -acting churches, which regularly had misunderstandings with quite differently operating churches in the former French and Portuguese territories.

In the Roman Catholic Church in 1975, there were seven African cardinals and 155 indigenous bishops. A bishops' conference for Africa and Madagascar was established in Accra, Ghana. The ancient Christian churches of Africa, the Coptic Orthodox Church of Egypt and the Ethiopian Orthodox Church, broke down their isolation to become members of the World Council of Churches. This increased their readiness to work together with other churches in their own countries. Moreover, the largest independent church in Africa, the Kimbanguist Church of Zaire, also became a member of the World Council. Co-operation between Protestant churches in national councils of churches was strengthened and slowly a number of independent African churches joined. Relations between Catholics and Protestants significantly improved. People were first Africans and believers, then members of their own churches. What is more, relations between the authorities and the churches called for as much agreement as possible.

A problem with many churches is that they have too many schools and hospitals, printing presses and agricultural institutes. The budget of these institutions is often much greater than that of the whole church and causes all kinds of management problems. The question arises whether these institutions really render Christian service to society or whether they are merely status symbols for the churches. Among the Catholics, many expatriates are still engaged in these institutions, particularly at the higher level.

The African authorities have a varied attitude towards these church institutions. In some countries they have nationalized medical services or at least have asked Christian hospitals to conform to national medical policy; in most cases they have also required them to respect the collective agreements for their hospital staff. Such demands can make medical care too costly for the poor.

The ideal of practically all African authorities is to gain control of the schools, since they understand the great ideological influence of education. This has led some countries (including even South Africa) to nationalize education. In many cases, however, nationalization has caused great financial and management problems. There are still countries in which Christian schools form an important part of the educational system; there are countries in which the authorities have asked the churches to take back the running and staffing of nationalized schools or have simply given schools back. There are also countries in which there is nothing but state education. Of course governments everywhere have the last word on the contents of the curriculum. There have been great efforts to Africanize school books so that children no longer receive a Europe-centred education.

Christian schools still form a great proportion of the total, but the same is not true of universities, which are almost all state-controlled. Whether education is cheap or expensive depends on the state's readiness to subsidize. Although African parents are ready to make great sacrifices in bringing up their children, there is a risk of making (especially advanced) education too costly for the poor. A general problem is that although the number of schools has tremendously increased, the number of children not completing primary education has also become very large.

There are other ambiguities in the church educational and service institutions. On the one hand, their leadership sometimes causes problems for the churches; but on the other faith missions, which strongly concentrate on preaching and conversion, are criticized for not co-operating in the renewal of the whole (converted) human being and his society. Moreover, some European governments subsidize Christian service, development and Christian education, since they have discovered that the churches reach the poor more effectively and that they are in a position to make better use of aid than the heavily bureaucratized government institutions with their multi-storey hierarchies. Conversely, it is easier for the churches in Africa to obtain financial support in Europe for their schools, hospitals and development projects than for their Christian witness.

As part of the general task of turning a former colony into a nation, language policy was very important for the governments. In order to avoid sharpening internal differences and to facilitate dialogue in the outside world, many countries have chosen the colonial language as their official language. In North Africa there was a strong Arabic movement, while a limited number of countries chose a large national African language alongside English or French. In Ethiopia, Amharic had always been the official language, while in South Africa, Lesotho, Swaziland and Botswana, large African languages have been recognized in education, the media and in government. In the same way, there are a few countries which have recognized a number of African languages: in Uganda, as many as ten. The churches, which everywhere use indigenous languages in their worship, are almost everywhere able to give their religious education in the African languages, but in the rest of their school teaching have to follow government policy. In the mass media, the press and television use the official languages. African languages can at most still be heard in radio programmes, especially in pop music, politics, and publicity. Most African literature is published in French, English and Portuguese; a limited amount is produced in the official African languages, while in all other African languages, only Bibles and Scripture portions are published, together with hymn books and to some extent catechisms and other Christian literature. It is true that church and government have often used the same materials for adult literacy programmes in African languages. But the general impression is that independence has meant little by way of cultural Africanization. On the one hand, people said they wanted to be truly African, but on the other they tried to obtain a full share of western culture (and also western economy and technology). And although the churches were permitted to become fully African, they have through their education mostly co-operated in this development. (See chapter 27.)

The governments of the independent countries have applied a policy of separation between church and state, everywhere except in a number of Muslim countries, especially in North Africa. Thus Christian evangelism is now forbidden in Morocco, Algeria, Tunisia and Libya. In Egypt there is still reasonable freedom of movement for the small percentage of Christians in the country. In West Africa, Christians in Muslim-dominated areas sometimes have to suffer discrimination by local or regional authorities, but the central government wishes to remain neutral in religious matters. In the Marxist and radical African countries, Christians and churches were at worst tolerated, not persecuted, as long as they kept to guidelines laid down by the regime. Only the unrecognized groups sometimes have difficulties with the authorities. These groups in some countries include by definition Jehovah's Witnesses, because of their negative view of the state.

In general it can be said that African governments wish to determine how large a place in society churches may have or obtain. Almost everywhere, except in Muslim countries, this place is reasonably large, except that the authorities practically nowhere appreciate the churches speaking out on politics. African church leaders are thus regularly able to speak much more frankly in great church gatherings outside Africa than in synods at home. There is also an African factor in this problem. In the old Africa, it was the task of priests to strengthen the position of the chief, the sultan or the king, not to criticize them.

Everywhere in Africa the church is perceived as indigenous and African. This is partly because much of church life takes place at a simple village level and partly because Christians played an important part in the political independence movements. Nowhere was Christianity seen as something which had to disappear along with colonialism. Even the white Christians' apartheid policy in South Africa had fewer negative effects than one might have expected, since the Christian voices in South Africa were not those of Botha but those of Tutu and Boesak.

The churches continue to grow, particularly because the followers of African traditional religions are convinced that these have no answers to the questions of the present day. They are joining the Christian churches, sometimes hundreds at a time. They are not converts, but potential Christians. Much will depend on the teaching and preaching which they hear in the churches and on the fellowship they experience in them. Especially in the cities, the number of new denominations is growing. This is partly the result of clashes between personalities or small groups in the structured churches and partly by the creation of new independent churches, for the well-known reasons of polygamy, links with the ancestors, faith-healing and the discovery of the Old Testament. They also arise through the witness of a new type of one-person missions from American Pentecostal circles. They break through tribal barriers to offer services in several languages. Psychologically they fit in with the loosening of tribal and family links in the large new cities. They offer a place of warmth and fellowship under the fiery leadership of a charismatic preacher. (See chapter 35.)

The established churches founded in Africa by missionaries in the nineteenth century are having a hard time. They are near the ordinary people because they use the local languages; they are scattered throughout over the country in many small villages and their evangelists, with their limited education, live close to the people. But their schools, especially their advanced education in the colonial languages, at the same time contributed to the alienation and superficial westernization of Africa. This applied also to the structures of their own church organization and their leadership. Among Roman Catholics, the problem is camouflaged by the presence of a still relatively high number of workers and financial help from overseas, although there is a desperate shortage of priests. Among Protestants, there is only a limited number of ministers having the same intellectual level as the new secular élite; most clergy have middle-school education and the churches are not in a position to pay the ministers on the same level as government employees. This all leads, in modern western terms, to a loss of status, though the real solidarity of the pastors with the simple and often poor believers is in itself not simple. It is remarkable that the new élite educated in French ways of thinking tends more to a reasoned distancing from the church and Christianity than those trained in the British tradition, since the Anglo-American intellectual tradition has always left room for religious conviction.

In Christian terms, on the one hand, the African fields are thus ripe for harvest, while on the other there is clearly a crisis in the quality of the pastors of the flock and the role of the far too western organizational structure of the churches. The preaching and the church have become African, but at the same time they share in the alienation and superficial westernization of the whole of society.

26

African Bible Societies

In 1932, after a successful staff conference of the BFBS, the NBSS and the ABS, it was agreed in principle that wherever more than one Bible Society was at work, there should be co-operation. It was also laid down that the aim must be to found overseas national Bible societies supported by local churches and Christians. Then, in July 1939, representatives of a number of Bible societies came together in the Netherlands to discuss co-operation. They were the four Bible societies which had international operations. In the spirit of the international mission conference of Tambaram: 'we have a Christian message for a non-Christian world, which in every place must take its own shape.' The participants agreed that they must work together to put the Bible in the hands of people everywhere. Thus it was decided to form a Council of Bible Societies.

Shortly afterwards the Second World War broke out, and six years later the world looked quite different. Europe had been devastated, as had parts of Asia and North Africa. The need for Bibles was enormous, since production had almost stopped during the war. As early as 1940, the English had asked the Americans to help in Africa wherever they could. After the war, continental Europe had the first claim on support. Britain (backed by Australia, New Zealand and Canada) and especially America came to help. Bibles were printed in dozens of languages, and paper was sent to Bible Societies in Europe. As early as May 1946, delegates of twelve Bible Societies met London to found the United Bible Societies. The English, but also the Americans, stated clearly that they were in favour of co-operation, but against a world Bible Society. They wanted to keep their big English and American fingers in the pie. The English maintained their worldwide ambitions, and feared pressure from a world federation to publish the Apocrypha while the Americans were reluctant to see others decide where their (large) funds should go.

In 1947 the Swiss Olivier Béguin became General Secretary of the UBS. He built it up step by step into a world organization in which all the work of the Bible Societies in the areas of Bible translation, production and distribution was co-ordinated. It appeared that the English, despite generous contributions from the dominions, could no longer support the growing worldwide operation, all the more since Canada and also Australia were pressing for more direct international responsibility. Moreover, it appeared that the Americans had much more money than they could use in their own international work, which was mainly in Latin America. An at least equally significant point was that the ABS, under the inspiring leadership of Dr Eugene Nida (who began work with the American Bible Society in 1943), had set up a modern translations department, which by making available specially trained translation consultants working alongside translators, could and did raise the quality of translations to a level which the English had never achieved. In this way the Americans came up with a contemporary version of what the Dutch had done for more than a century by sending to Indonesia 'language experts' specially trained both in theology and in linguistics. Finally, another significant fact was that the Dutch, but also the Scots and the Norwegians, were realizing that the churches and countries achieving independence should no longer be served in Bible work by agencies of western organizations. Here, too, there had to be decolonization.

Thus in 1950 the situation in Africa was as follows:

There was a joint Anglo-American agency in Egypt with sub-agencies in Sudan and Ethiopia. There were agencies in Nairobi for the whole of East Africa; in Salisbury for Central Africa, and in Johannesburg-Cape Town for South Africa. The whole of West Africa was still served from London and in Algiers there was an agent for the whole of North Africa.

The BFBS Annual Report noted total distribution of 620,761 Bibles and Scripture portions in Africa and support of 77 translation or revision projects. The ABS was willing to start an agency in Liberia. Literacy and the growth in education were emphasized and in the report on South Africa in connection with the white elections of 1948 the expression 'communist threat' was used.

Apart from Egypt, the Americans to the displeasure of the English had also helped American missions elsewhere with translation work and Bible production. They applied in their distribution a 'sales and purchase program' which meant that the mission in question under-took to sell the Bibles or Scripture portions at a price which people could afford and then to remit the proceeds to the ABS. In 1953, however, there came a first (small) breakthrough when an American called Nussbaum was appointed ABS agent in Monrovia, Liberia. In 1954 the BFBS placed secretaries in Lagos for British West Africa and in Abidjan for French West and Equatorial Africa. A year later, the Swede Anders Marthinson began to work for the BFBS in the Belgian Congo. For a number of years he was an inexhaustible supplier of success stories for the home front because he enjoyed writing. In 1955 the BFBS distribution figures for Africa were 1,539,082 Scriptures, including 588,000 Gospels. London had some kind of relation with translation work in 84 languages. Meanwhile, Dr Nida was gradually expanding the small ABS translation department in New York. In 1956 he called a conference of translators in Liberia.

After the mainly English expansion began internationalization. In 1957 Salisbury became a joint Anglo-Scottish agency for the Rhodesias and Nyasaland; in 1958 the Australians became partners in Nairobi. A Bible house was opened in the same year. In Abidjan and Lagos the Canadians began to share responsibility for the work. New agencies were set up jointly in 1959 by the Dutch and the English for the Bible Society in Cameroon, with a Dutch secretary, and in 1960 by the Norwegians and English in Madagascar, with the Norwegian Odd Telle in charge. The Swiss, Scots and English began together in Mozambique by appointing the Portuguese J.T. Leite as secretary in Lourenço Marques. Also before 1960 there were joint English-American agencies in the (Belgian) Congo, Liberia and Ethiopia. Especially between the English and the Americans there was constant rivalry over who would be responsible. Both societies appointed in 1961 new Africa secretaries: Frank Bedford for the BFBS and Paul Hopkins for the ABS. The breakthrough came in 1962 at a meeting of the BFBS and the ABS at Buck Hill Falls in the United States. There the 'Big Two' decided to co-operate in all African agencies, except in South Africa, where there had been an autonomous Bible Society since 1961. The Scots, Dutch, Norwegians and Swiss felt by-passed, but were nevertheless happy with this step, since now all the blank spaces on the map of Africa could be filled in and the organization was developing in a way more appropriate to the emergence of newly independent countries. For example, separate work had to come in Uganda and Tanzania, distinct from Kenya, and in Malawi and Zambia, distinct from Rhodesia-Zimbabwe.

The Dutch, however, had started in 1959 in Cameroon with the aim of preparing the ground for a national Bible Society in five years and the Norwegians were trying to do the same in Tananarive. The Americans, Scots and Swiss agreed with this strategy: apart from internationalization, decolonization was also needed. In 1963 a significant impulse was given to this movement by a three-day conference of national African church leaders in Limuru, Kenya, preceding a conference of Bible society secretaries from the whole of Africa. In Limuru the ABS, BFBS, NBSS, NBS and Norwegian Bible Society (NoBS) were also represented. African staff were already working in a number of Bible societies. At that moment, the BFBS General Secretary, Dr John Watson, came to Kenya convinced that the structure of joint agencies, agreed the previous year with the Americans, could still be built up for a number of years. However, when the Ugandan Rev. Asa Byara, later himself secretary of the Bible Society

The first African church leaders' conference, Limuru, Kenya, 1963.

in Kampala, thanked the mother Bible Societies for their service in spreading the gospel in Africa and expressed trust in the new impulse that the Americans would be able to give to evangelism with their Bible selections, but went on in the name of his African colleagues to make a strong recommendation that Bible Society work should become a matter for African churches and Christians, Watson understood the signal. With the hearty agreement of the representatives of the other 'mother societies', he declared a few days later to the secretaries that the whole Bible Society work must become a matter for the Africans themselves. Some secretaries, who thought that Africans were by no means ready for this, seemed inclined to rebel, but the old British Bible Society tradition of obedience to London won the day. At the BFBS Annual Meeting, Watson had explained the Buck Hill Falls agreement as a necessary cooperation of all forces in the face of the rapid growth in population. A year later, in the light of the Limuru meeting, he stated that in Africa the time had come for national Bible Society committees and African secretaries.

In these years of expansion, internationalization and Africanization, remarkable things happened here and there in Africa. In 1958 the 'million Gospels' campaign was launched, and in 1962 2,676,000 copies, especially of John, that most un-African Gospel, were distributed in many languages. In 1963 the UBS held a meeting in Tokyo which issued the slogan: 'God's Word for a New Age', with its aim of a Bible for each Christian household, a New Testament for each Christian, and a Gospel for everyone who could read. South Africa, on the basis of the Calvinist tradition, made an enormous contribution to the distribution of whole Bibles. The number of Bibles also doubled in Congo, while in 1962, Marthinson distributed New Testaments in 25 languages.

In South Africa the Bible Society was called from 1961 'Bible Society of South Africa, auxiliary society of the BFBS', but in Nigeria in 1960 the word 'British' was removed from its title, and it was called 'The Bible Society in West Africa'. In 1960 for the first time one heard reports of the prohibition of evangelism in Algeria, while the report on Congo in 1961 spoke of refugees from Angola. In 1961 new Bible houses were opened in Salisbury and Yaoundé, while Leite in Mozambique was able to obtain legal status for the Bible house only by registering it as a private bookshop called 'Casa di Biblia' belonging to the Portuguese citizen Leite in the Portuguese overseas province of Mozambique.

The Africanization of national Bible Societies began with the setting up of advisory committees. The first African secretary for church relations was the Rev. John Mpaayei, appointed in 1961 in Nairobi. In 1962 there followed the Rev. Henry Kachidza in Rhodesia and the Rev. Nkowane, intended for Malawi, who later worked in Zambia. In 1963 the Egyptian Dr Abd-el-Masih Istafanous was appointed as a second man in Cairo, and in 1964 the Rev. Jules Ramaroson in Madagascar. In 1964 the Rev. E. Mallo became secretary in Cameroon-Gabon, while the others assumed responsibility for their respective countries from 1965, in a single case in the face of almost public protest by the European predecessor. Bible offices or Bible houses were built in Sierra Leone, Ghana, Angola, the Central African Republic, Zambia, Malawi and Tanzania. In South Africa offices were opened in Botswana, Lesotho and Transkei.

Meanwhile, things were also moving in translation work.

During the war, Canon N.D. Coleman, a Greek scholar, was appointed translation secretary of the BFBS. In 1946–47 he went with Dr Nida of the ABS on a journey through Africa. On the way back to London via Congo, he was unfortunately killed in a plane crash. His successor was the Rev. W.J. Bradnock, who was later to cooperate, despite great hesitation, in bringing all translation work within UBS structures. In the course of a few journeys through Africa, Nida discovered how much translation work was in progress in Africa and how poor was the quality of many of the translations. Moreover the results of modern linguistics were being insufficiently used. He developed checking systems and worked for more training and help for translators.

While the English were still claiming total responsibility for all translation work north of South Africa, the ABS linguist Dr W.D. Reyburn began working with the American Presbyterians from 1956 to 1959 in South Cameroon to help Africans to reduce to writing languages smaller than Bulu and Bassa; the aim was to produce reading materials and possibly Bible translations in the smaller languages. In 1961 Reyburn returned to Yaoundé as a translation specialist under the joint umbrella of the Dutch, English and Americans, to become the first Bible translation consultant in Africa. In North Cameroon, he and the literacy specialist Dr Wesley Sadler held in 1961 the first Bible translation course for (mainly missionary) translators. In June 1962 the Dutchman Dr Jan Voorhoeve came as a second translation consultant. By then, the Netherlands had officially taken over responsibility for translations in Cameroon and Gabon.

By 1965 three American translation consultants were working in Africa. The ABS was assisting translation work in 108 languages, while Bradnock of the BFBS also travelled to Africa several times in order to assist translators.

In South Africa a full translation programme was worked out under the responsibility of the South African Bible Society.

This book is not the place in which which to tell the full story of the development of the UBS. I will therefore confine myself to those facts which were important for Africa.

With the British warning against a world Bible Society in mind, the Bible Societies saw an opportunity to develop the UBS into an efficient organization with modest headquarters first in London, later in Stuttgart, Germany, and now in Reading, England; and four regions, strongly independent in management and finance: the Americas, Africa, Europe-Middle East, and Asia-Pacific. There are two production centres, which on the basis of two funds provide financial and technical co-ordination to all Bible production: one in New York for the Americas and Asia-Pacific, and one in Stuttgart for Europe and Africa. Since the 1964 international conference with church leaders in Driebergen, Netherlands, it has become on world, regional and national levels a structure built on consultation and cooperation with the churches. Since 1969, the UBS Bulletin has published annual reports on UBS work throughout the world.

By 1967 all translation consultants were UBS workers. From 1950 there had been a common technical journal, *The Bible Translator*, and worldwide common administration of translation. Scholars worked together to produce new editions of the original texts in Hebrew and Greek and also in writing a whole series of handbooks for translators.

In 1968 the Roman Catholic Church's Secretariat for Christian Unity signed with the UBS a document entitled 'Guiding Principles for Interconfessional Cooperation in Translating the Bible'. This led in many places to cooperation with Roman Catholics.

Dr W.D. Reyburn, the first translation specialist of the Bible societies, Yaoundé, Cameroon, 1962.

From 1967 a world service budget was set up for all subsidized Bible society work. All societies, rich and poor, contribute what they can so that the sixteen self-supporting societies were not alone in financing the international work. In the rich part of the world, the many regional Bible Societies in the German Federal Republic developed into a single large and important German Bible Society. It was important for Africa that the four Bible Societies which had previously existed in France combined to form a single French Bible Society. For many years, the UBS had 23 member societies, but it now consists of 77 full and associate members, and Bible Society offices in another 34 countries.

National Bible Societies or offices which require financial support send their requests each year to their regional office, which for Africa is in Nairobi. Decisions on these requests are made in consultation. Then a global committee from the four regions, consisting of Bible Society staff and board members, decide the broad lines of the budget and the division of available funds between the four regions. What is interesting in this system is that in principle the rich do not decide on the allocation of funds for the poor. However, in practice the voices of the large Bible societies with long experience who make major financial contributions still preponderate.

In 1972 the UBS resolved to set up a worldwide programme of special selections for new readers (see chapter 27) and in 1980 a world translation programme was established. (See chapter 28.) There is growing concern for readers' helps alongside the Bible text and also for the use of non-print media such as radio and cassette recordings.

In Africa not only Africanization, but also filling the blank spaces on the map, remains no easy task. Finding and training qualified people for the posts of Bible Society secretary, distribution consultant, church relations secretary and administrator is sometimes difficult. The UBS regional centre in Nairobi is constantly at work in staff training. Although qualified cadres in some countries (and churches) are scarce, there is some progress in this respect. The staff who work in the Bible houses are a varied group consisting of ministers of various churches, teachers, accountants, former civil servants (even one former ambassador) and lawyers. There are also women secretaries and all Bible houses are now directed by Africans. In 1993 G. Bimazubute, the Executive Secretary of the Bible Society in Burundi, was murdered in a political row; in 1976, in the tense days before Zimbabwean independence, the Rev. Kachidza was imprisoned for a time. In 1977 the last European secretaries, Leite in Mozambique and Knight in Rwanda, left their posts.

In church leadership there has grown up a generation which has national and international management and administrative experience in Bible Society work. In 1965 South Africa became a member of the UBS and Cameroon-Gabon, Ghana, Madagascar and Nigeria became associate members. By 1992 there were 15 African Bible Societies in the UBS, including three associate members, and there were Bible Society offices in sixteen other countries. Relations between all churches and the national Bible Societies are generally good, showing that the Bible is important for the churches and that people realize that the Bible Society is the one organization able to provide Bibles at an affordable price in the languages which the churches want. In various countries, members of the independent churches and the Roman Catholic Church are on the Bible Society board. The financial contributions of churches and Christians are rather varied. When a new version is published, but also in emergency situations (for example in Uganda and at one period in Nigeria), contributions are readily made, but many churches have their own financial constraints and Bible Societies are still sometimes thought to have the old rich western institutions behind them. In many countries Bible Sunday is celebrated. Taking account of the great differences of income between Africans, some Bible Societies offer membership for a modest amount, and life membership for the new rich at ten times the price.

During the last 25 years money has almost always and everywhere been a problem for Bible work in Africa. The number of Christians is growing, but the number of inhabitants and also the number of readers is growing too so that there is constant high demand for Bibles and Testaments both in big languages with their common language translations and also in the smaller languages. Although grants for Africa from the world service budget grew between 1972 and 1986 from almost two million dollars to almost 10.5 million, Bible houses sometimes run out of stock of Bibles. Naturally this has partly to do with changes in rates of exchange and with inflation. An important cause of financial problems is that the currency of many African countries cannot be exchanged and transferred outside their own frontiers. In a number of countries money is thus regularly tied up, money which has come in through sales of Bibles, but which cannot be used for new orders from Hong Kong, Stuttgart or London. One answer is local production, but to produce Bibles on thin paper make great demands on local industry. In addition to South Africa, Zimbabwe, Egypt and Madagascar, where there has been Bible production for years, attempts to print Bibles are being made in a few countries, while in Zambia and Nigeria, the Bible societies are sharing in a (Bible) printing factory. It is possible in many countries to print booklets for new readers, Bible selections and Gospels, and sometimes even Testaments. However, when hard currency becomes scarce in a country, supplies of paper for printing, binding materials, and even ink may dry up. In Madagascar, Egypt, and even Ghana and Zaïre, there have been frequent problems of this kind.

Other factors contribute to insufficiency of stocks. In African cultures, people traditionally think no further ahead than the coming harvest. In the colonial period, the whites thought they were the only ones who could look ahead. The production of Bibles for Africa, however, requires about two years' planning. Requests have to be examined and accepted; printing sometimes takes place far away; harbours are sometimes choked with shipping; customs may be horrendously time-consuming and bureaucratic; sometimes transport within the country is also slow. Bible house staffs in Africa thus have to learn to look ahead.

Finally, a number of Bible houses handle large amounts of money. Since people are only human, there have been in African Bible houses, during this period of construction, a few cases where, either through incapacity or dishonesty, there have been financial mishaps. In this situation the local boards with the help of the staff in Nairobi, have carried out drastic purges.

The regional office in Nairobi has a staff of specialists in management, distribution, new reader publications, general publishing, and church relations. In the early years, most of these were non-Africans, but now the colour has grown darker. The first regional secretary in Nairobi was the Dutchman Rein W. Kijlstra, appointed in 1968. In 1976 the Ethiopian Ato Million Belete took over. He was succeeded in 1993 by the Rev. Daniel Bitrus of Nigeria. The old lines of communication with European countries are still better than cross-continental links between African countries. For example, Nairobi seems for people in West Africa much further away than London or Paris. Moreover there is still in Africa a great difference between French and English ways of thinking and acting. Nairobi does its best to serve the whole of Africa and especially to broaden the work in French-speaking countries; but the way of speaking and acting is still sometimes Anglo-African.

Africa naturally responded to the important impulses coming from the worldwide policy of the UBS. Common language translations, whether in European or African languages, were a great success. This was true of English and French, but also of Swahili and Afrikaans. The first edition of Bibles in 'new languages' is still quickly sold out almost everywhere. There is high demand for books of Bible stories for new readers. For example in Cameroon and Togo, there is great interest in Bible portions on cassette, while in Kenya and Madagascar there are opportunities for radio broadcasting. Although in some countries education is nationalized, there are means of distributing school Bibles, New Testaments, or booklets for new readers. In South African schools, there has been a great distribution programme for whole Bibles, but there are opportunities also in Ghana, Nigeria, Uganda and Zaïre. In Egypt, on several occasions thousands of New Tesaments have been distributed in the army. Everywhere, alongside church distribution people are trying to find normal commercial channels. The market mammies of Accra, Ghana, have for years sold Bibles on one afternoon a week. A problem in developing normal distribution channels is sometimes Bible smuggling from neighbouring countries where money is worth less; there are also some American organizations who find it necessary to pour into a particular country many thousands of Bibles at a time for free distribution. They do not realize that in this way they make God's Word literally worthless.

Folders containing one Bible story are mostly used for special campaigns and events varying from an international trade congress to a visit by the pope; from a big boxing match to the annual Fr. Laval pilgrimage on the island of Mauritius. Help is also naturally given at times of disaster, to refugees, and after wars. The Bible distribution channels in Zaïre were used during the years of conflict following 1960 to distribute food, and after all the miseries in Uganda, in 1982 the only means of quickly meeting the need for Bibles was to send two aircraft full of them. When Bible distribution in Nigeria came to a complete halt because people could not exchange money, a special UBS fund was set up in order to help the Bible Society replenish its stocks.

A secretaries' conference in Winneba, Ghana in 1967 marked out a new course for Africa. In 1972 followed the world assembly in Addis Ababa, and in 1982 the regional assembly in Nairobi.

During an evaluation of the working methods of the UBS and its regional centres, it was discovered that it was not a good arrangement for Lebanon and Turkey to be part of the Asia-Pacific Region and Egypt and the Maghreb part of Africa. There were particularly close links, mainly because of Arabic, between Lebanon and Egypt. Thus the NAWAT (North Africa, West Asia and Turkey) sub-region was formed and in 1986 it was decided to make this sub-region part of Europe.

The secretaries for the French-speaking countries, including some outside Africa, have held their separate meetings. France rendered very useful service in coordinating translation and production work in French.

In southern Africa, the South African Bible Society supported Bible society offices in Botswana, Lesotho, Swaziland and Transkei, and later in Namibia. All the work done in these countries was paid for by South Africa. Since 1976 all concerned have met in the annual Bible Society Council of Southern Africa. Even secretaries from the so-called front-line states have taken part on some occasions. In order to avoid giving the impression that South Africa was working in a paternalistic manner (the South African General Secretary, Rev. G. van der Merwe usually wrote the UBS annual report for these countries), the subsidy (paid by South Africa) now forms part of the budget and policy guidelines of the Nairobi regional centre.

Since 1987 the annual meeting has been called the UBS Assembly for Southern Africa.

In 1969 translation work was also regionalized. By 1992, the UBS was employing eighteen translation consultants in Africa, ten of them African, and two Roman Catholic, with a coordinator in Nairobi. Several others are in training with scholarships provided by the UBS. More than 200 translation and revision projects are needed. These include special translations for new readers, Gospels in new languages, New Testaments, Old Testaments and whole Bibles. Where Africans used to be mainly informants standing respectfully beside the missionary translator, now almost all translators are Africans. Because of the spread of theological education, many of them know Hebrew and Greek.

The number of translations has spectacularly increased. In 1992 there were Bibles in 122 African languages, New Testaments in 223, and Bible portions in 231 languages. In addition, in November 1991 there were portions and selections for new readers in 144 African languages. The technical processing of manuscripts takes place more and more in Nairobi, but also in Yaoundé, Kinshasa and Cairo. Through the UBS world budget, conferences, helps and sometimes also the translators themselves are subsidized. Primary responsibility for the translation work lies with the church(es) or mission(s) requesting the translation. Unfortunately projects often have to be postponed

New Bible House, Accra, Ghana.

because the UBS does not have sufficient funds or because the translators do not have enough time for the work. A significant number of projects, mainly in the larger languages, are carried on together with Roman Catholics. Nowhere has this created problems, though some Protestant translators may begin by thinking that Catholics think quite differently from themselves and must always be taught and watched.

Where the Wycliffe Bible Translators (WBT) have offices in Africa, their Bible translation organization works together with the Bible Societies. The WBT produces reading materials and translates (primarily the New Testament) in many small languages. Sometimes cooperation with the Bible Society consists in dividing the work, but in any case there is consultation. It also happens that the national Bible Society, at the request of a church, publishes Scriptures translated by WBT. (See chapter 28.)

In many countries, relations with the government are excellent. Some new Bible houses were built on ground given by the government and almost always they are opened by heads of state or prime ministers. In some French-speaking countries, the registration of the word 'Society' created problems, since in French this is a commercial term. The solution was to speak of an 'Alliance Biblique', a Bible alliance. In Algeria, Morocco and Libya, there has been discrimination for years against distribution of the Bible. Around 1970, Bibles were held in customs in Algiers for over three years; more than once the Bible house was forbidden for a time to import Bibles in Arabic without any reason being given. Christianity was deemed to be only for foreigners. In Morocco the entire Bible Society stocks were arbitrarily confiscated. After independence in 1974, the Bible house in Luanda, Angola was closed for a year. After independence in Mozambique, there were difficulties for years in obtaining permission to print, import or distribute Bibles. The situation there has improved insofar as the Bible Society has a warehouse once more; the import of Bibles and distribution through churches and bookshops are allowed. Local production is still impossible because of lack of paper, binding materials and facilities.

Elsewhere in Africa other problems arise from time to time, such as long delays in customs and new taxes suddenly introduced on imported Bibles; but in general, the Bible Societies everywhere enjoy freedom of action.

Part Two

27

The Book for Illiterates

André Philippe Byiong is a minister. His education consisted of a middle school certificate, four years of theological college and a year's study in France. He belongs to the Bassa, a Bantu people which lives between the capital, Yaoundé, and the port of Duala in Cameroon.

How had the Bassa come to that area?

Mr Byiong answers that question by telling the story of nine generations of his family, because an ancestor nine generations back was one of the leaders of the migration of the Bassa to the forest in which they live now.

The kingdom of Abomey in Benin is many centuries old. It is already mentioned in the ships' log books of European explorers from the sixteenth century, but it is much older still. That is proved by reliefs on the walls of the royal palace at Abomey. They tell a remarkable history going back for centuries.

Some of the kings are represented by an animal believed to typify their respective reigns. For example, a king with no foresight is represented by a pig, which can see no further than the ground beneath its feet: the king in whose reign the Portuguese first came to Abomey is represented by a Portuguese sailing ship.

To learn history in Abomey is to explain the meaning of the images in these reliefs: for Abomey had no writing. Elsewhere in West Africa, the Bambara and the Dogon also worked with pictures which record history. On a much wider scale, many African peoples have proper names which have a meaning. Such stories in pictures, or through names, do more than teach history. African village life is always a community of the living, the dead, and the still unborn. So in Abomey, these stories of kings were essential for discovering what life was about; for finding answers to questions about how and why things are as they are today; as models of how to behave now. Stories maintain life as it had always been. They mean continuity and stability, but they also provide a brake on change and renewal.

For centuries, the peoples of Africa have transmitted orally this history which was essential for their life. Their most celebrated story-

tellers are the Krio of Mali and Senegal. These *griots*, professional
story-tellers, have 900 years of history in their heads. In our times,
scholars have compared their stories with one another and with other
data, for example from archaeology. For the most part, the facts seem
to agree.

When, as early as the tenth century, the Ben-Hilleel appeared by
Lake Chad from somewhere in the north-east, they brought with
them, as good Muslims, their holy book, the Qur'an; but they did not
inspire people to reduce their own languages to writing. In the middle
ages, Islam reached Senegal via Morocco. There even grew up a great
'Kingdom of the Moors', which stretched from Mauretania to Spain.
On the southern edge of the Sahara, Tombouctou became a famous
centre of Islamic scholarship, with Qur'anic schools and libraries.
Bambara and a few other African languages were written down in
Arabic script. The same happened later with the Fulani and the Hausa
in northern Nigeria.

The orthography was technically poor and was used only for Islamic
religious treatises. Were the language and the script of the Qur'an
considered too holy for writing down the stories of Africa's own
cultures?

Still today lines of communication with North African Islam run
through the Sahara. Pilgrims go to Mecca and come back with books in
Arabic. It is doubtful whether they can read them because the
language is classical and the writing difficult (see chapter 37).

In the sixteenth century the European slave trade began to develop
on the west and east coasts of Africa. The Arab slave trade on the east
coast is much older. Trade has to involve communication. That
happened in English, Portuguese, Danish, Dutch and French: that is
in the languages of the slave merchants. When the king of Abomey in
Benin wanted to know more of the traders' language so that the
Europeans would no longer be able to trick him, he sent the son of one
of his courtiers to England to learn English. In order to go to school in
Europe the boy had to have a European name. He called himself
Lawson, after the captain of the ship he travelled on, whose name was
Law. The Methodist minister James S. Lawson, the former associate
general secretary of the All Africa Conference of Churches, came
from this family. But it was not English, French or Dutch which
became the trade language on the coast. For the purposes of trade, a
mixed language was developed, pidgin English, which in the eighteenth and nineteenth centuries was used even for written contracts.

On the east coast, Swahili, an African language with Arabic loan
words, developed as a trade language.

The fact that the European traders wrote things down did not give
the Africans the idea of doing the same with their own languages. Was
that because the coast peoples came to live more and more alongside
the Europeans and to think of themselves as their helpers? Or did

Africans consider their languages inferior to those of the powerful Europeans? Was it because society fell apart more and more under the effect of the slave trade, in which the coastal peoples, for reasons of self-preservation, became more and more the accomplices of the European traders? Or did Africans consider their languages inferior to those of the powerful Europeans?

There are two exceptions to this generalization.

In Liberia, some time in the nineteenth century, a Vai called Doalu Bukere had a dream in which he was given the task of putting his language into writing. He invented a peculiar script which never became widely used. In 1903, long after the slave trade had finished and the colonial period had begun, the German emperor Wilhelm II brought the Cameroonian Sultan of Foumban to Berlin as a living specimen of African folklore. On his return, Sultan Njoya called his *njies* or counsellors together to tell them about his visit to Europe. Njoya was a wise man. As leader of Bamoun he wanted to meet the German rulers on their own level. Njoya gave a long report on the whites' strange way of life in their cold, damp country, and then made two concrete proposals. He explained that the white rulers emphasized their status by means of large buildings so that the emperor had a palace and the people's representatives had a parliament. If the Bamoun wanted to play the white men's game, they must have the same. Then Sultan Njoya pulled out from under his *bubu* (his long robe) a piece of paper with a drawing of a German church in the Roman style.

The carpenters and artisans went to work and built in Foumban for Njoya and his *njies* a palace which was a mixture of rounded Roman arches and Bamoun artistic traditions with splendid wooden reliefs. This building still stands in Foumban: it is one of the most remarkable pieces of architecture in Africa.

The sultan's second idea was at least equally important. In Germany, Njoya had discovered the secret of the Europeans. The main reason why the Germans could invent and discover new things was that they had empty heads. 'In our heads,' said Njoya, 'there is no room, because they are full of things we have to remember. The whites do not have to carry this burden, because everything they have to remember is written down.' The sultan and his *njies* decided to make a script for the Bamoun language, because they wanted their heads to be as empty as the whites. They developed a script resembling hieroglyphics; in the end it had 250 characters and everything the Bamoun thought important was written down: history, laws, traditions. As late as the 1960s, there were still a few old men around who could read Njoya's writing.

Between 1800 and 1845 the first missionaries arrived on the coast of Africa. They learned the coastal languages and reduced them to writing in order to translate the Bible. The missionary pioneers were

Signs in the Bamoun script.

almost always also Bible translators: Krapf in East Africa, Moffat in the south, Crowther in Nigeria, Saker in Cameroon, and many others. Their work snowballed. In 1800 there were Bible translations in three African languages; now, in more than 500.

The motives of these first missionaries were very simple.

The African should be able to read for himself the story of God and man. In this way he would have no need of sorcerers and no need to consult ancestors either.

Africa was so big that as soon as possible the African himself must help to spread the Good News. He must therefore have the Christian gospel in his own language and the people must be able to read it. Above all the first generation of missionaries had generally only a short time to work in Africa. Most of them died within three years from tropical diseases. They themselves were, so to speak, not permanent, but a translation of the Bible would be.

The Bible societies helped in this translation work by producing and distributing the new translations. Many European Christians were happy to support this work because the fact of the gospel going 'to the ends of the earth' kindled their imagination. In many churches and missions one of the conditions for baptism became and still is passing a reading test. African Protestantism became so strongly the religion of the book that Roman Catholics paid attention earlier in Africa than in Europe to providing the Bible in the vernacular.

Thousands of people wanted to become Christians and learned to read. Their motive for doing so was to be able to read God's story for themselves.

In time the sheds in which the future Christians learned to read grew into hundreds of Christian schools. Yet even so, the missions did not teach all Africans to read. The continent was too big. There were too many languages and too many people. But by 1900, for example, a large proportion of the Hova on the plateaux of Madagascar were able to read. Before 1900 the American Presbyterians printed on their mission press at Ebolowa in Cameroon a hundred different books and booklets in the Bulu language. In the 1920s whole peoples in Zaire learned to read their own languages.

In 1960 the great independence movement began to bear fruit in Africa. At that time, more than 85% of adults were unable to read. Independent African governments, political parties and UNESCO were eager to do something about this. The citizens of an independent country, wanting to play a part in the big world, had to be able to read and were supposed to be eager to learn to read. With the children it succeeded. This was important in those many countries where half the population is under eighteen.

Parents who had never been to school themselves understood that their children had to be educated in order to 'get on'. They made great sacrifices for their children's schooling. In the 1960s, education developed by leaps and bounds so that now in most countries between 60% and 100% of children between six and twelve go to school and up to 25% of the national budget is devoted to education. Unfortunately quite a few children do not complete their schooling. They are able to read a little, but do not become what is called 'functionally literate'.

Before the Second World War, 90% of all education in Africa south of the Sahara was Christian. More than half the schools still are. All that began under sheds built so that people could learn to read the Bible in their own language.

For the other half of the population, those over eighteen, there came literacy campaigns. Readers were prepared and instructors trained. The aim was to teach people to read in six weeks. But this aim was not reached.

Africans in the rural areas (and that means 80% of Africa's millions of inhabitants) saw no point in it. Why should they learn to read? You had to buy an expensive newspaper every day and unless you happened to live in a village on a main road or a railway newspapers always arrived too late anyway. It was much better, when you had sold your crop, to buy a transistor: the radio was always up to date and you didn't have to learn to read. People who live below the breadline are only prepared to learn something – they are only ready to change their lives – if they see an immediate advantage. Sultan Njoya knew that. His motive for reading was to become like the whites. The missions and Bible Societies knew this too. Their motive was to enable people to read God's book for themselves.

Learning how to read, here in Chad, as the start of total life improvement.

The turning point was a big UNESCO conference in Teheran in 1965. The slogan became: 'Learning to read as a starting point for total life improvement.' The call was for cooperation between governments, UNESCO, churches, industry and business. The authorities, private organizations and commerce must address the problems together.

There are examples of projects which succeeded. Literacy campaigns combined with agricultural improvement: teaching how to read instructions for manuring in order to produce bigger crops. Literacy campaigns in industry, providing an opportunity for unskilled workers to become better paid skilled ones. Reading combined with information about medicine, hygiene, and farming in Togo, resulting in more surviving and healthy children. Literacy programmes in Tanzania as part of the government's total rural development. Church literacy projects in Ethiopia which became part of the army and police training programme. These literacy campaigns played a significant role in the emancipation of the Ethiopian army so that Mengistu was able to find support for his revolt among the ordinary soldiers. Literacy programmes were shown on television in Kenya.

The number of illiterates is gradually diminishing, as reading is seen as the start of total life improvement. But the major source of information is still the radio. It is unlikely that the whole present generation of African adults will ever learn to read.

It is even doubtful whether the rapidly growing population of Africa will ever as a whole learn to read. There are some who do not complete their schooling. There is the influence of radio and, in the cities, of television. Large-scale literacy development has begun in Africa at a time when in Europe the Gutenberg era, the period of the printed word, is giving way to the electronic era of the ear and the image. For years Muslim organizations have understood these signs of the times and have sent out the entire Qur'an free of charge on long-playing records to all radio stations. African Bible societies, too, are working with Bible portions on cassette.

Another problem received great attention at the Teheran conference. It became clear that between the first reader and the newspaper or the novel a kind of bridge literature was needed. Otherwise there is too big a jump in language and practice and also in the quantity of letters. After the readers there are needed little books with well-known popular stories and simple booklets with information, for example, about diet and hygiene; books about agriculture with many illustrations; a practical guide on how to repair a bicycle.

Experiments in Liberia, Tanzania, Ethiopia and elsewhere, have shown that reading material is needed which interests the new reader and which he enjoys reading.

At their world assembly in Addis Ababa in 1972, the Bible societies decided to set up a programme for new readers consisting of leaflets and booklets containing parts of the Bible. These were planned to help people to learn to read and improve their reading in five stages until they could understand the New Testament in common language. The simplest of these booklets have short sentences, large letters, and many illustrations. The later series become progressively more difficult.

The principles of the series are: to use relevant Bible selections in special translations; to have illustrations which make the text more accessible; to publish in all big languages and all languages in which there are literacy programmes. All this is done in cooperation with the churches and where possible with the authorities.

In 1975 there followed a working conference in Nairobi to assess progress in this programme in Africa. It appeared that the programme was functioning in nineteen countries and 55 languages; 40 booklets had been published, 25 new ones were in the press, and translations for 78 more publications were ready. It was agreed that illustrations were best made locally in order to make connections with the indigenous culture. Booklets containing several stories seemed to work better than leaflets with only one Bible story. Efforts were made to do all the production locally wherever possible. The translation always had to be checked to make sure that it was a real translation in simple language and not a paraphrase. The programme was successful among adult new readers, most of them young people who had not finished primary school, and even in the schools themselves.

Churches and missions naturally wanted to include as quickly as possible in booklets for new readers those Scriptures which they considered to be the heart of the gospel. Research among readers had meanwhile shown that in Africa it was also necessary to choose passages from the Old Testament and that these were greatly valued. In 1991, over 2.5 million portions and over 911,000 selections for new readers were produced.

From a missionary and Christian point of view, these are the first steps towards the whole Bible. The publication of these special new reader Scriptures enables the Bible still to have a place in literacy programmes. This approach is however criticized in some quarters on the grounds that the Bible consists of the sacred texts of the congregation and the church and that these must not be popularized as literacy materials. This is in fact the old Roman Catholic argument that the Bible is only the book of the church for use within the church (see chapter 36); or even the Islamic argument that the language itself is holy so that the Arabic of the Qur'an cannot be really translated (see chapter 37). Muslims and indeed Jews find it necessary and normal that their children should learn sacred texts by heart in the original. This discussion is irrelevant to Africa as long as the parts of the Bible used are stories, since in Africa important things in life were and are handed on in the form of stories. This means of communication is still alive and well. The proof is the hundreds of thousands of simple Christians who cannot read or have forgotten how to read, but who remember many Bible stories and their entire hymn book as well, because story-telling and singing go together. Bible stories as an aid to literacy are therefore not only practically useful and African, but still help people who want to learn to read to understand God's Word also. And when learning to read becomes the start of total life improvement, the message of the Bible has to have its place in that process.

28

The Book in Babel

In Africa about 1800 languages are spoken. That means that there are 1800 ways of speaking and communicating which other people do not understand. That is an unscientific definition of language, but linguistic theories often contradict one another so that a pragmatic description is the most usable. Moreover the scientific classification of these languages is not yet perfect. Families of so-called related languages are distinguished, but sometimes racial classifications and linguistic distinctions are confused.

There are in Africa some big languages, such as Hausa and Fulani in West Africa, which are spoken by millions of people. Rwanda has one language for six million people. But in Cameroon, there are 125 languages for twelve million people, so that the 5% of the population of Africa who live there speak 15% of the languages of Africa. It could be that the Bamileke, in the west of Cameroon, are the clearest example of the African Babel. The Bamileke know fifty dialect families. There are dialectal differences from one village to the next and people who travel more than five kilometres from their homes no longer understand one another. In the markets of this region the language of communication is pidgin English.

In the old days, the peoples and clans of Africa were self-sufficient and lived in relative isolation from one another. Contacts were minimal. In certain areas, women were stolen from other, weaker peoples in order to increase the number of potential brides. In other places, a kind of silent bartering took place: food or other objects were left at a certain spot and later taken away by another people, being replaced by goods of equal value. Migrations and wars also brought peoples into contact with one another. The emigration of one part of a people could lead to changes in the language, as between French and French-Canadian or between Dutch and Afrikaans.

Since all these peoples and clans felt themselves closely related to their ancestors, there was intense pressure to preserve their own identity. In such a situation it is not easy for trade languages, spoken and understood by several peoples, to develop.

A language only spreads beyond its own borders when isolation is broken down. This may happen in various ways.

1. The leader of a people may set himself up as a conqueror, defeating surrounding peoples and bringing them permanently under his authority. This happened in about AD 200 around Lake Chad; in the eighth century in the areas now known as Senegal, Mali and Niger; in Zimbabwe from the thirteenth century, and similarly in Nigeria, Benin and Ghana. Somewhat later there arose the pastoral kingdoms of Rwanda and Burundi. Within a kingdom a language served as a means of communication for a larger group of people. Sometimes it was the language of the conqueror, sometimes the language of the conquered.

2. In the fourth century some Malays crossed the Indian Ocean. They conquered the largely uninhabited island of Madagascar and developed their culture on the high plateaux together with rice growing on terraces. Their appearance and life-style are those of the Batak of Sumatra. They bury their dead in monuments which are much more imposing than the houses of the living, monuments exactly like those around Lake Toba in Sumatra. That is how Madagascar came to have a Malay language, Malagasy.

3. The Arabs came even before Christ from the Arabian peninsula to trade on the east coast of Africa. Muhammed taught the Arabs not only commerce but also conquest. From the ninth century, Arab city states were set up on the African coast: Mogadishu, Malindi, Mombasa, Zanzibar and Mozambique.

   Trade in gold, ivory and slaves brought prosperity to these cities in the twelfth century. These city states produced a mixture of Arabs and Africans speaking a trade language, Swahili, in which a Bantu core was mixed with Arabic influences.

   That is how the first big trade language in Africa was born. Now it is spoken by more than fifty million people from Katanga in Zaïre to the coast of Kenya, and from Uganda to Tanzania and Mozambique.

4. Islam is not only a religion, but also a culture and a language. The spread of Islam in North Africa meant the spread of Arabic. 70% of all the Arabic speakers in the world now live in Africa, mainly in North Africa. They speak Arabic dialects and for those of them who can read, the printed word of books and newspapers is rather close to the classical Arabic of the Qur'an.

5. In the fifteenth century came the Portuguese. Bartholomew Diaz reached the southern tip of Africa in 1488. He was followed by Dutch, Danes, French, Britons and even German Brandenburgers. Their interference on the coasts of Africa covers three centuries of the slave trade during which about twenty million people were taken from Africa to the Americas. This, together with the Arab

slave trade on the east coast, caused the complete disruption of African culture and life, up to a thousand kilometres from the coast.

This at the same time involved the birth on the west coast of a second great trade language, pidgin English, a language with many English, but also some Portuguese and even Dutch words, together with a Bantu structure. Around 1840, contracts and letters were written in pidgin and the language was used from Senegal to the River Congo.

6. Even before the colonial period, a few languages spoken by small peoples along rivers grew into trade languages covering a much wider area. We do not know whether this happened through increased communication through the slave trade or through internal development. One such language is Sango, now the official language of the Central African Republic, but formerly the language only of an insignificantly small people living on the banks of the Oubangi. It is probable that Sango was accepted in the Oubangi markets just because the original Sango speakers were such a small and politically unimportant group. Choosing their language for trade could not disturb the balance of power in the region.

From 1792, missionaries came to the coasts of Africa. They were the first Europeans who did not live either on their ships or in a fort on the coast, but among the Africans. They were the first whites who wanted to learn the African languages and reduced them to writing in order to preach the gospel and translate the Bible into these languages. From their ranks came the precursors of African linguistics: men like Krapf in Ethiopia and Taylor in Congo. They did not know how many languages there were in Africa or how many people spoke them. They were looking for big languages, but depended solely on God's guidance to find them. Krapf thought that Oremo, the language of the Galla, was the language of black Africa. Rebmann began in Kenya with Swahili, but had no idea how important a language it was. Samuel Crowther took Yoruba in 1848 and the Germans in Togo chose Ewe. Moffat began in South Africa in 1825 with Bechuana, while the English began with Malagasy in Madagascar and the Scots in Nigeria with Efik. Yoruba, Ewe, Swahili, Bechuana, Malagasy and Efik indeed proved to be big languages. But Alfred Saker in Cameroon in 1845 chose Duala, a small coastal language, and the British and Foreign Bible Society in 1815 brought out a Gospel in Bullom, another small language in West Africa. In 1879 the Americans in Gabon printed John's Gospel in Dokele, another language of a small people. Most of these languages were given only one Gospel. Other small languages, such as Duala, but also larger languages such as Bulu, spread far beyond their original frontiers through the influence of

Christian education and missionary Bible translation. In this way there developed a number of 'church languages' in the midst of the African Babel.

In translating the Bible into large languages, such as Swahili in East Africa and Nyanja in Nyasaland, the translators discovered that there were great dialectal differences within these languages. In such situations efforts were made to produce so-called 'union versions'. That means that translators tried to make a written language which would be a kind of highest common denominator of all the dialects. Sometimes this artificial written language was a great fiasco, because the intended readers rejected it: but in other cases, the union version was a powerful stimulant to develop a single written language for the speakers of all dialects. This happened for example with Swahili and Nyanja, and also with Igbo in Nigeria.

The language choices made by the pioneer missionaries sometimes had far-reaching consequences for the work of the missions. For example, American Presbyterians in southern Cameroon tried to use Bulu as a means of communication with several peoples. But the 25,000 Ngumba rejected Bulu and in 1929 set up their own Ngumba speaking church, which still exists as the Eglise Protestante Africaine. In 1929, Norwegian Lutherans began missionary work in northern Cameroon. The dominant group in this area was the Fulani, a Muslim pastoral people. In order to steer clear of Islam, the Norwegians decided to begin work in the language of the Mbum, non-Islamized serfs of the Fulani. But these Mbum had no status in the community; they were a minority people speaking a minority language so the church remained small. The Lutherans now work in other languages and the Bible is also available in Fulani. Comparable examples could be given from other countries than Cameroon of the unexpected consequences of choosing a particular language.

Putting languages on paper and translating the Bible was mostly the work of missionaries helped by African informants. None of the missionaries was trained in African linguistics, for such a discipline did not yet exist. At Fourah Bay College in Sierra Leone, the first European secondary school in Africa, young Africans were taught Hebrew and Greek with a view to Bible translation and Krapf had a similar ideal in Ethiopia. But only a limited number of missionaries knew the biblical languages, Greek or Hebrew. The quality of the translations was very uneven. In orthography, some brilliant solutions were found, but sometimes completely wrong ones. There were even missionaries who came to Africa with very limited intellectual equipment and worked in difficult conditions, but nevertheless developed into gifted translators who made monumental translations of the Bible. The Bibles in Malagasy and Bechuana are impressive examples of this.

The writings of the missions and the Bible societies give little insight into the contribution of African co-workers to the translations. Their part was certainly fundamental, since they were the ones who knew their own language. But the mission and Bible Society documentation was not generally concerned with recording history, but with arousing interest and support in Europe. Since the pioneer European and American translators were concerned on the one hand with giving the Bible to grateful Africans in their own tongue, and on the other hand with painting a picture which would raise money, data on African translators and co-translators are somewhat scarce.

The real translation problems were and still remain very diverse. Most African languages are tonal. That means, for example, that a high 'a' often gives a word a different meaning from a low 'a'. When these tones are not reproduced in writing, the language is unreadable, since 'bak' with a high 'a' means something completely different from 'bak' with a low 'a'. Some translators have found rather complicated solutions to the problems of orthography. For example, in Mundang, a language spoken near Lake Chad, Greek letters were added to the Roman alphabet. Other languages were written in the international phonetic alphabet.

Taking account where possible of UNESCO rules and the results of scientific linguistic analysis, translation consultants of the United Bible Societies have advocated the most practical solutions of orthographical problems. Where children learn French as the official language at school, the spelling of their own language must be as much like French as possible. The same applies to English in English-speaking countries and Portuguese in countries where Portuguese is the official language.

A second point is to try to develop an orthography which can be typed on a normal typewriter or word processor. In addition to the normal alphabet, a limited number of other signs may be used by replacing little used characters on the keyboard such as £. $. %. . ãnd ! If more characters are used than exist on, or can be fitted onto, a normal keyboard, typing and production of texts in that language becomes more difficult.

A quite different question is what is to be done with objects, such as animals and plants, which the intended reader does not know. What is to be done with the word 'snow' in languages of the Sahel? Or with 'shepherd' in an area, where, because of sleeping sickness, no herds can be raised? Or with 'vineyard' where vines are completely unknown? Or, to make things even more difficult, what is to be done with the snake in Genesis 3 in a culture in the Central African Republic where the snake is sacred? In most cases, these questions were and still are answered by choosing similar objects, animals or plants from the African setting. For example, the bear in Duala becomes a chimpanzee and the vineyard in a Zaïre language becomes a citrus plantation. In a Lake Chad language, the Holy Spirit is called God's shadow.

A third translation problem, perhaps the most difficult one, has to do with abstractions. This involves a difference between the biblical and the African ways of thinking. Fulani, spoken from Senegal to Lake Chad, has twenty different words for 'beautiful'. A flower is beautiful in a different way from a mountain and a woman beautiful in a different way from a cow. The same word cannot be used for them all. There is no single word for 'beauty'. Beauty is always related to a particular object: a girl, a flower, or a cow. What westerners express as the abstraction 'beauty' is only known to the Fulani with an accompanying noun: the 'beautiful' woman. The same is true for many abstractions such as righteousness, love, grace, and sin. How then can such biblical concepts be translated? The answer sometimes requires long research and discussion and sometimes there is no complete solution. In Bassa (Cameroon), for example, Protestants used the Greek word *charis* for grace and Catholics use the Latin word *gratia*.

It is remarkable that when African countries became independent, their language policy did not really change. On the contrary, many countries' national governments were at first hesitant in stimulating their own languages, since these emphasized the differences between peoples within the frontiers of a country and showed that the old colonial frontiers were badly drawn. Moreover, African countries (understandably) wanted to play a full part in the wider world and in the United Nations where French and English were official languages. Thus most countries in Africa chose English, French or Portuguese as their official languages. The only country south of the Sahara which did the opposite was Tanzania, which chose Swahili as its first and English as its second language. In a number of countries, official African languages took their place alongside the recognized European language. The number increased either when the national consciousness grew to feel that the recognition of African languages was no longer politically dangerous or when the feeling for African culture became stronger. At present Swahili is also officially recognized in Kenya, while Zambia has Chibemba, Nyanja and Tonga; Malawi Nyanja; Uganda has ten recognized African languages; in Rwanda Ruanda and in Burundi the related language Kirundi; in Madagascar Malagasy; in Zaïre Kikongo, Kituba, Lingala and Zaïre Swahili; in Nigeria Hausa and Fulani; in Togo Ewe; in the Central African Republic Sango; in Senegal Mandinka, Soninke and Wolof; in Somalia Somali and in Ethiopia Amharic.

Botswana has Tswana, Lesotho Southern Sotho, Swaziland Swazi, while in South Africa, in addition to English and Afrikaans, Northern and Southern Sotho, Tswana, Swaxi, Zulu, Xhosa, Venda and Tsonga are officially recognized languages.

Finally, in North Africa the whole of the Maghreb has become strongly Arabized, so that French has become the second language and in Egypt English.

In addition to Arabic, which is a fully cultural language in all areas, a great number of the large recognized African languages have a considerable production of 'reading materials' for education, in the press and sometimes also in novels and plays. These languages also play an important part in radio and television. A number of regionally recognized languages, for example in Uganda, are either used as the medium of instruction, for radio, in one newspaper and in literacy and development programmes, but have no printed literary products of their own. Scientific publications are published in very few of the officially recognized African languages. Official languages, regionally recognized languages and sometimes even other languages, it is true, play an important part in the rapid growth of pop music of various kinds: in advertising jingles; in political slogans in praise of the leader; in worship; and in love-songs and 'easy listening' music. However, the vast majority of writings by genuine African authors are published in European languages. This, I think, has to do with the European education of the African writers, and with their attempt to reach a wide market. It is nevertheless striking how the themes change. For years, novels written by Africans were concerned with the pros and cons of life for Africans under the colonial misunderstanding, while today's books are mostly critical analyses of how present-day society is going to the dogs.

There is in Africa generally a growing concern for indigenous languages. This includes interest in the hundreds of smaller African languages. Some African universities have established departments of linguistics; UNESCO makes a contribution through international conferences, for example on the orthography of languages spoken across political boundaries. But however much the authorities may wish to do so, they seldom have concrete plans, let alone the financial resources to develop these smaller languages in print and through the media. The most that happens, as far as the authorities are concerned, is that the smaller regional languages function in the reception classes of primary schools, as a bridge to larger languages in literacy programmes, and as languages understood in government offices. On paper little more is done. These languages may be also improvised for radio and are used in pop music. The economic motive of the viability of publications in a given language often play a central role, both in government and in commerce. In Africa as in other parts of the world, what matters most in deciding whether and how a language will be used in printing and reading is not the number of speakers, but the status of the language, the love of the language, and the consciousness of its own cultural heritage.

In addition, one might even say in contrast, there is a quite different development in the big new cities of Africa. When cities began to grow, people from a particular ethnic group went to the city and lived as far as possible by themselves. But this no longer works, because the cities have become too big, and the people too poor. The growing number of mixed marriages between partners from different groups shows that the big city is no longer an agglomeration of villages. In the melting-pot of the big cities of Africa, poverty is winning the battle against tribalism. There also, 'languages' are growing up which are simplified forms of African languages or Africanized European languages. Such languages are spoken at home and at table with the children. If people read at all, they do so in the official language learned at school.

Where in this Babel do the churches stand as communicators of the gospel? The Protestant churches have always worked in the African languages and still do so in their preaching and worship, but also in their teaching and membership training. They have at their disposal Bibles or New Testaments in more languages than those officially recognized. Sometimes they work with a Bible in one of the official languages, with impromptu translations being made for speakers of the smaller languages. There are also churches which have not only the Bible, but also a hymn book, a catechism and all kinds of devotional and development literature in their own language. They have good distribution channels for these books and newspapers. But there is also a large number of churches in which the production of vernacular Christian literature is slowing down or has dried up altogether. This happens because of lack of funds or technical problems with production or import; it can also happen because of insufficient concern for and commitment to one's own language.

The Bible societies have large tasks ahead of them. In many places in Africa, the old missionary Bibles are being retranslated by indigenous translators. For this, they are using special handbooks developed by the UBS, and they are assisted by UBS translation consultants. In many cases they are busy translating the Old Testament to complement the New Testament which they have already. The strategy behind this is the 1980 UBS resolution to work for a complete Bible in common language in all languages with more than a million speakers and in all other official languages. The Bible societies give priority in all these translations and revisions to the so-called functional equivalent principle; that is, they aim to make, not a word-for-word translation, but to transfer the entire content and meaning of the message in today's language. Only in this way can the difference in thought and culture between the Bible and African thinking be bridged; except in Egypt and Ethiopia, Africans, unlike westerners, did not have a Jewish and Greek background. In this type of translations, the receptor or target language is more important than the source language. Decisions regarding this type of translation are made by the churches in the area, who are to make and use them.

At the first big conference of Bible Society representatives and church leaders at Driebergen in 1964, the German Protestant Bishop Dibelius called for Bibles with notes, 'for we in Europe no longer understand the Bible.' At the same time, John Gatu of Kenya pleaded for Bibles with notes 'because we do not yet understand the Bible.' Because the word 'notes' makes one think of dogmatic interpretation, the Bible Societies prefer to speak about 'readers' helps'. People are now working in many countries (for decisions are always taken at national level) towards simple readers' helps in all editions for use in evangelism, while in the big languages, in addition to or as part of the common language Bible, attempts are made to produce study Bibles with full historical, linguistic, geographical and other helps beside the biblical text. It has proved possible, not only for members of different Protestant churches, but also for Protestants and Roman Catholics, to cooperate in making such helps without encountering doctrinal problems. The old Bible Society principle of 'no note or comment' has been modified.

In addition to complete Bibles in the bigger languages, the Bible Societies are cooperating in translations in smaller and completely 'new' languages. This always happens at the request of local churches or missions. National Bible Societies are also ready to participate in new reader programmes (see chapter 28). But as for Bibles in big languages, Bible Society help is limited to scientific, technical and financial help for the translators. Technical help includes a steadily increasing role for computers and text processors, with electricity provided by solar panels in places far from the large centres. Once the translation is complete, the Bible Society guarantees to publish it at a price which people can afford.

Since 1962 the Wycliffe Bible Translators have also been working in Africa, often under the name Summer Institute of Translators (SIL). The SIL is an organization independent of any church; its task is to translate the Bible into all the languages of the world, so that people may meet Christ in their own language. The SIL workers have traditionally made their own translations, but for some years have been increasingly emphasizing in Africa the training of African translators. In practice the SIL is active in small languages with not more than 100,000 speakers. They have made a list of all languages in Africa spoken by people who are themselves asking for a translation of the Bible. The list includes 30 languages with 50,000 to 100,000 speakers; 25 with 25,000 to 49,000; and 55 languages with 1400 to 25,000 speakers.

It is certainly true that throughout the world there are peoples and smaller groups who would like a Bible in their mother tongue, because that makes their little language important. But this costs a great deal of time and energy and it is very probable that in such small languages nothing more than reading books and the New Testament will ever be printed. History shows that the Bible goes its own way, but without a clear relation with church work or church building that way comes to a dead end. The situation is quite different in areas where SIL helps in the translation work at the request of the local churches. Wherever the work of SIL fits into the UBS strategy, the two bodies co-operate in Africa.

Because SIL does not want to be a missionary organization or a church, but simply to enable God's word to make its own way, in a few African countries SIL has signed contracts with the authorities for linguistic research, and cooperate in literacy work. In this way, linguistically speaking, they render to Caesar what is Caesar's, so that God's word can be translated.

Under a variety of names, SIL have offices in Nairobi, Kenya; Yaoundé, Cameroon, and a number of other African countries. They are working in Africa in a total of 200 languages. The Bible societies in Africa are also deeply involved in a trend in exactly the opposite direction, namely the growth of big languages, especially in the large new cities. In 1966 there appeared the first New Testaments based on the functional equivalent principle: they were in Spanish and English. These editions have proved an enormous success in the secularized western world, but also in Africa. (By 1992, almost 36 million copies of the entire Good News Bible had been distributed worldwide). Older people in Africa whose speech was influenced by the classical King James Version which they had learned at school found it hard to accept the new translations, but young people saw the relation between the language of the modern Bible and that of their school books and radio and television. The Bible in 'français courant', today's French, is also a great success, for example in a city such as Abidjan. In the cities, the big African languages are also growing. This is true, for example, for Swahili in East Africa and for Kituba in Zaire. Since many children do not complete their schooling, the number of functional illiterates is increasing. This means that in the big languages, such as English, French, Portuguese, Swahili, Kituba, Shona, Kinyarwanda, a common language translation is needed, and also a series of booklets with Bible selections for new readers. Even the translation in today's Afrikaans, for the white and coloured people of South Africa, has sold over a million copies.

As elsewhere in this book (see chapter 37), Arabic is a separate problem. A Bible translation close to the language used in school, in newspapers and on television is in fact urgently needed, since classical Arabic is too difficult; but many Christians have learned from the Muslims such reverence for sacred books that they lean more towards a classical, and therefore less easily understandable, Bible. A study

Bible in classical Arabic, with many readers' helps, is being made, and is likely to prove a striking success.

All this confirms that the churches, and therefore also the Bible Societies, have a great deal to do in this African Babel. Unfortunately, it is necessary for this work to be based on a strict scale of priorities, and this not for reasons of principle but on purely financial considerations. In some respects, SIL follows a different translation strategy.

Finally, whatever language is used in church and in evangelism, everything now and in the future depends on the choice and commitment of African believers themselves. The history of African teaches that to be a Christian, to meet the Father of the Lord Jesus Christ, only truly happens when this meeting, encounter, and conversion happen in one's mother tongue.

29

The Book in the Colonies

In Africa they tell the story that the missionaries came and said, 'Let us pray.' After the Africans had finished praying, they opened their eyes and saw a book in their laps; it was the Bible. But their land had gone.

The Europeans, however, did not realize that the Bible was also the time-bomb with which one day the African would in turn blow up their colonialism.

We have already told how, between 1790 and 1845, missionaries settled on the coasts of Africa. They fought the European and Arab slave trade and dreamed their dreams of converting the whole continent. Missionaries became explorers, going to find out how and where a chain of mission stations, an Apostles' Road, could be built to take the Good News to the ends of Africa. The most famous of them, David Livingstone, Moffat's son-in-law, became the first to travel right across Africa. People were fascinated by these explorations to discover unknown worlds. The effect on the European public at that time was like that of space travel in our day. People's minds became filled with a strange mixture of romantic inquisitiveness, derived from Rousseau, about the 'noble savage' and the Christian call to go and save the poor heathen 'out there'. That is why missionary societies and Bible societies, and also geographical societies, aroused so much interest. When Livingstone was lost in the African interior, it was a newspaper which financed Stanley's search for him, for fine stories about Africa were always news. Thanks to men like Livingstone and Stanley, but also John Hanning Speke and Captain Richard Francis Burton, Heinrich Barth, Gustav Nachtigall and Mungo Park, the sources of the Nile, the course of the Niger and the Congo, and the great waterfalls of Africa were discovered and mapped.

The slave trade on the coast and by sea had largely ended by that time, but missionaries in particular reported on the horrors of slave transport in the interior, which was continuing and even growing. Zanzibar appeared to be supplied from as far away as Nyasaland and

Katanga. Livingstone started to plead for the African to be protected not only against slavery on the coast and at sea, but also in the interior.

This humanitarian appeal gave some European countries an excuse to interfere. The Belgian King Leopold II found Belgium too small. He hired Stanley to set up for him a kind of private kingdom on the River Congo. In Germany, Bismarck was more concerned with power in Europe than with far-off lands; but the Woermann trading company in Hamburg managed to convince the Chancellor of the value of a colonial adventure. Britain and France wanted to maintain their traditional trading links with various places in Africa, while Portugal did not want to lose what was left of its old glory. The British and French were not interested in settling in Africa, since for them Africa still mainly offered ports of call on the way to more profitable places in the Far East and America; but they did not wish to see Belgium's and Germany's position in Africa strengthened. Both Protestant and Roman Catholic missionaries, including Cardinal Lavigerie, the founder of the missionary order of the White Fathers, pleaded for intervention in order to put an end to the misery of the interior slave trade. There was a threat of serious conflict over the colonial activities of the Belgians and Germans; the French were also concerned about British activities in Egypt. So Bismarck called a conference on Africa in Berlin at the end of 1884. All interested European parties attended, including the Turkish sultan. The British did not trust the French, and the French felt the British had stolen a march on them by their interference in Egypt, where the French had built the Suez Canal. This helped Leopold II to obtain at the conference the blessing of the European powers on his 'International Association of the Congo', the purpose of which was to suppress the slave trade and further free trade in the Congo basin. The result was that the European countries, and also the Turkish sultan, recognized the treaties which Stanley had made on behalf of Leopold II with a couple of hundred African chiefs along the River Congo. The same recognition was given to the German trading agreements on the coasts of Togo, Cameroon, Tanganyika and South-West Africa. It was important for the missions that freedom of religion was recognized by all participants in the conference. Missions would be free, everywhere in Africa, to carry on their work of founding churches and schools. This applied not only to Catholics and Protestants, but also (because of the sultan's presence) for Muslims.

After that, it was easy for Cardinal Lavigerie to persuade Leopold II to organize another big conference in Brussels in 1889–90, finally to abolish the slave trade. An international agreement for the abolition of the slave trade was signed in 1890. This agreement recognized the need to set up fortified posts inland to combat the slave trade. These could also protect mission stations.

All this looked, and partly was, idealistic; but the consequence of
the Berlin Conference and the Brussels Act was that the African
continent was divided between the European powers, and modern
colonialism began. Sometimes frontiers were set by literally drawing
lines on a map, so that in some places one African people would find
itself living in three different countries. Africa became Belgian,
German, Spanish, Portuguese, Italian, British and French. Only
Liberia, the land of the returned slaves, and Ethiopia, the old
Christian kingdom, remained independent.

Many missions in Uganda, Bechuanaland, Nigeria, Congo and
elsewhere were thankful that now the slave trade within Africa itself
could be stopped and the gospel could spread safely. Especially in
France and in Britain, public opinion was keenly interested in the
colonies. Politically important was the Suez Canal, which the Frenchman Ferdinand de Lesseps had built and which the British were to
govern. There the British discovered the value of linking the economic
activities of trading companies with diplomacy. In southern Africa
they found gold and diamonds, proving that Africa was more than a
continent of ivory and slaves. Finally, the role of enthusiastic individuals should not be underestimated. The aim of people like George D.
T. Goldie in Nigeria, King Leopold II for the Congo, and Cecil J.
Rhodes in southern Africa was to obtain large colonial possessions for
themselves or their homelands.

Meanwhile the first industrial revolution had begun in Europe. It
required both raw materials for the factories and markets for industrial
products, so the colonies became both suppliers and customers. In
addition, health care in Europe improved so that the population began
to grow. More work and more opportunities were needed for more
people.

All this meant that between 1885 and 1890 (not earlier) colonial
administrations were set up all over Africa and modern colonialism
developed.

Its distinctive features were the following:

1. After the various territories had been occupied, sometimes with the
   use of force, the African population was told to stay where it was
   and keep quiet; tribal wars were henceforth forbidden. A minimal
   administration was set up, sometimes on a military basis, trying to
   use existing African administrative structures such as village chiefs,
   sultans and kings. The colonizer was looking for the cheapest
   solution. In some areas, such as northern Nigeria, this 'indirect
   rule' gave fresh status to the local feudal rulers. As early as 1903 the
   French parliament resolved that colonies would not be subsidized
   by the home country.
2. The colonies were suppliers of raw materials. Copper came from
   Katanga and Northern Rhodesia, gold and diamonds from South

Africa and the Congo. Then there was hardwood from West Africa, and rubber, but also new agricultural products such as cotton, sisal, cocoa, coffee, bananas and tobacco. The simplest solution was to develop single crop territories, in which, as far as possible, one product would be produced: sisal in Tanganyika, groundnuts in Senegal, coffee in Uganda, cocoa in the Gold Coast, and so on.

3. Roads and railways, harbours and later airfields were built, as they became necessary to meet the colonizer's needs. The local population was often forced to help in building the roads and railways. This forced labour was one of the most hated aspects of the colonial administration. In the Belgian Congo, Angola and Mozambique, the population was also pressed into service on plantations.

4. Western medical care was introduced. The colonizer organized campaigns against the major diseases and encouraged the missions to take responsibility for basic medical care. Major diseases such as sleeping sickness and smallpox were suppressed; but never throughout the colonial period did medical care make the transition from curative to preventive medicine. Although mortality figures remained high, there was general and significant progress.

5. The colonizer needed junior civil servants, and sergeants for the army, who could read and write. Hence modest developments in education were encouraged. The missions played a great part in this, as we shall show later in this chapter.

6. Planning and decision-making for the colonies took place in a ministry in the home country; Africans had no influence on them. The colonies themselves were run by omnicompetent Europeans. This was true, not only in administration and economic activities, but also in the missions. It was the period of paternalistic missions 'out there', and mission boards in Europe with a feeling of superiority, anxious to do what was best for the 'natives' entrusted to them.

Thus there arose in Africa a society of misunderstanding in which Europeans decided everything in an incomprehensibly European way. Their symbols were a soldier, a policeman and a European administrator, trader or missionary, people who called Africans everywhere by their first names and kept them waiting on the verandah until the European was ready to come out to see them.

Within this general picture, each colonizing power had its own ways. The Germans were hard. Early in the twentieth century in Namibia, then South-West Africa, the Herero revolted, and the Germans tried to exterminate the entire people. Yet the Germans were also strong on the theory of colonization. In mission, they developed the concept of 'people mission', mission to a whole people. The worked out a language policy in which one big African language was chosen in each region for primary education, with German for secondary education. After the First World War, their colonial activity came to an end so that they were never able to put their theories into practice.

The French wanted assimilation. Their administration was strongly centralized, just as in Paris. They occupied Algeria in order to end piracy, to expand France, and to fulfil a 'civilizing task'. In the Sudan, they met British competition and lost. Years later, Cecil Rhodes was to report to Queen Victoria: 'We left the sand to the French.' In black Africa, the French offered Africans a stake in French culture. They were therefore not interested in African languages, which they called 'dialects'. They prohibited education in the vernacular and introduced a French curriculum, complete with the rivers of France, French history, and reading books which featured little Jean playing in the snow. A Frenchified African élite soon shared in the administration of the colonies. Generally speaking, conservatives and Catholics in France were in favour of colonization and socialists and later communists against it.

Even anti-clericals generally saw the value of Roman Catholic missions in the colonies. When the French occupied Madagascar, and later when the League of Nations gave them Togo and Cameroon as mandated territories, the Protestant Mission de Paris had to assist non-French missions on the spot against discrimination by French colonial administrators, proving by their work and their manpower that mission in France was not only a Roman Catholic concern.

The British never developed a general colonial policy: in each territory, they took things as they found them. In Egypt they intervened for political reasons, and in South Africa for economic reasons (gold and diamonds). In other places they often acquired their colonies and protectorates under pressure from public opinion at home or at the demand of a trading company or a missionary society. In cultural terms their colonization assumed that it was an honour to be part of the British Empire in its political, economic and also religious greatness. 'Learn a bit of English', it implied, 'so that you can talk with us, but for the rest, remain yourselves, since you have the misfortune not to have been born in the British Isles.' The greatest honour an Englishman could give an African was to grant him a British passport.

King Leopold II saw his Congo purely as a source of profit. Its main product was rubber. People there were so shamefully treated that the international community, partly on the basis of reports from Protestant missionaries, forced the king in 1908 to transfer his private kingdom to Belgium. Belgium had no colonial history and the Belgians had no real colonial ambitions. So they behaved in the Congo like normal Belgians. They exported their language controversy to the Congo. In the early 1960s, the Kinshasa (then Léopoldville) telephone directory was in two languages: French and Flemish. The Belgians entrusted education to the Catholic missions and clearly discriminated against the Protestants. They were active in organizing basic technical instruction, but began much too late with higher education.

Portugal's 'overseas provinces' served as visible proof of her past glories. The home country was poor and its colonies merely a source of profit. A co-operation agreement was signed, handing over education to the Roman Catholic missions. They were to turn the colonialized population into Catholics, but also into good Portuguese. Since the Berlin conference, Protestants unfortunately had to be tolerated, but they were subjected to permanent discrimination. When risings and a war of liberation against Portugal broke out, the colonies had only 35,000 *assimilados*, that is, officially recognized black-skinned Portuguese. There were however no African clergy, and among a thousand pupils at the secondary school in Lourenço Marques in Moẓambique, there sat thirty Africans.

The colonizer did not resolve the tensions and problems between Africa's many ethnic groups and sub-groups. Tribal wars were prohibited, and for two generations the mutual oppositions were put on ice. In the growing cities and the new industrial areas, the various peoples learned to live alongside each other, but often not with each other.

Dr Kwame Nkrumah, the first president of Ghana, once said that God had blessed West Africa with the mosquito. The mosquito indeed prevented Europeans from settling permanently in West Africa. They only came there for a time, whereas they settled as colonists in places where there were no mosquitoes: Europeans and Asians in East Africa and southern Africa, Portuguese in their colonies, French in Algeria and Tunisia. The colonists were a great problem for decolonization in the 1960s.

In the colonial period, both Catholic and Protestant missions had an ambivalent image. The pioneers before 1885 lived, struggled and died alongside Africans. Now the various missionaries came to stand between the African and the colonizer, sometimes as the righteous defender of the African, but sometimes also as an extension of the colonial administration.

The temporary shelters under which the first missionaries taught Africans to read the Bible in their own languages grew into Christian schools with European curricula required by the colonizer. For him that was the cheapest solution, since the missions wanted both to contribute to African development and also to train leaders for their own schools and churches. The Catholics, whose religious orders had plenty of cheap man- and woman-power at their disposal, were particularly active in school work. One might say that the schools enabled them to catch up on the Protestants. In 1945 90% of all education in black Africa was still Christian, and even in a country like Egypt the best schools were Christian.

In the countries in which African languages were allowed to be used in education, the New Testament or the Bible held an important place among reading materials. They were plentiful and cheap, thanks to Bible Society subsidies. As a result the Bible knowledge of the average African Protestant was greater than that of the average West European Christian. Where education had to be given in the colonial language, the French Bible translation of Louis Segond or the classical King James Bible was used. Biblical English and French could be traced for a long time in many Africans' speeches and letters. The Portuguese refused to use African languages. They accepted only diglot editions of the Bible with Portuguese on the left-hand page and the African language on the right.

In the colonial period, European power was clearly present even in the most remote parts of Africa. According to African thinking, the God who stood behind the Europeans must also be powerful. It mattered less whether the Europeans honoured or dishonoured God in their daily lives. When, in such a situation, the Protestants made particular efforts to translate the book of the God of the Europeans and make it cheaply available, the Bible became very popular in Africa as a source of information about the background of the colonizer's power, as the book of white magic. It also became a source of consolation and hope for forced labourers working on the roads and railways; as a signpost for uprooted people in the cities and the new industries; as something to hold on to in a society based on misunderstanding.

For all the missions, the colonial administrator corresponded to what the Letter to the Romans called the powers that be, ordained by God. Sometimes the administrators thought of themselves as having received from God the task of civilizing the poor heathen; for a superior Christian religion was too easily linked with a superior western culture. For some missions, perhaps at certain times for all, the colonial government was seen as an administration whose actions had to be constantly tested against the biblical standards of stewardship and justice. The situation varied, depending on the mission and country in question and on the concrete circumstances.

After the Second World War, it became widely recognized that expressions like 'missionary society' and 'missionary congregation' were not found in the Bible. Two or three gathered together in Christ's name were enough. Sometimes it was the missionaries themselves who came to see this; sometimes African Christians. Towards the end of the 1950s, most Protestant missions became autonomous African churches and many Roman Catholic dioceses came to be governed by African bishops. This happened before political independence. The ideals of the mission pioneers became a reality: churches became self-governing, self-propagating and self-supporting. They preached the

Shop Name: WESLEY OWEN/CROYDON [18] A/c No. : 965014 76

Title: ON THEIR WAY REJOICING 1995

Author: SCHAAF, YPE

Publisher: PAT

Retail Price: £7.99 Vat Rate: 0.00% ISBN: 0-8536.4561-2

Subject: G02 CHURCH HISTORY Supplier: STL

Order No.: 612628 (1)

Date: 09/01/95

Qty Required: Your Ref: 070195FH 3551

gospel themselves, they administered their own churches, and they found their own finance.

When later African countries attained political independence and began to build their own structures, it became clear that two generations of colonization by Europeans who felt themselves superior were still exercising a great influence. The new elite which assumed the leadership professed with their lips that they wanted to find their own answers to modern challenges, but in fact they tried to build European societies in Africa, or at least aimed at full participation in northern technology and economics. Yet the colonial period had been too short for true westernization, and this is an important cause of the problems of Africa today.

As we have said, the role of the Christian churches and the Bible in all this has been ambivalent. On the one hand the Bible and the Christian churches offered answers to the questions and uncertainties which had arisen in the colonial period, and the Bible and the church made these answers easily available in the languages of the people. On the other, churches and missions also supplied Bibles in European languages, thereby promoting alienating western education with its feeling of superiority and its so-called objective scientific pretentions which end in secularization.

30

The Unique Forerunner

In the colonial period, Togo and Dahomey were called the Latin Quarter of French Africa. In both countries, quite a few Africans had been educated to a modest middle-school level and had administrative jobs with the colonial government and in trading companies from Dakar in Senegal to Brazzaville in the Congo. After the wave of independence in 1960, a large proportion of these clerks were sooner or later force to return to their home countries in order to make room for local people. In Togo and Benin (then Dahomey) this caused additional employment problems.

As early as the 1920s, people from Dahomey also worked as junior officials in Abidjan, Côte d'Ivoire. Among them were Christians which had come into contact with the gospel at home, in Cotonou or Porto-Novo, through a British Methodist mission. In 1924, these migrant workers in Abidjan wanted to build a church in order to hold services in their own language. They had problems with the French colonial administration about the official recognition of their church and about buying a piece of land.

One of their missionaries came over from Dahomey to try to settle the matter. The minister in question was called William J. Platt. He turned to a French lawyer for legal advice. The lawyer asked which group of Protestants he had come to see in Côte d'Ivoire. Missionary Platt replied: 'The only Protestants there are in Abidjan, the *petits fonctionnaires*, junior officials, from Dahomey.'

Then the French lawyer told him that there were thousands of Protestants in Côte d'Ivoire who had no missionaries to instruct them in the teaching of the Bible. Representatives of these people had recently been to see him with a thick roll of bank-notes, asking him to go to Europe and bring back missionaries. He had refused.

Platt settled the legal problems of his own fellow-believers from Dahomey and went to look for these other Protestants. In the primeval forest of southern Côte d'Ivoire, he found in many villages a kind of churches where people met on Sundays. These buildings contained English Bibles which the people could not read. Sermons were preached in Fanti (a Gold Coast language) and songs translated into Fanti were sung. There were even churches with belfreys. Everyone said that they were waiting until the promises would be fulfilled. Platt estimated that about 50,000 people were involved.

The founder of this waiting community was a Liberian called William Wadé Harris. Later, one of Platt's French colleagues went to meet him in a village in Liberia. His story, complemented by information from the waiting Christians in Côte d'Ivoire, was as follows.

Wadé Harris had been a sailor. In his travels along the West African coast, he had come into contact with Christianity in Lagos, Nigeria. He was converted, and after a long time as a sailor and as a farmer in his home village in Liberia, the Lord called him to go and spread the message of the Book which he had learned to love. So Harris set out on foot, clothed in a long white garment, with his English Bible in his left hand and in his right hand a wooden staff surmounted by a cross. In the villages of Liberia, no one wanted to listen to his story, so he went further afield. In the Appolonia district of the Gold Coast, and also in the villages of southern Côte d'Ivoire, God granted him the power to touch people's hearts.

Harris's message and mission were very simple. First he told the people, burn your fetishes because they are idols. Secondly, believe in the saving cross of Jesus Christ; and thirdly, believe in God's book, the Bible, which one day white people will come to explain to you. Wadé Harris preached in pidgin English, the trade language of the west coast. When people wanted to exchange their fetishes for Harris's wooden cross, he refused to break his cross in pieces and distribute the pieces, because he did not want Christ's cross to become a new fetish. Harris also refused to replace the traditional healers by going to cure the sick. He stood by what the Book said about Christ. An estimated 100,000 people burned their fetishes and were baptized in groups of five with water from Harris's calabash. They were not told precisely in what the Good News of the Bible consisted. They were not told the biblical meaning of baptism. Harris knew too little about it himself. He simply said: 'No more fetishes; no more traditional healers; but wait for the white men who will explain the book about Christ.'

Harris remained three months in the Gold Coast and about two years in Côte d'Ivoire.

When, in 1913, he first came to Côte d'Ivoire, the bush dwellers were just having their first contact with French colonialism. In all villages workers were recruited by force to lay a railway to the south. This forced labour had given rise to disturbances in some places. Traditional powers were opposed to this break-up of village and primeval bush society. There was unrest. In other words, the world

changed with the coming of the railway. The traditional healers and
the powers of their own society, which so to speak lived in the fetishes,
had not been able to withstand this break-up; they had lost the battle
against the new powers. This opened the way for the white answers to
the questions of life, for a new gospel. Yet Harris's message was not
only new; it was not just about a God whom Europeans would make
known; it came over also as a truly African message.

The French were impressed by the integrity of this man with the
white robe, the wooden cross, and the Bible. Yet they were very
apprehensive about an organized movement. First they let the prophet
from Liberia go on his way; then they arrested him, but the
French governor released him. But still, shortly after, he was gently
escorted to the Liberian frontier. On the way, he baptized two of his
guards.

Two years later, in 1916, Harris tried to return to Côte d'Ivoire. This
was in the middle of the First World War, and he was not allowed
entry. So Wadé Harris came to the conclusion that his God-given task
had ended and he went back to farming in the village where he had
been born.

In 1913, while Roman Catholic missions were already active, but
there was no Protestant work in Côte d'Ivoire, Wadé Harris with his
evangelistic motivation had been the first to reach people with the
Good News. Thousands had built houses for God and waited until
Platt found them in 1924. Then the British Methodist mission, which
was certainly not rich, had to take a difficult decision. Although the
work in Dahomey was by no means finished, a few missionary
workers, together with thirty Christians, including some evangelists,
were transferred from Dahomey to Côte d'Ivoire, in order to make
Harris's promise come true for the waiting thousands.

This meant slowing down the work in Dahomey. In southern Côte
d'Ivoire, the Methodist Church is the largest Protestant denomination.
Next comes a Harris Church which perhaps mixes the Bible more
strongly than Harris would have wished with African traditions.

Bible translation work began immediately in 1925 in Adjukru,
Ebrie, Atchi and Dida. It was a difficult task and it went slowly. At the
time of writing, the Christians in southern Côte d'Ivoire have New
Testaments in nine languages, of which six have been published since
1980. The first complete Bible, in Gouro, was produced in 1979.
Alongside these translations, the Bible in *français courant* (Today's
French Version) is also used.

Later Platt became for many years a general secretary of the BFBS.

As for the Gold Coast, British missionaries in the early 1920s found
much greater openness to the gospel in the Appolonia District than in
other parts of the country. An African minister reported to the mission
that this was because a movement started by Wadé Harris was behind

it. Here too the mission sent people, this time from Axim, to give answers to those who were waiting.

Wadé Harris's white robe, his cross and his Bible meant for thousands, at a time of growing uncertainty, the beginning of liberation.

31

Free from Slavery

For centuries, three words summed up the reasons for non-Africans' interest in Africa. These were gold, ivory and slaves.

Slavery already existed in the time before Christ; Greek and Roman society and economic life turned on the work of slaves. These included Germans and other 'barbarians', but also Africans brought in via Egypt and North Africa. Long before Mohammed, the Arabs became the great slave traders. Later, the Qur'an gave rules and conditions to regulate slavery, but did not forbid slavery itself. The first supply routes for slaves from Africa ran through Senegal, Mauretania and Morocco to Algiers on the west, and from the Sudan via the Nile to Alexandria on the east.

The Christian conscience opposed slavery on the grounds of the equality of all human beings before the Lord; this was emphasized in the church. Yet until the middle ages, even monasteries in Europe had slaves; as late as 1542, a pope defended this practice. In the same period, other popes protested against slavery in the territories of Africa and America which Europeans had recently discovered.

But more and more labour came to be needed in the sixteenth century in the Americas for the sugar plantations which the Europeans were setting up, at first with local labour. Most of the Indians did not prove suitable for this work, so someone had the idea of bringing negroes from Africa to do it.

The transport of many millions of slaves from Africa to the Americas became one of the blackest pages in the history of the commercial expansion of Europe. About every fifty years the slave trade was accompanied on the one hand by loud and clear Protestant and Catholic protests against this inhuman trade, and on the other by theological discussions about whether a negro was really a human being.

The first European slave route ran from West Africa to North and Central America. It was followed by routes from Angola and Mozambique to Brazil. For many years, the Dutch triangular route was notorious and very profitable. Dutch products were taken to West

Africa; there slaves were obtained for America; and then the ships returned from America to the Netherlands with sugar and cotton. Fort Elmina in Ghana (then Gold Coast) played an important part in this.

For centuries, one of the largest and most horrible centres on the east coast, for both Arabs and Portuguese, was the island of Zanzibar, now part of Tanzania. Portuguese, Dutch, British, French, Danes and Germans all helped to write the black pages of three centuries of slave trading. Nor was the slave trade in Africa confined to Arabs and Europeans. Slavery was also practised in African society itself. But slaves were never, or only rarely, sold. It was the Europeans with their commercial methods who corrupted these traditions. They armed the chiefs and kings of the coastal peoples and forced them to hunt slaves in the interior for the Europeans. African leaders who refused knew that their own people would be taken away. Some leaders co-operated in order to have a share in the profits from this trade in human beings.

The European slave trader made his deliveries wherever there was a demand: to the sugar plantations of Brazil, the West Indies or Louisiana; to the mines of South America; and also to the sugar plantations of the island of Mauritius in the Indian Ocean, and the farms of the Cape of Good Hope.

Scholars estimate that in three hundred years Europeans took between ten and twelve million slaves from Africa. Including those who died on the way to the coast, or during transport to America, the total is between eighteen and twenty million.

As time went on, the demand for African labour became ever greater so that the slave hunters had to go further and further inland in order to 'capture' young, strong men and women. The Arab slave trade on the east coast was almost as extensive as the European. Around 1820, raiders were hunting for slaves as far as Katanga, almost in the heart of Africa.

At the same time, reports from pioneer missionaries about the destruction of African societies because of these slave hunts were beginning to reach Europe.

In 1742 John Woolman, an immigrant newly arrived in Philadelphia had, as an apprentice clerk, to draw up a contract for the sale of a negro woman. It made him think, study and read. As a Quaker he came to realize that the sale of human beings cannot be either humane or biblical. God's creatures must not be used and sold like tools. In 1758 he succeeded in convincing the Quaker Meeting in Philadelphia of the truth of his insights. The first anti-slavery action committee was set up. A teacher called Anthony Benezet kept its records. He had pamphlets published and got influential people on both sides of the Atlantic to write them. As a result the movement of protest against slavery began in an area where people could see for themselves, every day, both the inhumanity of the slave trade and the humanity of black servants and labourers.

In England too protest movements began in Quaker circles with efforts to change people's way of thinking about slavery. In 1783 an action committee was set up; it began by distributing in England Benezet's pamphlets from Philadelphia. The problem was seriously studied. In 1785 Thomas Clarkson won an Edinburgh University Latin essay prize with a treatise against the slave trade. In the following years, there appeared a stream of booklets, essays and studies on slavery and the slave trade. The spokesman for the anti-slavery movement was William Wilberforce, a Member of Parliament. He gathered around him a small group of parliamentarians from various parties which came to be called 'the Saints'. The motivation for their struggle was humanitarian and biblical, but their methods were very modern: speeches, documentation, pamphlets, books, petitions, questions in Parliament. In 1788 Parliament failed to approve a first bill for the abolition of the slave trade. But the Saints ensured that, each year until 1834, the slave trade reappeared on the agenda. Business and other vested interests organized resistance so that in 1790 a bill for the abolition of the slave trade was defeated in Parliament by 163 votes to 88. The Saints responded by organizing 500 petitions throughout the country. In 1792 they won their first victory: a motion for the gradual abolition of slavery was passed. Despite the French Revolution and the war with France, the Saints continued their campaign, and in 1807 they finally succeeded: both Houses of Parliament approved a law abolishing the slave trade. On 1 March 1808 the law took effect, making the slave trade illegal throughout the British Empire. The navy was given the task of enforcing the law.

Since the prohibition of the slave trade meant merely that no more Africans were enslaved, the Saints went further. The millions still living in slavery had to be freed. In 1822, Thomas Fowell Buxton took over from Wilberforce the leadership of the campaign in Parliament. The motives for this continued action were clearly stated in the title of a book which Wilberforce had published in 1823: *An Appeal to the Religion, Justice and Humanity of the Inhabitants of the British Empire in behalf of the Negro Slaves in the West-Indies*. And in England in 1822 religion meant biblical Christianity. In 1824 and 1830 there appeared the two volumes of James Stephens' *The Slavery of the British West-India Colonies Delineated*.

In 1825 Zachary Macauley became editor of a newspaper called *The Anti-Slavery Reporter*. Parliament passed in 1823 measures for improving the situation of the slaves. They had no effect, because the slave owners proved recalcitrant and uncontrollable. In 1823 also dozens of petitions were drawn up and signed. By May the Saints were able to announce that one and a half million signatures had been collected. A 300-strong delegation went to see the Prime Minister at 10 Downing Street. They came from all over the United Kingdom: from the Isle of Wight to Scotland and from Wales to Harwich. They came from all classes of society and from both the Church of England and the free churches. This protest from the entire country made such an impression that in August 1833 Parliament resolved to abolish slavery itself. On 1 August 1834 the Saints won their greatest victory: both the slave trade and also slavery itself were prohibited in the British Empire. Parliament set twenty million pounds aside as compensation for the slave owners.

Meanwhile, since 1807, the British Navy had been active in controlling shipping off the slave coasts and bringing back to Africa slaves found on ships at sea. In what is now Sierra Leone, Freetown was set up as a town for freed slaves. Even before the success of the Saints' campaign in Britain, Denmark had abolished slavery. After 1834, the other European countries followed. The United States resolved to abolish slavery in 1862, but in the United States, abolition only became effective after the Civil War which lasted from 1861 to 1865.

Yet all this did not yet mean the end of the slave trade in Africa. Throughout his journeys across Africa, Livingstone encountered slave raids, for example in what are now called Malawi and Zaire. In his famous speech in the Senate House in Cambridge in 1857, he spoke in fiery words, pleading for opening Africa to 'Christianity and commerce'. He believed that only the gospel, together with the economic development of Africans themselves, could put an end to the slave trade.

His speech made a great impression, but nothing happened. On the west coast it is true that by about 1860 the slave trade had largely disappeared, but at the same time about 60,000 slaves a year were still being sold, mainly by Arabs through Zanzibar and other East African ports. In 1872 the Sultan of Zanzibar signed an agreement abolishing slavery on his island, but on the coast and in the interior the wretched trade went on. Livingstone and his associates now obtained support from the Roman Catholic side in the person of Cardinal Lavigerie, Archbishop of Algiers, the founder of the White Fathers and one of the great nineteenth-century mission pioneers. He began a campaign against slavery in the Roman Catholic countries of Europe. The intentions of Livingstone and Lavigerie were honestly Protestant and honestly Roman Catholic. They wanted to spread the gospel and were concerned for God's African creatures.

On the suggestion of Lord Salisbury, an anti-slavery conference was called in Brussels in 1890 by King Leopold II. The participants signed an agreement prohibiting slavery and the slave trade; extending European administration in Africa in order to exert control; and limiting the export of weapons to Africa. This was all very humanitarian and Christian, but it legitimized the occupation of Africa by the European powers.

The pioneer missionaries were very thankful for these developments. Finally, Africa would be free from the misery of the slave trade. Finally, the missionaries could devote themselves in peace and safety to the preaching of the gospel. Finally, more than a hundred years' struggle against slavery were rewarded by the coming into being of a secure Africa.

The missionaries praised their Lord for his great deeds. And that is how modern colonialism began in Africa.

The Bible played a great part in this whole drama of slavery.

Defenders of slavery quoted Bible texts to their own advantage.

The Quakers and the Saints read in the Bible that people can and must not make slaves in God's name.

Livingstone had learned from the Bible that the gospel must be the beginning of a total improvement of life. Hence his plea for Christianity and commerce for the Africans.

On the American plantations, the slaves found comfort in the Bible; they learned to bear their heavy cross through this vale of tears, dreaming and singing in their spirituals about heaven and the blessings of the hereafter.

When these slaves were freed, some of them went to spread the Good News in their old African homeland.

32

Free from Sin and Death

The great God made heaven and earth: a flat earth with the dome of heaven over it. The great God made the sea and the rivers, the fishes and insects, the birds and monkeys, the snakes and cattle. He also made the first man and woman and instructed them to govern the earth.

But in making the earth and everything on and in it, God made one mistake. He set the dome of heaven too low over the earth. That is why God forbade the woman to pound maize, for this is done with a long stick in a wooden pot, and the danger is that during the pounding the top of the stick would bang against the dome of heaven and break it!

For a time everything went well; but women are women, and one unhappy day, a young woman started to pound maize. The worst happened: she punched a hole in the dome of God's heaven. Then the great God became angry and went off. Since then men and women can no longer reach God.

Among the peoples of West Africa, there are many versions of the story of the creator God who went off in a huff. All of them are attempts to explain why there is a creator God whom people cannot reach.

From the time God went away, human beings have to bring presents to the tombs of their departed ancestors in order to obtain advice. They have to learn from the stories of their ancestors' lives so that the wisdom of their answers can help people understand how to face the challenges of today. People have also tried to solve the problem that God cannot be reached by giving names to the rain, the river, fertility and everything else on which they depend so that people can speak and act by rituals and sacrifices in such a way as to force things into a viable balance. Another way is to learn all the rules for life and society, and to observe them strictly for these rules have kept the world of yesterday in being. Finally, for questions and problems which cannot be settled in other ways, there is the traditional healer, the so-called 'medicine man', who with his psychological insight, his knowledge of the past, his conjuring tricks and sometimes his paranormal gifts, but in any case also his knowledge of herbs and potions, must have the answers. All this has to do with life here and now, involving the dead who gave life, the living who keep life in being, and the yet unborn who are to carry life on. For to live means to struggle in a hard and dangerous world to maintain and strengthen one's own vital force.

There are as many variations on this theme as there are peoples living on the African continent. But in broad outline, this is what life is felt to be by followers of what are called African traditional religions.

Islam, the religion of Muslims, is a quite different story, which will be told in chapter 37.

The missionaries' message, for Africans trying to strengthen and maintain their life–force, was very simple. It is true that someone had once banged a hole in God's heaven. Christians call that the Fall. Only God did not go away in a huff; he did not leave humanity to its own devices; he sent his own Son to earth to free us from sin and death. God is not only our creator; he is also our Father. He understands all our languages. To speak with him is called prayer, and people can do this without ancestors, spirits or powers, also without a sorcerer. And God is with us to the end of time, when Christ will return to set up his kingdom of peace and justice. This good news, this gospel, can be found in a book called the Bible. People can read in it for themselves the story of the God who is Immanuel, God with us. We are going to translate the Bible for you in your own language and teach you to read your own language.

That is how the first missionaries became Bible translators and writers of reading books. That is how they came to build shelters against the sun and the rain, places where Africans were taught to read their own languages. In that way, the Bible as the story of God's dealings with the human race, a story they could read for themselves, became important in Africans' lives. Christians became readers, people of the Book which they could read for themselves without sorcerers or priests or other go-betweens, because the God of the Bible had become a man among men. He spoke Bulu and Nyanja and Yoruba and Dinka and all the other languages.

All too often, the priest or sorcerer had become in African village society a tyrant or a cunning manipulator, dictating to people or terrifying them. The message of the Bible made people free from the power of priests and sorcerers.

In African villages, many people die young, mostly in small and simple huts. This means that from their early youth, people experience death existentially: it happens before their very eyes. The traditional religions tried to strengthen the vital force, but in the face of death all they could do was to try to keep the spirits of the dead under control, and where possible to use them. In contrast to this, the Bible said that death had been conquered, that the Lord had risen. Africa's own religions knew where human beings had come from, but not where they were going. The Bible did know: it told of a Lord who was the way, the truth and the life.

There was another important factor too. The gods and powers of the traditional religions are each tied to a particular place. They live in particular rivers, on particular mountains and in particular heavenly bodies. The ancestors too are each bound to a particular place, the place where they are buried. When a whole people decides or is obliged to move (and that often happened in Africa), they also took something of their gods and powers with them; and further, they came up with a new story in order to explain all about the removal. But in the colonial period, many individuals moved to work in the ports, mines or plantations. They also could become soldiers in the colonial army or servants in a white household or petty clerks. What then were they to do about the powers and the ancestors on whom they depended in order to remain alive? These remained at home in the village. It may seem strange, but the traditional African religions are not mobile. But Christianity is! You only have to look at the missionaries who have come to Africa from so far away. Christians meet God in a book that they can take with them wherever they go. The same is true of Judaism and Islam. All three are book religions, religions of wandering peoples, who as herdsmen could not tie themselves to particular places on this earth, but must either have a holy stone in Mecca as a goal of pilgrimage once in a lifetime, or Jerusalem as symbol of the city with golden gates in the new earth which will have above it a new heaven. Faith in the God who goes with his followers, whose Book they can take with them, could offer comfort and hope to the uprooted African slaves in the Americas. Meanwhile, in colonial Africa, the religion of the book also became, for hundreds of thousands who voluntarily or under pressure went to work far from their own village and ancestors, a lamp for their feet and a light on their path.

It has been a miracle that the founders of the missionary societies saw clearly that the preaching of Christ 'to the ends of the earth' was only meaningful if the Bible was made available in people's languages. On the other hand, African traditional religions proved fertile soil for the message that sin and death had been conquered and that people might speak directly with God and read about him. Christians believe and trust that God's work continues in this world, but on this earth the message about the Lord only really touches people when it offers answers to questions they cannot answer for themselves.

Of course, in the colonial period more practical motives were also involved. 'The whites are all-powerful, so their God must be powerful too.' 'In order to become like the whites, who can do everything, I must also get hold of their God.' 'The whites' Bible gives me access to the basis of their knowledge and power.' With such arguments colonialism became a kind of ally in the spread of Christianity.

That time is past: the Europeans have lost prestige through the Second World War, and African countries are now independent. The missions have grown into autonomous churches, some of them very large; they cannot be dismissed as a kind of neo-colonialist western survival. The availability of the Bible in many African languages has played a great part in this 'Africanization' of the gospel.

The traditional religions are in steady retreat, since they have no answers to the questions and challenges of the present time. This can be shown in a practical way. In the 1960s, a survey in Kenya showed that the followers of traditional religions had the lowest level of education and the highest rate of unemployment, and thus the lowest income. They were also the last to get a radio set.

Perhaps even more important than the financial or educational background is the fact that it no longer looks good to be a follower of an African traditional religion. As a result, whole villages and whole peoples are in the process of making a choice between Christianity and Islam. Since independence, the last thirty years have seen the Arab countries taking a more powerful place in the world so that Islam has ceased to be on the defensive. It has become self-confident. It presents itself in Africa as the religion brought, not by whites, but by Africans themselves. It is true that in some countries, tens of thousands of people, sometimes entire villages or a whole people at a time, choose Christianity. Their 'conversion' is primarily pragmatic. They do not want to fall behind socially, educationally, economically and sometimes also politically. They are not so much Christians as potential Christians. The content of their faith will largely depend on the quality of the preaching and teaching which they receive and from the worship and fellowship of the churches which may welcome them. It is crucial that the church should meet the questions and expectations of these thousands in a way which is both African and Christian. It goes without saying that the Bible, as the revelation of God's way with his people, in a language they can understand, at a price they can afford, is essential in the process of creating and developing faith.

33

Free from Oppression

The first Christian secondary school in Cameroon was a teachers' training college in Foulassi. This is where the American Presbyterians began to train their first church and school leaders. Like many secondary schools in Africa, the one in Foulassi had a boarding department. In 1950 it had among its pupils some who wanted to serve the church as teachers or preachers, but also young people who were dreaming of quite different careers. Yet the future was not clear: Cameroon was a French mandated territory under the United Nations with no immediate prospect of independence. When the governor visited the school, the pupils waved French flags and sang the *Marseillaise*, including words like 'fatherland' and 'tyranny'. Since teaching in the school was as French as in Verdun or Montpellier, they knew what 'fatherland' and 'tyranny' meant; civics, literally 'instruction civique', was part of the curriculum. This is a typically French subject which includes national economics, elementary sociology and patriotism. So Cameroonians at Foulassi learned precisely what a town council, a parliament and a president were. But they learned this in French terms, because Cameroon was a colony which did not have town councils or a parliament. Civics was taught in Foulassi by an American-naturalized Swiss minister called P. Chazeaud. A man born into the Swiss federal tradition, who had learned about American democracy, was teaching French civics in a colonial teacher training college.

When the course was over, Chazeaud asked his pupils to think about what they had learned and to give their personal reaction in the next lesson. That evening in their dormitory, they composed a song as their African reaction to French civics. Next morning, since the tune did not flow very well, Chazeaud sat down at the piano and helped his students to polish the song they had written. The whole school sang it. It soon became more widely known and was duly banned as subversive by the French authorities.

On 1 January 1960, this song from the Foulassi school became the first national anthem of independent Cameroon. Chazeaud was one of the first Europeans to receive a high Cameroonian decoration.

Chazeaud, like the other missionaries, had not come to Africa to engage in politics, not to mention helping to compose national anthems. They came to preach the gospel. Their schools were a way of preparing Christian leaders for their churches and for society. But more than that happened in teacher training colleges like the one at Foulassi, and also in ordinary secondary schools, which grew in numbers after the second world war. Because the colonial rulers wanted local leaders with European-style training, the curricula were European so that the pupils came to know the ideas and history of Europe. Civics included the establishment of the British parliament and the liberty, equality and fraternity of the French Revolution. That is how European-prescribed teaching in Africa caused a movement towards political awareness.

Foulassi, like many other institutions, was a Christian school. That means that the pupils heard the gospel of Jesus Christ who freed them from sin and death. Some pupils were moved by this message; others asked questions; others, again, accepted the Christian gospel. But even they began to think. Christ, says the Bible, sets us free from sin and death. 'For eternal life', said the missionary. But what about here on earth? Are only Europeans to be free on earth? Do not Africans, from a Christian point of view, have the right to govern their own country and work for its development?

Questions could also arise in discussions about the biblical concept of justice. Did that fit the colonial situation, in which, at best, white foreigners decided what was good for blacks, and at worst, colonial rulers oppressed the colonized? Christian leaders in Southern Africa draw the conclusion from the story of Israel's exodus from slavery in Egypt, that it contains a promise of liberation for the black and coloured people of South Africa. They too are led out of the whites' house of slavery into a promised land.

So the Bible became a book which motivated people not only to be converted, but also to work here on earth for a promised land. The missions had mainly preached a personal, spiritual and ethical gospel, but in African society, where life is total, the spiritual and the social, the present and the future could not be separated. So the Bible had to become also a book about the change of the whole of society. In the growth of political consciousness and national aspirations and in the struggle for independence, Christians played an important part.

What follows is by no means a complete list, but one may mention as examples Julius Nyerere, the ex-President of Tanzania, who began as a teacher in a Catholic school; Kenneth Kaunda, the former President of Zambia, a son of the manse, who despite his criticisms of the churches remains a convinced Christian; Moise Tshombe in Zaire, who was a Methodist; Dr Akanu Ibiam in Nigeria, Dr Kofi Busia in Ghana, Charles Assale in Cameroon, were and are Christians. In the resistance movements against the Portuguese in Angola, many soldiers had a New Testament in their knapsacks. The untimely murdered leader of Frelimo, Eduardo Mondlane of Mozambique, was brought up by missionaries and married a missionary's daughter. Ronald Mugabe, the President of Zimbabwe, calls himself a Marxist, but he comes from a Catholic school; and Joshua Nkomo and Ndabaningi Sithole are Christians, like Nelson Mandela, President of South Africa.

Elsewhere in this book we have said that the Bible contains time-bombs which help Africans to get rid of the whites who had stolen their land. That is true; but the different Christian traditions have different attitudes to social and political involvement.

Roman Catholic thought is strongly hierarchical; in the middle ages, the pope fought the emperor, the highest secular power. On the other hand, Catholics were not pioneers in helping ordinary people to gain a voice. Current Latin American liberation theology may thus be seen as a break with Roman Catholic tradition, and Rome has therefore problems with it.

Towards the end of Luther's life, when the wars of religion were bringing great misery to Germany, he became more and more inclined to believe that churches and Christians should always respect the authorities as ordained by God. Much later, this view had the dreadful consequence that the great majority of German Lutheran churches recognized the Nazis' Third Reich as the authority ordained by God, which must therefore be obeyed. A small minority in the German Confessing Church took the opposite view and was duly made to suffer by the Nazis. But this helped the Lutheran churches of Namibia, at the 1977 Assembly of the Lutheran World Federation in Dar-es-Salaam, to convince their brothers and sisters of the rightness of a different view of secular authority. Bible in hand, they insisted that the South African occupiers of their country could not be the authority ordained by God which must automatically be obeyed.

Among the Reformers, Calvin was the man who reformed not only the church but also society in the city state of Geneva. Calvinists have always tried to follow through Christian principles both in their personal lives and in society. A remarkable list of examples could be drawn up in Africa too. The Mau-Mau secessions in Keny, and the Bassa and later Bamileke risings in Cameroon around 1960, took place in areas which had Calvinist churches. Eastern Nigeria, the area of the Biafran rising, is the land of the mainly Calvinist Igbo. In Angola and especially Mozambique, where there were resistance movements against Portuguese colonialism, there are also large Calvinist churches, while in South Africa, both the hard core of the white régime and also the opposition of people like Dr Allan Boesak, are Calvinist.

Finally there are the faith missions which, because they belong to the second wave of missions in Africa, work mostly in the hinterland. They had absolutely no interest in society and politics, because they were too concerned for the eternal salvation of the individual and many of them lived in the conviction that Christ would soon return. Typically, few of them were interested in starting schools. It is therefore all the more surprising that now, in some of the mainly Baptist or Pentecostal churches which arose from their preaching, African pioneers have begun, with the Bible in their hands, to draw out the social consequences of the gospel by becoming involved in agricultural development and training. This is happening in Burkina Faso and elsewhere.

The growth in political awareness aroused by the European school curricula imposed on Christian secondary schools by the colonialists, and by the time-bombs in the Bible itself, never took concrete political form in or through the churches themselves. Churches and missions were not political movements. As we have said, missionaries had not come to start political campaigns. So those who had come to political consciousness through the Bible and Christian teaching had to go elsewhere to find content for their political convictions. This sometimes happened in political parties with which they came into contact during advanced studies in Europe; sometimes also through political literature.

In this, the writings of Karl Marx were more influential than the programmes of European socialist or communist parties. These were seen by Africans as too bourgeois and European. What they were looking for was an ideological basis for an African programme. In any case, the result of all this was that schools like Foulassi produced both Christian leaders and fiery Marxists, skilful politicians and sincere freedom fighters. It is a fact that much political and social involvement of churches throughout the world today has been inspired by the way in which Africans read the Bible in a setting of total thought and action. Colonial régimes did not realize what they were doing when they imposed their European curricula on pupils who would become the new African élite.

Nor did Chazeaud and the other missionaries realize what they were doing when they taught that Jesus Christ was the saviour and redeemer from sin and death. For them the gospel was first and foremost a spiritual message which had consequences for the sick and hungry, but no more than that. African Christians went and still go much further, just by reading what the Bible says about salvation and liberation, exodus and deliverance, justice and oppression.

Nationalist thinking began to develop before the Second World War, particularly among small groups of African students in Europe. In London men like Jomo Kenyatta, in Paris the Senegalese Leopold Senghor, and also West Indians, played a part in this. After the Second

World War the movement grew, under the inspiration of developments in India, Pakistan and Indonesia. Had not all Africans who had served in the allies' armies been fighting for freedom? During the war, promises were made: in 1944 by de Gaulle in Brazzaville, while the British had said of the Gold Coast that it should become the first black dominion.

The Protestant and Roman Catholic missionaries had started something in Africa with their secondary schools. Since the schools themselves and the colonial rulers gave no answer to the questions which were being asked there, the students looked for answers in Europe. The first question of the African students was: 'Who are we? Where do we find our identity?' What European anthropologists and missionaries had written about Africa and the Africans cannot be true. They described a continent of naked primitive people, living in an endless circle, without a history, with a special psychological background called 'primitive mentality'. Was that the Africa of Benin and Zimbabwe, ancient Ghana and the Almoravids, the kingdom of the Buganda and the Zulu kingdoms? Was that the Africa which had given the world jazz, beat music, blues and spirituals? Was that the Africa whose masks and pictures had been the great source of inspiration for modern western art?

In 1938 Jomo Kenyatta published in London an anthropological study of his own people, the Kikuyu, entitled *Facing Mount Kenya*. This book already showed that the question of land ownership must lead to conflict (the later Mau-Mau rising). In Africa itself, a start was made in the Gold Coast, where Kwegyir Aggrey (1885–1927) played an important part in founding Achimota College (later Achimota School) in the 1920s. This school wanted to train Africans in personal and equal co-operation between black and white, for, Aggrey said, we need one another just as much as black and white keys on a piano. The conceptions of this pastor and teacher were new in the sense that he consistently upheld the equality of Africans and Europeans. The next step was taken by Frantz Fanon of Martinique, who at the end of his classic book on (de)colonization, *The Wretched of the Earth* (1961), says: 'Let us resolve not to imitate Europe; let us bind our brains and muscles together in a new direction.' The Third World had to begin a new history of humanity.

Behind his plea for a new way there was an attempt in Paris to articulate African culture in philosophical terms, using the word *négritude*, being black. The proud consciousness of being black was born in the United States about 1920. Via Haiti and the West Indies, it reached Paris, where Senghor, Aimé Césaire and Léon Gonthran Damas gave substance to the term *négritude*. In London, also in the 1930s, students spoke of the 'African personality'. Later, this kind of thinking took on a new, American form as 'black power'.

Key words in this African philosophical thinking were emotion, total thought, vital force. In a remarkable book called *Bantu Philosophy*, Placide Tempels, a Belgian Roman Catholic missionary from the Belgian Congo, tried to systematize African thinking in scholastic terms; his book had great influence for some years. Africans were also discovering their own history, behind such names as Bornou, Kanem and Benin, Ghana and Mali, Zimbabwe and the Kikongo Kingdom. Young African intellectuals rejected Europe-centred history writing and anthropology. They began decolonization on the scholarly level. They publish poems and novels. Africans were searching for themselves, for their own authenticity. The poem written in 1956 by Bernard Dadié of Côte d'Ivoire has become a classic; it includes the lines:

Je vous remercie Dieu, de m'avoir créé Noir
d'avoir fait de moi
la somme de toutes les douleurs.

(I thank you, God, for having created me black; for having made of me the sum of all sufferings).

Yet the studies, the poetry and the novels which began to appear in the 1950s were more than a search for Africans' own roots and identity. They were also concerned with the future of an Africa which must be free and independent. This raised a second question: What foundation does Africa's own history and character provide for the independent nations of tomorrow? What can the common life of the village, the chief as representative of the ancestors, the village council as the place for putting right everything which disturbs village society, the structures of the kingdoms of the past, contribute to the Africa of tomorrow? The nationalist students of the 1950s tried to analyze European political and economic systems and test them against their own African world.

Capitalism did not appeal to them; the mercantile, and later the industrial, capitalism of Europe had among other things created colonialism. What place was there in African society for the tough, individualist approach of the free market? Capitalism means that the strong always become stronger and the weak weaker. How does that work in a continent where, by western standards, the vast majority of people are counted among the weak? Moreover capitalism presupposes the existence of capital which Africa lacks. Capitalism thus means permanent dependence on European and American creators of wealth.

Nor did western European socialism attract them. The British Labour Party and the French socialists were too bourgeois, too concerned for their own welfare. European socialists were not much concerned with the Africa of tomorrow or with the Africans' struggle for freedom.

The theoreticians of the Kremlin began about 1956 to be interested in Africa. In 1960 the Moscow Africa Institute opened, and its director Potehkin came with a blueprint for Africa. He sensed that the classical Marxist story did not fit in Africa; for who were the capitalists against whom the proletariat had to unite? The proletariat had to be united against both the colonialists and the neocolonialists. Moscow would support this struggle in every way possible. It was also clear that in the newly independent countries the state was going to play an important part, for lack of any other cadres. Communism believed in central planning of the economy; it was therefore important to infiltrate the state apparatus responsible for economic planning.

But African intellectuals of the 1950s were not taken in by propaganda stories. They had already had the experience of studying at the newly founded Lumumba University in Moscow. And the Soviet bureaucracy was deadly. Just one visit to the satellite countries of East Germany, Poland, Hungary or Czechoslovakia was enough to unmask as a lie the story of a Russia which had never had any colonies.

Africans returned to the sources, to the books of Marx and Engels themselves. They were studied particularly intensively in Paris. Could the communal aspect of communism relate in a modern way to African village life? Could the revolutionary element in communism become a starting-point for the changes needed for the liberation and modernization of Africa? And there were much more difficult questions: Is the African view of a community of the living, the dead and the yet unborn compatible with an analysis of society in which everything is reduced to economic and materialistic data? Who in Africa are the proletarian and the capitalist, without whom no class struggle is possible? Proletarians there are in plenty, but is the capitalist the sultan or the expatriate? How can it be the European or the American, when half of them are missionaries? What is more, Marxism is atheist, and there is no room for atheism in Africa.

The result was that the future leaders of the political freedom movements worked out their own ideas and published them in books. Leopold Senghor of Senegal, Kwame Nkrumah of Ghana, Kenneth Kaunda of Zambia, Julius Nyerere of Tanzania, Tom Mboya of Kenya, Eduardo Mondlane of Mozambique, Ndabaningi Sithole of what is now Zimbabwe, all wrote books with a kind of blueprint for the future of their countries. In these books they all tried to take the structures of their own African society as a starting-point. These African starting-points were combined with socialist concepts, because they related to the communal life-style of the African village. Most books advocated a co-operative approach and strong state influence in agriculture, land use, energy provision, banking etc. Building on African traditions of simple survival, some found ways of combining all this very pragmatically with a wide measure of freedom for private enterprise. On an international level, these books pleaded for the necessity for African countries to be independent: the struggle between East and West was a problem for rich countries.

The ideologies and programmes with which the countries becoming independent in the 1960s began did not, however, produce lasting democracies in the western sense. In a number of cases, the presidents became a kind of superchiefs or enlightened despots, ruling their countries with one party within which the various peoples and also the various viewpoints might encounter and find one another. In other countries the largest ethnic group supported a military leader who could impose his will on everyone. Everywhere a part was played by the artificial frontiers from the colonial past and by the fact that many countries had been created in the past by Europeans only in order to further their own interests. In Africa south of the Sahara, Côte d'Ivoire became the symbol of a distinctly free-market approach and Tanzania the symbol of African socialism. But Nyerere's self-help principle, aiming to spread the population by building new villages and developing initiatives in agriculture and industry, supported by an administrative apparatus including the nationalized banks and trading companies, sank into a morass of bureaucracy, impotence and corruption, because of structural poverty.

From 1972, there began in Madagascar a movement for a kind of socialism in which the basis of society would be a modern form of the old village communities or *fokonolona*. The manifesto of the Malagasy Socialist Revolution soon became known as the *boky mena*, the Red Book. Inspiration was drawn from the works of Lenin, Marx, Ho Chi Minh and even the North Korean Kim Il Sung; but great stress was also laid on Malagasy patterns, notably in education. It is remarkable that President Ratsiraka repeatedly illustrated his speeches with concepts and stories from the Bible. Madagascar is so influenced by Christianity that national construction has to proceed with reference to the Bible! Nevertheless, the decentralized socialism of this great island did not succeed in bringing welfare to its people. Just as in Tanzania, there are internal reasons for this, but both countries are also poor and have suffered from the oil crises and the fall in prices of raw materials on the world market.

A whole series of countries has tried a system which they called socialist and which excluded the exploitation of one person by another. Power must belong to the people – which however did not mean the population. The people consisted of those who were educated and trained, those who formed the party, which has the task of forming the whole population. Education was therefore very important and racism and tribalism were suppressed. Radio, media and instruction must make an important contribution to education.

During the period of the Cold War, the Soviet Union did its utmost to make socialist friends in Africa. But the countries which called themselves socialist in Africa were always Marxist in their own way.

The only country in Africa which has tried to carry through an Eastern European form of communism was Ethiopia, where a USSR-type constitution was set up with a single party, a central committee and a Politburo. It is remarkable that this happened in a country which was structurally very similar to Russia. Communism was first intended for the oppressed workers in the mines and factories of Europe after the first industrial revolution; it had success in 1917 in the Russian peasant society with a feudal background, where the nobility and the hurch held the levers of power. Similarly, in the Ethiopia of Haile Selassie, all power was held by the imperial family, the nobility and the church, while the people consisted largely of landless peasants.

As for the Chinese, their entry into Africa was seriously misguided. On his first trip to Africa, Cho En Lai, China's Foreign Minister, stated in Nairobi that Africa was ripe for the revolution, whereupon President Jomo Kenyatta enquired what revolution he was talking about. Kenya had already carried through the revolution of liberation from British domination.

The Chinese opened in quick succession a number of embassies, which just as quickly had to close because they became centres of political agitation and propaganda which the African governments could not accept. Later the Chinese came back more cautiously, among other things with economic aid for Congo and Zanzibar, and by laying the new railway track linking Zambia with the coast at Dar-es-Salaam in Tanzania. The West had refused to finance the railway. In Tanzania, Chinese ideological influence became considerable for a time because President Nyerere was very impressed by the Chinese people's efforts to build up their country without external help; and one of the most important features of Nyerere's socialism was self-reliance. Notably in Swahili, the official language of Tanzania, much communist literature was distributed in the 1960s. And the Chinese Red Book looked from the outside just like the pocket edition of the New Testament!

All this has now passed into history. China is concentrating all its efforts on building up its own country and has given up its ambitions for military, or even purely ideological, expansion of the communist gospel.

Now the great message of communism with its classless society has failed in the former Soviet Union and throughout the world. China, Cuba, and the South African communist party have become the residues of an outdated ideology.

Throughout the world, pragmatism and realism now reign. As for developing countries it has been discovered that development is impossible without a democracy which guarantees the participation of all, together with critical checks on the rulers.

Marxism is no longer the answer for the whole world. People are choosing the way of democracy and the time for great ideologies has passed.

What about Africa?

A Nigerian writer has said recently that the concept of the 'African personality' (what in French is called *négritude*) is ridiculous. Why should a negro reflect philosophically about the fact that he is a negro? Does a tiger think about his being a tiger (his *tigritude*)? Has the African personality movement been more than an incident in the movement of emancipation?

European concepts covered with a bit of African dressing will not further the development of Africa. In our days we see in Africa, on the one hand, the final stage of all kinds of dictatorships and on the other the emergence of a realistic pragmatism in order to overcome the economic problems.

Two things are becoming clearer and clearer:

1. The condition for the healthy development of a country is a democratic system which enables the people at any moment to call those in power to account.
2. Basic for the development of a country is the readiness of its own population to make a physical, intellectual, social and moral effort.

In Africa, there are thus movements towards a multi-party system and realistic economic reconstruction. Although Africa's great difficulties today have external causes such as the economic power of the rich countries, drought and the spread of Aids, people are also speaking of a second liberation, this time not from foreign colonizers but from the new African élite of profiteers. In countries like Zaïre and Benin, church leaders are acting as mediators in political change.

Of course, there are still questions and risks. Will multi-party democracy lead to the political and social conscience which is indispensable for survival, or to a rebirth of tribalism?

In the process of democratization and reconstruction, church leaders in a number of countries are playing the role of mediators. The Zaïre theologian Kä Mana has tried to define the task of the churches in this situation by elaborating his 'Theology of Reconstruction'.

34

The European Book

When in an African village you ask an old man with many years' experience behind him, what is 'good', he will tell a long story about someone who lives two villages away by the river, or at the cross-roads, or by the very big tree. The conclusion he draws from all the details he gives about what this man does or does not do is that this man is good. The wise old man does not give an abstract definition. Goodness consists above all for him in a good man who lives or lived in his world. When this wise old man takes the Bible in his hands, the letters of Paul have little to say to him. They are too abstract; he does not hear them speaking about people of flesh and blood who have their own personal names. Christ, the caring God in human form, does speak to him; so do the Gospels and the Acts of the Apostles. He feels at home with people of flesh and blood, who experience and do things: people like Peter, John the Baptist and Zacchaeus. He is fascinated by the Old Testament stories about the patriarchs and Moses and David. In the Bible's Book of Proverbs, he discovers proverbs like his own. Parables make him think of his own fables with a moral. He experiences in his own life the Psalmists' wrestling with God in joy and sorrow, in need and liberation.

In the church his favourite preacher is the one who tells stories, not the abstract exegete of difficult passages.

Insofar as the New Testament reflects a Greek world, it is foreign to Africans. The Greek separation of body and spirit, being and action, faith and action is strange to them. In the Jewish world, the world of the Old Testament, Africans feel at home. Partly, but not only, because the pastoral peoples of Africa still have the same problems as Abraham, Isaac and Jacob, in finding water or a tomb. Not just because he recognizes stories about presents, dowries and polygamy, or about the fertility gods, the Baalim, on the high places. Not even because of the land of milk and honey, or because of great droughts which are seen as punishments. Africans recognize themselves in the Old Testament's whole way of thinking, because it is all-inclusive. In Hebrew the word *dabar* means both word and act. This all-inclusive thinking is the basic pattern of African life, which sees work and religion, life and thought, feasting and fasting as parts of a single whole.

The first generation missionaries often considered Africans as blind heathen; but they lived so close to them that pioneers such as Crowther, Krapf and Moffat translated Matthew and then Genesis, Mark and then Exodus into African languages. Later things changed. There came faith missions, mainly from British and American revival movements, concerned only with the spiritual: bringing lost souls to Christ the Saviour. They were apolitical: they had no time or energy for the body or for this world. They began no medical work, no agricultural projects, and sometimes not even schools, because what mattered was souls. They worked in holy haste, because the Lord might return tomorrow to save but also to judge. They worked hard on translations of the New Testament, but were less interested in the Old. The example of the polygamist Jacob could have a bad influence on converts from whom monogamy was consistently required. In some languages they wrote hymn books in which the name of God did not occur; the hymns were all about Jesus. It was not for nothing that this development took place in the colonial period, in which the pattern of thought and action was completely prescribed by the white European (and American) with their superiority complex.

Even in our days the Wycliffe Bible Translators have been doing precisely the same too long with their policy of translating only the New Testament.

In the colonial period, everywhere in Africa, American, German, Norwegian, French, Alsatian, English and Scottish village churches were built, depending on where the missionaries came from. Protestant ministers went about in clerical gowns (which were the academic gown which Martin Luther wore as a professor of Wittenberg University in Germany) and Roman Catholic priests said mass in Roman, European robes. Dancing and drums were forbidden in church; they were bound up with the rejected powers of the past. Because of the climate, they were replaced by miserably moaning harmoniums and American organs. Hymn tunes remained European; only the words were translated. The same was done, for example, with the hymns of Sankey and Moody. And all this was dropped into a culture in which rhythm is much more important than melody. The rhythm, the beat, amplifies the beat of the heart, the beat of life itself. (It is remarkable that now, young people all over the world completely understand this). When a church constitution had to be made for the Presbyterian Church of Cameroon, American missionaries translated the orders of the United Presbyterian Church of the USA straight into Boulou, complete with special provisions for Massachusetts. The Roman Catholic missions made their own contribution by distributing large numbers of German pictures of a blond German Madonna and Christ.

Towards the end of the 1960s, a group of Christians from the village of Baffia in southern Côte d'Ivoire under the leadership of a teacher became well-known through their Ivoirian version of the Parable of the Prodigal Son. They even went on television. They played with white-powdered faces, because they said: 'People in the Bible are white.'

It remains not surprising that Africans should think like that. Didn't it say 'British & Foreign Bible Society' on the title page of almost all the Bibles they had received?

It is however remarkable that the Bible came to be considered as a 'white' book, since it is not a European book at all, but the story of events which took place in the Near East; and also since the churches in Egypt and Ethiopia, to name but two, are much older than many European churches.

Yet the missionaries can scarcely be blamed. In Christian Europe and America, they were set apart in solemn commissioning services to take the gospel of redemption to 'heathen lands afar' where 'thick darkness ruleth yet'; where 'primitive natives live in tribes in the interior.' These 'heathen lands' were not like other, normal countries: they were colonies and protectorates to which Europeans were taking 'civilization'. Even if these missionaries wanted to learn more about the background of these 'primitive natives', they read phenomenologists of religion such as Strauss and Lévi-Bruhl and Van der Leeuw, who from their European studies had invented the theory that the African had a primitive mentality, quite different from Europeans' way of thinking.

In southern Africa, the Bible became a 'white book' in a quite different way. This had to do with the fact that in southern Africa there arose a Christian white tribe, concerned above everything to preserve its own identity.

The Christian church in the far south of Africa did not begin with a missionary society's initiative to take the gospel to the ends of the earth, but in the Christian conviction of Dutch farmers, who settled there from 1652 to grow vegetables and ensure fresh water for the crews of ships passing by the Cape on their way from Europe to the Dutch East Indies. Their church was the Dutch Reformed Church, ecclesiastically under the Amsterdam presbytery, and financially under the United East Indies Company. Soon there landed on the Cape slaves from the Dutch East Indies and parts of Africa, and the whites also mixed with local Hottentots and Bushmen. Children of these unions were baptized and received into the church, as were indigenous converts. There was even a rule that a slave who was baptized must be set free. Some slave-owners were therefore not particularly interested in the conversion of their personnel. The small Dutch colony did not grow quickly, but around 1688, it was increased by the arrival of almost two hundred French Huguenots. They strengthened the Boers' Calvinist convictions and were assimilated in a couple of generations. In the course of the nineteenth century the same happened with German immigrants.

In 1806 the Cape became British and thus, in the eyes of many Boers, politically and intellectually liberal. British missionary societies began to work among the Africans. They treated the Africans as equals. The Bible Society formed an auxiliary committee, and in 1845 this became an agency in Cape Town. Some Boers were little interested in distributing the Bible also among the black and coloured population. When, in 1833, the British abolished slavery, many Boers said that this was enough. Between 1835 and 1837, a total of 10,000 Boers loaded their ox-wagons for the Great Trek and founded their Calvinist republics of Transvaal and the Orange Free State, because of what they called 'the intolerable teaching that heathen blacks and Christian whites must be treated on equal terms.'

In 1857, the Synod of the Dutch Reformed Church passed an important resolution. It stated that it is humane and 'biblical' that heathen converts should be received into existing congregations, but that 'because of the weakness of some', it may sometimes be necessary to set up separate churches for the converted heathen. The man who introduced this resolution was the Rev. A. Murray. He was one of the Scottish ministers who had come to strengthen the Dutch Reformed Church. The Scots were good Calvinists, but they were also strongly influenced by the English revival preachers. They opened the eyes of the Boer churches to revival and thus also to mission. Mission first took shape in the work which the Dutch Reformed Church began in Northern and Southern Rhodesia and in Nigeria. The wish ('because of human weakness') to set up separate churches for coloureds and blacks was linked with greater concern for mission. In this way, from 1881, there arose also separate Reformed churches for blacks, Indians and coloureds in South Africa itself.

In 1899, when the British tried to annex the Boer Republics too, the wretched Boer War broke out, which the Boers lost in 1902. Economically and politically they were poor and powerless. Culturally they felt themselves in language and development inferior to the hated British. In this setting arose their movement for social, economic, political, ideological and spiritual emancipation, which was crowned with success when in 1948 the (Boer) nationalists won a general election. Their struggle had cultural aspects. As early as 1871 they set up the secret True Afrikaner Society, which wanted to make the Afrikaans language, a dialect of Dutch, into a language of culture. After the turn of the century, the Second Language Movement brought a flowering of literature in the language of the Boers, which they now called Afrikaans. In 1914 Afrikaans conquered the schools, and in 1916 the Dutch Reformed Churches. In 1918 Afrikaans became a subject taught in the universities, and in 1925 the official language alongside

English. In 1933 the Afrikaans Bible was published, and in the following year the metrical Psalms.

As already mentioned, this was more than a language question. Nationalists describe the development as follows: God's hand brought Dutch Calvinists to the Cape; enabled the group of free burghers to grow into a people; freed them by the Great Trek from the degeneracy of anglicized and liberal Cape colonial society; preserved them from black attacks (the blacks were the Canaanites in the promised land!); and established them in the freedom of republican independence. But the Evil One continued his attacks on the chosen Afrikaner people; British imperialism pursued them; a century of injustice culminated in the Boer War, which brought in its train the loss of independence, and thus poverty, oppression and anglicization. Only through courageous faith and uncompromizing obedience to their calling can the Afrikaner people have a future. In this belief the Afrikaners set themselves apart, organized their own nation and finally in 1948 won the election against their liberal British opponents. Thereafter, with unbending faith in the rightness of their conceptions, they built South African society on the model of separate development, under white national Christian Afrikaner rule. They themselves called this the policy of separate development; the rest of the world called it apartheid.

The ideology which lies behind this policy and this emancipation was founded by the white South Africans on the Bible. The division of the human race into races, peoples and languages is a conscious act of God. See the list of nations in Genesis 10 and 11. The history of the people of Israel teaches us that only a people which maintains its identity in blood, customs and belief can fulfil God's calling. Just as a man must keep himself holy before God, so also must a people. And 'holy' means 'separate, apart'. Paul may have been a Roman citizen, but he was proud of being a Jew; he had a distinctly national pride.

Even the *baasskap* (mastery) of the whites over the blacks and coloureds was explained on the basis of the Bible. In the Bible people are of equal value (before God), but not alike. The Bible provides standards for masters and servants, each in their own position. See Ephesians 5. At the national people's congress of 1947 in Johannesburg, a 'comprehensive policy of racial separation, apartheid in every area of life' was adopted. It issued the following statement:

The Congress expresses its conviction that, on the basis of Christian guardianship, the task and responsibility of the white race is:

To provide necessary protection for the non-white racial groups.

To place them in such a position that, both materially and spiritually, they may have all the resources necessary eventually, in an independent and responsible manner, to manage their own affairs and work out their own salvation.

The non-Reformed Protestant and Anglican churches of South Africa, and also the Roman Catholics, rejected racial separation from the beginning. The black population gave its own varying answers. On the one hand, it set up independent African churches; on the other hand, tension increased between the white Dutch Reformed Church and its fully-grown children, the Reformed churches for blacks, Indians and coloureds (see chapter 35). It is remarkable that the denominational family of which the white South African Reformed Church is a member, the World Alliance of Reformed Churches, declared apartheid to be a sin.

The Dutch Reformed Church is now withdrawing from its biblical defence of apartheid. Its last synod accepted a report rejecting it.

The Boers of South Africa have applied the Afrikaans tribal concept consistently to their own people group, which is of Dutch, French and German extraction. The Afrikaner tribe has tried to do this in a Christian way, based on the Dutch Calvinist sense of sovereignty in its own circle; this was accompanied by the conviction of having been called by the Lord to perform a great task. But German roots have always been influential among the Boers: they have been haunted by the concepts of 'national soul' and of the superior 'Herrenvolk' or master race. One may mention, on the organizational level, the 'Ossewa-brandwag', the Fascist organization in South Africa.

Some claim that religious arguments have been used only to maintain the dominant place of the whites in the economic and political spheres. Were not the Boers poor and powerless at the beginning of this century? Having obtained all the power, they felt themselves threatened by the mass of the new powerless poor: the growing black population. Many observers are thus convinced that fear is at the bottom of white politics. South Africa has now started to break down apartheid and to give the non-whites a full share in state and society. The first democratic elections ever have been a success and Nelson Mandela is now president. But it will be clear that a complete conversion of the Boers is needed.

The Bible and the Bible Society have played a remarkable role in this whole situation. For years, white South Africans have tried to use Bible texts to justify their principles of racial separation. South Africa has become the country in which Christians opposed Christians, basing their arguments on the same Bible.

The translation of the Bible into Afrikaans was of great importance for the emancipation of the Boers, while the Bible in African languages taught the Bantu and coloured peoples to link salvation and liberation and deliverance from need with an exodus from oppression.

Over the years, the white Boers have given more and more money for the Bible. The Bible Society of South Africa has built Bible houses in Transkei, Botswana and elsewhere, and has made great efforts to translate, and where necessary revise or retranslate, the Bible in the languages of the peoples of South Africa. That was a logical consequence of the white Christian ideology that each people must remain itself, even in relation to God; hence each people must have the Bible in its own language. Just as the Boers as Afrikaners found themselves through the translation of the Bible into their own language, so may the Xhosa and the Zulus and all the other peoples.

35

The African Book

To meet Christ in the Bible in Africa naturally means meeting Christ as an African. One may ask if this happened in the early days. The first Christians in Egypt were Jews, Greeks, and perhaps Egyptians living in Alexandria in the setting of hellenism, the general culture of the eastern Mediterranean area; while the Christians of North Africa, now called the Maghreb, were Latin-speaking colonists. The struggle to win for Christianity a place in the Greek Neoplatonic thought of Alexandria, and the Donatist controversy about rigorism among Christians in Carthage, were not confrontations of real Africans with the message of Christ. However, some historians have seen in the Donatists' radical gospel an African way of resisting Roman thought. The situation changed when the Egyptian farming population along the Nile became Christians, and when Christianity later went up the Nile through Nubia into Ethipia. The Coptic Orthodox and Ethiopian Orthodox churches, and also the vanished Nubian churches of Sudan, were the first examples of African Christianity.

In Egypt there were some remarkable features. The first was the individualism of believers, proved by the large number of bishops, and also in the fact that the monastic movement began with individual hermits who withdrew into the desert to pray. We cannot tell whether the fact that monasticism began in Egypt is connected with the contrast between the rich land of the Nile Delta and the infertile desert close by, or with the Egyptians' mentality, or with both factors.

The second remarkable factor is that both Egypt and Ethiopia have something of the radical thinking of North Africa (or should one rather speak of the 'other than human nature' of the old Egyptian gods?) Both churches became monophysite; that is, they believed that Christ had only one, divine nature, and not two natures, divine and human, as the western church confesses.

In Ethiopia the Old Testament also had its own influence on the Christian church, because the Old Testament was known there before the coming of Christianity. Believers of both churches have had for centuries their own proper pride. The Copts feel that they are the true

Egyptians, while the Ethiopians consider themselves to have been set apart since the time of King Solomon as God's special people.

When, at the beginning of the nineteenth century, modern missions began to enter Africa, Coptic and Ethiopian Christians were thought by the European and American missionaries to belong to sleeping churches, which had to be awakened by the revival movement. That did not work, because neither Copts nor Ethiopians had much respect for European Christians. The ancient Orthodox churches of Africa began to change as soon as they were treated as 100% equal members of the World Council of Churches, and taken seriously alongside other churches.

Where, from the nineteenth century, the preaching of the missions had an effect, and people were given the Bible in their own languages, there came sooner or later the need for their own encounter with Christ. In the African view of life, everything hangs together, and life is a question of carefully maintained balance. Against this background, the three aspects of the missions were well received: first preaching, Bible translation and teaching; second, care for the sick; and third, total life improvement. The type of faith mission which exclusively stressed a personal relationship with Jesus and concentrated completely on personal salvation with its eyes on the early end of the ages was often felt to be not of this world. The African feeling for life calls for religious practices which will strengthen the life-force here and now.

Both Roman Catholic and Protestant missionaries' attitude to the first African converts' traditional religious practices was very negative. They wanted complete separation from the religious past; thus dancing and drums, secret societies and traditional rites of initiation were banned. Even the 'medicine man's often excellent knowledge of herbs and natural medicines was rejected. A certain maturity seemed required, together with a certain distance from the old life, before valuable elements from the old life could be re-evaluated and re-integrated.

Today, a dance round the church led by the minister in his gown once again forms part of the celebration of the eucharist of the Bamileke in Cameroon. From the beginning, the Africans sang hymns introduced by the European missions in their own rhythm; but now that rhythm, together with narrative songs and drums, have become common in most churches, even complemented by modern trumpets and electric guitars. In the Roman Catholic churches of Africa, the Second Vatican Council's decision that the eucharist should be celebrated in the language of the people has brought great changes. As for the 'medicine man' with his herbal knowledge, many people already went, and still do go, to see him on the sly. Moreover, one of the reasons for the creation of independant African churches all over the continent lies in the need for Pentecostal laying on of hands, with prayer for the healing of the sick. For sickness is more than a bodily failing; it has to do with the (spiritual) state of the whole person. And what is more, if the Lord and his disciples healed the sick, why should not we be able to do so in his name?

Africans' confrontation with the content of the Bible was more difficult.

For a long time, the attitude of many African evangelists and even ministers could be summed up as follows: teach me from the Bible what may and may not be done and then I shall become a new spiritual village chief, upholding the Christian law. Church councils and regular meetings of synods, when they had to deal with matters of discipline, often took on the character of a palaver, in which it was never truth which was in question, but rather the quality of the speeches for the prosecution and the defence. In this setting, sins 'counted' only if they were proved. This raises the question: What is the value of preaching about sin and grace in a world where sin must be proved to be sin, otherwise it did not count? Behind this lies a still more difficult problem. In much African thought, moral wrong or sin is assessed by its practical consequences. If the consequences are removed, then immediately it ceases to be wrong. Prayer thus becomes a confession of innocence. You do not pray for forgiveness, but for evil to be turned away; for guilt in Africa has always been rejected. When something goes wrong, there is always an explanation, which may be found for example in the spirits of the ancestors or with an enemy. How then can one forgive? To think as Christians means at this point making all things new.

Many Africans believe that the sacraments help to strengthen their vital force. Protestants may well say that the Lord's Supper is a memorial, but the Bible says it is the body and blood of Christ, so to eat and drink that must surely strengthen the vital force!

An important ethical problem was and still is polygamy. Christian marriage is supposed to be monogamous, but what is to be done with the wives of a polygamist who becomes a Christian? And what is to be done with a whole polygamous family whose members want to be baptized? Must all wives but one be sent away? If so, where? What status will they have in the community? Must not love prevail over law in this situation? Another aspect of the matter is that among many African peoples, life only becomes meaningful when the future is ensured by the birth of a son. When this does not happen, may one take a second wife to put things right? It is remarkable that on questions of marriage and offspring, African Roman Catholic priests are often particularly strict. Is this a reaction to their own celibacy, which to African thinking appears a great but not unnatural sacrifice?

In relation to marriage and the continuation of the race, many Africans also see the ancestors as a problem from a Christian point of view. Life binds together the dead, the living and the yet unborn.

Roman Catholic prayer for the departed fits in better with African thought than the Protestant view, which is limited to believing in and waiting for the resurrection. Moreover, Christ said: 'I am the way, the truth, and the life.' Does that mean that the fathers, who did not know Christ, did not know God either, and thus have no part in salvation? In African thinking that cannot possibly be true, since people are inseparably bound up with their ancestors. In any case, Africans recognize in the Genesis accounts of the ancestors of the human race the stories their own peoples tell about where where their ancestors came from, and where the world came from and how.

Questions of law or prophecy; ethical questions about marriage and posterity; theological questions to do with the fathers and the creator God: these are in many parts of Africa the central points of the African confrontation with the Bible. Whether one speaks of contextualising or indigenization, a meeting between indigenous thought and culture on the one hand, and the gospel on the other is legitimate, and happens wherever the church is active in mission. In this discussion, Protestants shy away from the word 'accommodation', which Roman Catholics sometimes use, fearing adaptation of the gospel. Others, however, strongly believe that it is not right to preach a timeless gospel of grace for sinners of all times. Indigenization of the Gospel is one of the consequences of the incarnation of the Word, and translation of the gospel in people's own languages is an indispensable instrument of indigenization.

When Africans began to read the Bible, and particularly the Old Testament, for themselves, they became convinced in various parts of Africa that the God of the Europeans was not concerned with the existential problems of the struggle for life, and the consequent need to strengthen the vital force; he was rather the God of a new élite, which was learning to read. In Uganda, one name for Christians was *umushomi*, readers; and the Zulus in South Africa used the same word *isikole* for school and church, while the pastor and the teacher were both called *umfundisi*. Church and school were almost completely identified.

It is true that the great revival movement in East Africa was an attempt, by penitence and personal conversion, to evoke deeper faith among ordinary people. But in various places, this led to the creation of Christian communities of people who wanted to be both fully African and fully Christian. Sometimes they kept the organizational structure of the church from which they had separated, but sometimes this was also africanized. These churches wanted to be Christ's clan, God's extended family, in which they would experience warmth and fellowship. They wanted to build dance and feeling, prayer and healing into a life-giving liturgy. The church was seen as a new fetish, which offered more than the old one, and thus made the old superfluous. The mission churches often merely added something to African life, but left African traditional life too much undisturbed. The independent churches did not make this mistake: they insisted that the old fetishes must be burned. The independent churches fight evils which have always been there, such as the infertility of some women; but they also fight the modern evil of alcoholism. They want to take seriously both traditional Africa and the changing modern Africa.

More independent churches arose among Protestants than among Roman Catholics. The reasons are that Protestants were always more divided, had a more decentralized administration, and have more Bible translations to give points of reference for their own encounter with African life. However, since the decree of the Second Vatican Council on the use of the vernacular in church, the number of independent churches has also risen in Roman Catholic circles. Another factor is that the Roman Catholic structure makes it impossible for the village evangelist ever to be ordained priest and to administer the sacraments in the villages.

Three other important aspects of the independent African churches must be mentioned. The first is that women, including women prophets, often win greater prominence than in the 'main stream' churches. Second is the fact that almost all independent churches make room for polygamy. Third, they all offer a truly African way of life to people with little education, who feel threatened by the changes, for example of urban development. The leadership in these churches is often hypnotic, in the style of the old chiefs. Of course, here and there people are badly treated by charlatans and profiteers who misuse their charisma for their own power and profit. And of course there are also independent churches which are so African that they have done away with central aspects of the gospel.

One of the largest independent Christian communities in Africa is the Kimbanguist Church in Zaïre, the People's Republic of Congo, and Angola. It arose from the revival preaching of the Baptist healer and prophet Simon Kimbangu. Belgian priests convinced the colonial authorities that Kimbangu was dangerous. The Protestants protested little or not at all. Kimbangu was convicted in 1921 and died thirty years later in prison. His followers were persecuted by the Belgian authorities with the result that the movement grew and grew. In 1957 it was officially recognized. Now the Kimbanguist Church is a member of the World Council of Churches and has a couple of million members. The Kimbanguists try to be an African communion of saints on earth. They pay great attention to teaching and social activities. It is remarkable that the Kimbanguists, throughout the conflicts which followed the independence of Zaire in 1960, consistently maintained a pacifist stance in the name of Christ.

A large independent church in West Africa is the Church of the Lord (Aladura), founded in Nigeria in 1930 by a Yoruba catechist called Josiah Olunowo Oshitelu, following a series of visions.

In South Africa, the story of African theology and the independent churches is different.

Very early, even before 1900, black messianic movements arose in reaction to white supremacy and power. They forged links with black American churches and became known as Ethiopian or Zionist churches. But black messianism did not begin in South Africa. In 1700, in the Kingdom of Kikongo, the prophet Donna Beatrice was given by the king the status of a black Christ (see chapter 6).

Now in South Africa the independent churches have more members than the mission-founded churches. The number of movements runs into thousands and is constantly increasing.

Alongside purely African Christian churches, there are all kinds of syncretistic sects which, sometimes in strange ways, mix African and Christian elements. One reason for the growth of these churches and movements is the establishment in South Africa, because of industrial- ization of enormous black townships in which people often feel uprooted. For them these truly African churches become the place where they experience safety, confidence and fellowship. Another reason for their growth was that churches were for a long time one of the few forms of organization in South Africa which are legally open to the so-called 'non-whites'. This means that the independent churches play various important roles in community life.

Moreover, africanization is going on also in the churches founded by Roman Catholic and Protestant missions. These have to some extent the same characteristics as African theology in other parts of the continent; but they are specially influenced by the fact that many South Africans classified as Bantu and coloureds have felt themselves oppressed by a political system in which a white minority decided what is good for the whole country.

African liberation theology has emerged under the inspiration of American black theologians such as James Cone. This theology reads the Bible as a message of liberation from oppression for the South African blacks. The theology of South African Boers is situational and African Christians want to have their situational theology too. Christ stands with the poor. He wants to free the oppressed from their alienation from God and from their slave mentality. Black theology is looking for conceptions of God which are not the mirror of white authoritarianism. It is an open question whether this last type of theology is really African, or whether it is the African form of something which is appearing in many parts of the world, namely theological and biblical reflection on oppression and the denial of human rights.

Whether in African or black theology, independent churches or messianic movements, the Bible in African languages is an indispensable condition of this whole struggle to find an African Christianity. Translation consultants of the Bible societies advocate functional equivalent translations which pay particular attention to the receptor language so as to bring the message of the Bible as close as possible to the situation of people in Africa. To do this the New Testament is not enough; in African thought, the Old Testament becomes a dictionary of the New.

Finally, in terms of organization, the new national Bible Societies of Africa already included leaders of independent churches in their work and their boards at a time when national Councils of Churches hesitated to do so.

36

The Book of the Church

In the Roman Catholic Church, a basic motivation for missionary work was given by the great philosopher and theologian Thomas Aquinas (1225–1274). In his *Summa Theologica*, he stated that mission must be *implantatio ecclesiae*, the implantation of the church in the different peoples, as a saving institution in its hierarchical structure. Whereas the Protestant missionary goes out to proclaim the Good News, the Catholic missionary's first task is to found a church. This applies equally to the Capuchins, who went to the Kikongo kingdom in the sixteenth century in the wake of the Portuguese; to the new missionary efforts after the setting up in 1622 of the Congregation de Propaganda Fide, the coordinating organ of all mission work from Rome; and to the new wave of Roman Catholic missions in the second half of the nineteenth century.

Gregory XVI, the first great missionary pope of the nineteenth century, who reigned from 1831 to 1845, wrote shortly before his death an instruction on the education of native priests. In 1869, the First Vatican Council approved a plan whereby, in overseas areas, a Vicar Apostolic appointed by Rome governed the church until a bishopric was created. The missionary orders were under his authority. The desire to train local priests was one of the reasons for the Catholic missions' great stress on education. Yet the education of priests in Africa developed much more slowly than the training of Protestant ministers, because celibacy for priests was not only a severe, but also a completely un-African demand. After Dom Henriques of the Kikongo kingdom in 1518, the first African bishop was consecrated in Uganda in 1939. In 1993 there were 497 bishops including 113 expatriates, and 8 African cardinals. In 1994 Africa had 44 senior seminaries with 14,649 students. There were 20,768 priests, still including 20 per cent expatriates. This means that the number of non-African ministers in the Roman Catholic Church in Africa is much higher than the number of Protestant missionaries.

The first training institute for Roman Catholic missionaries was founded in 1658 in Paris. Roman Catholic missionary work in Africa (beginning in Senegal and Liberia in 1843, and in 1851 in South Africa) had a strongly French character. The most important founders of missionary orders were Cardinal Lavigerie, Archbishop of Algiers, who set out to convert Africa with his White Fathers, and Jacob Libermann, who was of Jewish descent. He reorganized in 1848 the Congregation of Holy Ghost Fathers, which had existed since 1703. Its task was to be the conversion of the black peoples, because 'God's time has come'. In 1900, 70 per cent of all Catholic missionaries in Africa were French. In 1930, that proportion had halved: not because the French contribution had decreased, but because more missionaries had come from other countries. By that time there were more than 7500 French Catholic missionaries, whilst the Italians, Germans, Belgians and Dutch each had more than 2000. After 1939, when the Germans (once again) had to withdraw because of the war, their places were mostly taken by Americans.

The Roman Catholics also turned their attention to the ancient churches of Egypt and Ethiopia. In 1862 Pope Pius IX founded the Congregatio pro Nepotiis Ritus Orientalis, which opened in Rome seminaries for the eastern rites, and in 1917 a separate Holy Congregation for the Eastern Church was founded. Its task was to unite with Rome the eastern churches offering them partial freedom, for example in liturgy and in church language. That is why there is also a Coptic Catholic Church in Egypt.

Roman Catholics have increased greatly in numbers in Africa. There were about two million of them around 1900, five million in 1930, 27 million in 1965 and 92 million in 1993; they are supported by missionaries of more than fifty different orders and congregations. This growth was greatest in the Belgian, French and Portuguese colonies. In the period of decolonization, tensions arose in Zaïre, and especially in Angola and Mozambique, between the church and the new governments, since the Roman Catholic Church in these countries had identified itself too strongly with the colonial administration.

In our times, the Second Vatican Council, which began in 1962, stressed the idea that mission is entrusted to the whole church. Popes Benedict XV, Pius XI, and especially Pius XII, with their encyclicals *Evangelii praecones* (1951) and *Fidei donum* (1957), prepared this new missionary thinking of the council. In *Evangelii praecones*, Pius XII wrote: 'The ultimate aim to be striven for must be that the church should become strong among the nations, and that it should be given its own hierarchy, chosen from among its own priests.' At the council, for the first time, a great number of African bishops were present. Alongside the church as a saving institution to be set up in each nation, one can also read in the council's documents about 'the people of God moving towards the manifestation of the Kingdom of God, characterized by preaching, communion, brotherly love and righteousness.' A clear consequence of the missionary task of the whole church is, according to the council's document *Ad gentes*, the missionary task of the local church. The church's centre of gravity is also moving towards the third world, as Europe becomes more secularized, and the church and Christian faith grow in Africa.

Yet the Roman Catholic Church suffered from one psychological disadvantage, now that Africa was almost completely independent. The head of the church has his headquarters in Rome, in Europe, and it is he who appoints the men who, in independent African countries, hold pastoral, spiritual, and also administrative power in the church: the bishops. This means that the Roman Catholic Church is less indigenous than the Protestant churches, which do not have a supreme head somewhere in the rich and formerly powerful part of the world. Rome is trying to overcome this psychological disadvantage by making an effort to indigenize the church in liturgy and theology, without deviations from Catholic teaching. So when a bishop in Zambia called Emmanuel Milingo, in line with African tradition, but also appealing to Jesus as the great healer, practised healing by prayer, he was promoted out of the country to Rome. On the other hand, the present Pope John Paul II tries to act as pastor of the whole world church, undertaking many journeys, partly to listen carefully on the spot, but also to present correct Roman views in the course of these journeys. In addition, national bishops' conferences have become more important; there is also a conference of bishops of the whole of Africa and Madagascar. The organisation in April 1994 of a synod of the African bishops in Rome, and not in Africa itself, proves that Rome wants to keep things in hand.

It is clear that a world church can work on the basis of a broader strategy than completely indigenous churches. One has the impression that for a long time, Rome saw the Lovanium in Kinshasa as the axis of Roman Catholic thinking in Africa. Since Zaïre's politics of 'authenticity' has put an end to the Lovanium as a Roman Catholic university, the pope, during his last visit to Cameroon, has promised a Catholic university for Yaoundé.

It is remarkable that this essentially centralized church, which for centuries had Latin as its language of communication, was from the beginning so open to the culture and thought of the peoples among whom it wished to plant the church.

In 1548 a New Testament was printed in Rome in Ge'ez, the church language of Ethiopia. Between 1645 and 1865, the Capuchin Fathers collected all the information they could find about the life and thought of the Kikongo. During this period they published six books on Kikongo cultural history, and four books on the language, including a grammar, a dictionary and a catechism. When De Propaganda Fide was founded in 1622, one of its instructions to missionaries was that they should devote themselves to language studies so as to be able to preach and translate in local languages. As early as 1623, it was decided to issue the Bible in Arabic; this was done in 1671. The

Vatican was given its own printing press, which by 1643 had worked with 23 different alphabets. But it is remarkable that for a long time, there was also within De Propaganda Fide a conservative trend which did not want to publish scriptures in local languages.

In the nineteenth century, Cardinal Lavigerie forbade 'his' White Fathers to speak French among themselves. They had to communicate in the language in which they were doing their missionary work. New arrivals on the mission field were given six months to learn the local language. At the same time, Libermann charged the Holy Ghost Fathers not to despise African thinking because they were Europeans. They therefore had to learn the Africans' languages. The first Catholic missionaries in Liberia began to learn Grebo, and later, in 1848, Bishop Jean-Rémi Bessieux of Gabon prepared in Pongwe a dictionary, a catechism, and a life of Christ. In 1855, Alois Bobes, Franz Riehl, and the African priest Gerald Sok produced on the mission press at Ngazobol, near Dakar, a set of Bible readings for Sundays and weekdays translated into Wolof.

The general policy of Catholic missions in Africa became that of translating what was necessary for founding and building up the church. That included the catechism and the Bible readings which, following the church year, were used in celebrating the mass. The next step was often a life of Christ and/or a book of Bible stories.

Protestants and Roman Catholics agree in saying that the illumination of the Holy Spirit is necessary for understanding the Bible. But the Protestants say, on the basis of the priesthood of all believers, that the Spirit works directly in each reader of Scripture; whereas Catholics claim that interpretation has been entrusted to the church and its tradition. They therefore allow Bibles to be supplied to church members only if they are provided with notes approved by the church. The Roman Catholic Church has thus never withheld Bibles from church members, but it has set Holy Scripture within the church as guardian of salvation. Catholic Bible translations have been made in the national languages of Europe, for example in Dutch, so that even before the Reformation, large numbers of people had the Bible in their own language. Rome has always given Scripture a place, within tradition and the church's teaching office, as a means of salvation; also within the missionary task of building the church in all parts of the world.

The available data, which are difficult to assemble and therefore incomplete, give the following picture of Catholicism in Africa. From 1850, the Roman Catholic missions translated and published in at least a hundred languages Bible readings for the church year, the catechism, Bible stories from the New (and sometimes also from the Old) Testament and/or lives of Christ, and used them in churches and schools. In addition, in the 1930s, in at least 26 of these hundred languages, one or more Gospels were translated and published, together with a New Testament in at least eight languages, and a Bible in four. These four are Arabic (as early as 1671), Malagasy (1938), Lingala (1949) and Swahili (1960). It is remarkable that these Roman Catholic Bibles and New Testaments are all in languages in which a 'Protestant' Bible had played a great part in the growth of a large church. That is true of Malagasy, Swahili in East Africa, and Lingala in Zaire, but also Luganda, the language of the first evangelization of Uganda; for Sesotho in Lesotho, and Shona in what is now Zimbabwe. In other words, when the Roman Catholic missionaries did more than what was strictly necessary for the church's (Bible) teaching, and translated whole books of the Bible, it was mostly in a situation of competition with the Protestants, who in the big languages had long had the whole New Testament or even a Bible. In this way, as early as 1818, the monks of the Monastery of St John the Divine in Lebanon published the set Bible readings in Arabic in two parts, which were often reprinted; while as an answer to the Protestant Van Dyck Bible of 1865, a revision by the Dominicans of the old Catholic Bible in Arabic appeared in Baghdad between 1875 and 1878, and between 1876 and 1880 a completely new translation of the whole Bible was made by the Jesuits with the help of Maronites in Beirut.

The same competitive situation (Roman Catholic missions in many places began after the Protestants) sometimes also determined the Catholics' choice of language. In East Cameroon, the Presbyterians were working in Bulu even among peoples who were not Bulu, but who understood a little of the language. One of these peoples was the Ewondo. The Catholic mission discovered that the Ewondo despised the language of the Bulu. So they went to work in Beti, the language of the Ewondo, with the result that a large part of the Ewondo are now Roman Catholics. In the same way, the Catholics discovered, when they began missionary work in West Cameroon fifty years after the Protestants, that the Basel Mission was using two languages: Duala on the coast, and Bali (Mungaka) inland. Except among the true Duala, and especially among the Bali, these two languages are decidedly not liked. Thus the Roman Catholic mission (and, for that matter, the American Baptists) used a trade language, pidgin English, throughout the area in church and school. Similar strategic choices were made in other countries too.

The Bible naturally became involved in the mutual recriminations of the different missions. Protestants claimed that Rome pushed the Bible under the carpet, while Catholics said that Protestant freedom with the Bible caused divisions.

The place of the vernacular in education caused major discussion within the missions, notably in the French and Belgian colonies.

The first thing to be said is that, partly in order to withstand the Protestants, but even more with a view to training catechists, teachers and later priests, church and school had to be closely linked. The

school was seen as an important means of evangelization. A threefold
distinction was made. First, there was tribal education, which was
entirely through and for life in traditional society. Second came
European schooling which the colonizer wanted to be in his own
language so that the African could serve his purposes as a petty
official. Third, there was the mission's religious education, which, it is
true, addressed the African in an individual and thus un-African
manner, but in order to bring the individual into the community of the
church, so that, strengthened and fed by baptism and the other
sacraments of the church, he could found a Christian community.
Religious education therefore had to take place in the African
language.

In the 1920s, in the French colonies of West and Equatorial Africa,
a sort of compromise was reached between Roman Catholic (and also
Protestant) missions on the one hand, and the colonial administration
on the other. Officially, in the (subsidised) schools, only French would
be used, but the vernacular was allowed in religious instruction. But
the colonialist had no means of knowing what the school understood
by religious instruction. In their efforts to bypass the Protestants with
their schools, which had succeeded all over Africa in the thirties,
Roman Catholics became the great disseminators of the colonialists'
European language – and this despite their interest in African
languages. Africans, especially those who believe that the language of
the colonizer is indispensable in order to get a share of the European's
power and knowledge, were grateful for this policy. By signing a
contract with the colonial government whereby they were paid for
taking charge of education as a whole, the Roman Catholic missions in
Portuguese territories became the bearers of the Portuguese (language) policy, and in the Belgian Congo the promotors of broad basic
training in the national language, in which Flemish, alongside French,
was not forgotten. In Madagascar, the Roman Catholic missions were
more the disseminators of French, while the Protestants there were
more strongly the disseminators of Malagasy. In the British territories,
language policy was less of a problem. Yet there remained something
ambiguous in Roman Catholic mission policy. On the one hand, it
wanted Africans to use their own languages as a means of remaining
themselves over against the disintegrating individualizing and atomiz-
ing of the colonial culture. But on the other hand, it contributed to
alienation by using education in the colonial language, and with
curricula from the colonial homeland, to form an African élite. That
was even true of purely church education. In 1940 the curriculum of a
junior seminary in Ouagadougou, Upper Volta was completely French
in language and content.

At the end of the 1950s, there came great changes both in relations
with the Protestants and in relation to language and the Bible.
Ongoing africanization in the churches led in many places to more

openness and understanding between Protestants and Roman Catholics. The establishment of independent national governments also called for joint policy, for example of hospitals and schools. People felt themselves Africans first, and Catholics or Protestants second.

In 1959, the Jesuit Dr Walter Abbott in the United States and Father Walbert Bühlmann in Switzerland began to plead for co-operation in Bible work. Abbott came to the Secretariat for Christian Unity in Rome, while Bühlmann cooperated in the first book on the role of Holy Scripture in Catholic missions, published in 1966 in German, in Switzerland, with Johannes Beckmann as editor.

The mission tradition of vernacular work and the movement in some European Roman Catholic churches towards greater use of the Bible were both reinforced by the decision of the Second Vatican Council that in future the eucharist should be celebrated in the language of the people. That meant doing away with Latin as the language of the church, which psychologically for the Third World was a significant gesture towards the inculturation of the church. It also meant for Catholics the need to pay great attention to the translation of the Bible, since the Sunday readings all came from Scripture. Why not use the experience of the Protestants with their Bible societies? In discussions held in 1967 it became clear that Roman Catholic and Protestant biblical scholars had so much in common that it would be possible to work together in translation. The only question that mattered now in translation was: 'What does the original text say?', not: 'What does the church or my theology want it to say?' There was also agreement that Bibles must have reader's helps, which should have an informative, not a dogmatic content. Some Bible Societies (including the BFBS) thus to some extent abandoned the old principle of Bibles 'without note or comment', since notes approved by Rome no longer had to be of a dogmatic nature. Finally, the problem of the deuterocanonical books, which most Protestants call the Apocrypha, seemed soluble. These books: Judith, the Wisdom of Solomon, Tobit, the Wisdom of Jesus Sirach, Baruch, the Epistle of Jeremiah, 1 and 2 Maccabees, Greek Esther and the additions to the Book of Daniel, were all written in the period between the Old and New Testaments. It was therefore decided that interconfessional editions of the Bible should print these books in a separate section between the Old and New Testaments. The results of these discussions were recorded in an official document signed by representatives of the United Bible Societies and the Secretariat for Christian Unity. In 1987 these guidelines for interconfessional translation were revised, since a new situation had arisen in biblical scholarship. On the initiative of the UBS, working groups of Protestant, Orthodox and Catholic scholars had set to work to provide better editions of the original Hebrew and Greek texts. These have now been published and are used in translation work in Africa.

For Roman Catholics, however, it was not just a question of using the vernacular in celebrations of the eucharist. Vatican II had underlined the place of the Bible in the whole life of the church and believers. This led in 1969 to the foundation of the World Catholic Federation for the Biblical Apostolate (WCFBA). This organization became the meeting-place and the coordinating point for all Bible work in the Roman Catholic Church, specifically in three areas:

1. Encouraging the translation, publishing and distribution of the Bible.
2. Making and providing helps to the better understanding of the Bible's content with a view to preaching, catechesis and the liturgy.
3. Stimulating activities and meetings to encourage reading, studying and meditating on the Bible.

All these developments made the Bible fully open in Roman Catholicism, remaining the book of the church.

In 1965 there took place in Enugu, Nigeria a conference of church leaders convened by the governor of Eastern Nigeria, Dr Akanu Ibiam. Its purpose was to set up a Nigerian Bible Society. When the question arose as to what people from what churches should be members of its board, the Africa secretaries of the UBS, Paul Hopkins and Frank Bedford, discovered that there were Roman Catholics attending the meeting. Since high church Anglicans also went around in cassocks, they had not realized this at first. Bedford hesitantly said to Dr Ibiam that people in England had not yet reached the point of including Catholics in the board of the Bible Society, whereupon Ibiam answered gently: 'We're not in England here; we're in Nigeria.' And in fact Anglicans and Presbyterians, evangelicals and Catholics became members of the board.

This story is typical of the African drive with which, in many countries, Roman Catholics started to cooperate in Bible society work, sometimes by bishops becoming ordinary members of the society, but also regularly, by bishops or priests functioning as board members. Here and there, however, the sores of old conflicts remain so that more time is needed either at regional or national level. In 1975, new cooperation began in Madagascar, and in 1987, two Roman Catholics became members of the national Bible society committee. In 1964 the bishops of Zaïre decided that in future the eucharist would be celebrated in the following languages: Lingala, tshiLuba, kiSwahili, kiYombe, kiKongo, kiSanga, baNgala and chiBemba. Similar decisions are made in many countries. Where people do not have their own translations, they use for the lectionary readings editions of the Bible Society (sometimes specially printed for the Catholics, as happened for example with the seTswana Bible in South Africa), or they translate them themselves, or they discuss making a new translation with the other churches in cooperation with the Bible Society. There is thus great interest in many places, on the Roman Catholic side, in projects for common language translations. Important inter-confessional projects include Today's Arabic Version, which involves not only Catholics and Protestants but also Copts; Today's Swahili for East Africa, Hausa for Nigeria, Zulu for South Africa, and Malagasy. Generally speaking, there is Roman Catholic participation, or in any case interest, in practically all translation projects in official languages and large church languages.

In 1976 a Tanzanian priest became the first UBS translation consultant in training.

Sometimes cooperation fails or causes great problems. This can arise through differences between traditional Catholic and Protestant spellings of proper names. This was the case in Madagascar. Difficulties can also arise where people use a completely different dialect of a language in church. For example, the Romana in Zaïre decided to make their own Lingala translation of the Bible.

A practical problem in cooperation with Catholics is that the Roman Catholic Church has no tradition of giving money for the work of the Bible Society. The solution has to be for Catholic dioceses to share in the translation costs; as in other churches in Africa, Roman Catholics are also to be encouraged to ask for prayers and gifts for Bible society work.

In 1975 the Bishops' Conference of Africa and Madagascar asked the WCFBA to found a service centre for Africa, and in 1981 the Bible Institute for Catholics in Africa and Madagascar (BICAM) started work in Nairobi under the authority of the continental bishops' conference. The centre issues a quarterly information bulletin in English and French, and twice a year a more substantial pastoral bulletin, also in English and French, which includes theological and exegetical articles on the Bible. Once a year, the centre also publishes a prayer booklet with Bible readings, and people are working on a series of commentaries on the Sunday readings. BICAM organizes, on its own premises and elsewhere (for example in Malawi, southern Sudan and Côte d'Ivoire) conferences on the use of the Bible. Finally, BICAM advises on Bible translation projects, and cooperates in this work with the UBS and Wycliffe Bible Translators.

The January 1986 issue of BICAM's newsletter 'The Biblical Apostolate' contained the following statement: 'Discovery of the Bible set people aflame so that groups for Bible study and prayer sprang up like fire in the dry savannahs of Africa. This fire of God's Word is spreading daily at all levels of the church in Africa.'

37

The Book from Heaven

As early as the tenth century, 'the book from heaven', the Qur'an, came across the Sahara to tropical Africa. At that time, Christians in Egypt were oppressed and the Christian Roman emigrants from North Africa had almost disappeared.

By that time, the Islamic Ben Hilleel had reached Lake Chad, while Islam was also reaching tropical Africa by a western route through Morocco and Mauretania to Senegal. In Senegal, there arose one of the largest Muslim kingdoms of the middle ages. In the name of Allah, the Almoravids conquered North Africa, Portugal and Spain; in 732, these 'Moors' were turned back with the greatest difficulty by Charles Martel near Poitiers in France.

Islam has been called the youngest child of Judaism, because Mohammed on the Arabian peninsula not only had contact with Christians and sought relations with Jewish communities, but was also clearly influenced in the Qur'an by the Bible, particularly the Old Testament.

'Islam' means 'the religion of submission', and 'Qur'an' means 'what must be recited and preached'. Islam asks its followers to observe a few simple basic rules, and in addition has a developed system of commandments and prohibitions. Islam has no priests, but it does have Qur'anic teachers and theologians. Within Islam, there are many different schools and tendencies.

The Qur'an was written in Arabic; more precisely, it was dictated to Mohammed by an angel. Hence the language of the Qur'an is also holy. As a result there has been much discussion among Muslims about whether the Qur'an can be translated into another language. Another point is that Arabic, as the language of the Qur'an, cannot change. In the course of centuries, this has had remarkable linguistic consequences for the whole Arabic-speaking world.

A literary language has grown up on the basis of the classical Arabic of the Qur'an.

This has also become the language of science. From early times Islam has stimulated not only legal studies, but also the natural sciences, and has given rise to a rich literature. Centres of learning came to flourish, not only in Mecca and Medina, but also in Cairo, in Baghdad in what is now called Iraq, in Seville in Spain, and in Tombouctou on the other side of the Sahara. This scientific and literary language, strongly influenced by the Arabic of the Qur'an, is more classical than the English of the King James Version or the German of the Luther Bible. Alongside this there has grown up a kind of general purpose Arabic used in teaching, journalism and modern literature. An important difference between this modern literary language and the classical Arabic of the Qur'an and scholarly writings is that the modern language is written without pointing, that is unvocalized.

This kind of Arabic is also mostly used for subtitles on TV and orally on the radio. This general purpose Arabic functions at school and in the media throughout the Arabic world; but for daily communication among themselves, people speak local dialects of Arabic, some of which are close to the official language, but most are quite different. These popular languages are not usually published or written.

This means that the Arabic world has a classical literary language and a general purpose language, both of which are so different from the language spoken in daily use that they have to be learned at school. The advantage of this remarkable situation, which as we said above is rooted in the holiness of the Qur'an, is that the whole Arabic world can be reached with a single written and printed language.

Tombouctou, once an important centre of Muslim studies, is now a sleepy town in the steadily growing Sahara. Yet the transit routes through the Sahara are still channels of communication for knowledge and for pilgrims between Africa and the Muslim centres, using Arabic as a vehicular language.

Until the colonial period, Islam spread in Africa south of the Sahara in three ways.

The first was the conversion of rulers to Islam. In this, Muslim scholars from Tombouctou acted as go-betweens at the courts of the rulers in question. This was élitist Islam; in most cases, the people slowly followed their rulers. This happened in the middle ages in the West African kingdoms of Mali and Gao to the west, and Kanem and Bornu by Lake Chad; also, at the beginning of the twentieth century, in Cameroon among the Bamoun. Their sultan chose Islam in 1913, and now 80 per cent of all Bamoun are Muslims.

The second way in which Islam spread was by military conquest, followed by forced conversion to Islam. That happened in 1076, when the Almoravids conquered Kumbi, the capital of the old kingdom of Ghana, in what is now Mali. In the same way, the Fulani waged 'holy wars' in the name of Allah in various parts of northern Nigeria and north Cameroon, leading to the setting up of great sultanates and emirates. Nevertheless, there has been only limited spread of Islam through 'holy wars'.

In both these processes, the tsetse fly played a part. The Muslims always came on horses and with camels, and these died from sleeping sickness brought by the tsetse fly. For a long time, therefore, the tsetse fly marked the frontier of Islam in Africa, so that pastoral peoples became Muslim, but not the farmers.

The third method of expansion is still important: it is through Muslim traders who settle among non-Muslims, and Muslim herdsmen who come into contact with animist farmers. These foreigners often marry girls from the other group. To a certain extent, they live like the others, but through their conduct, their visible practice of daily prayer and their economic success, they pass on their Muslim faith. Without any missionary organization behind them they show by their lives that Allah is great.

In the precolonial period, Arabs and Persians established themselves on the east African coast as far as Zanzibar and beyond. They built harbours and founded sultanates in a kind of city states. The appeal of their Islam was limited, because their main activity was the export of slaves to the Arabian peninsula.

Within a period of twelve centuries, gentle pressure and the occasional use of force has reduced the Christian population of Egypt to 7 per cent of the whole. In North Africa during the twelfth century, the last remnants of the Christian emigrants disappeared, and the Berbers and Tuaregs were quickly islamicized. The Berbers even played an important part in the growth of the Almoravid Kingdom. In the fourteenth century, in Sudan to the south of Egypt, Islam was imposed by force, while in the sixteenth century the Ethiopian Christians halted Islam with great difficulty, with the help of Portuguese military support which arrived just in time.

In the nineteenth century, when the Christian slave trade ceased, the Arab slave trade on the east coast continued. The slave traders went further and further into the interior. They went to Katanga in Zaïre, and Livingstone met them in what is now Malawi.

Africans accompanying pilgrims across the Sahara on their way to Mecca also regularly 'disappeared'. They were sold in Saudi Arabia to cover the costs of the pilgrimage. Around Lake Chad such disappearances appear to continue to the present day.

The 'law and order' of the colonial period made possible the extension of migration of Muslim traders in West Africa as far as the coast, and in East Africa into the interior. This helped the spread of Islam.

Moreover, for reasons of economy, the colonial government used in many places the system of indirect rule, giving African rulers a place in the regional administration. Thus, in northern Nigeria, northern Sudan, north Cameroon or Zanzibar, where the local ruler was a Muslim sultan, the British or French put a brake on missionary expansion in their territories, or even prohibited it, in order to remain on good terms with these rulers, though often many of their subjects were not Muslims themselves.

In East Africa, after the long period of the Muslim slave trade, Islam came to have a more human face. Some of the workers who came from (then British) India to lay railway tracks were Isma'ili Muslims. They settled in Kenya, Uganda and Tanzania, and under the leadership of their Aga Khan, with his strong social convictions, they contributed to the establishment of hospitals, social institutions, and later even newspapers.

This whole development produced a situation in which now, 70 per cent of all Arabic speakers live in Africa.

After independence, in many African countries the expansion of Islam underwent another change.

In Morocco, Tunisia, and especially Algeria, Islam and Arabic had become symbols of opposition to colonial occupation. After independence, the major part of education in these countries became Arabic, while the return to France of the 'pieds noirs', the white colonists, reduced the Christian churches to very small groups. The churches were seen as communities of foreigners. In Algeria, the Berber peoples, who feel themselves culturally threatened, vigorously oppose arabization.

After the independence of Sudan, the Muslim majority in the north tried to arabize and islamicize the non-Islamic and partly Christian south. In 1972, after ten years' civil war, the south gained internal autonomy. Now relations are again very strained and there is fighting between north and south. The north does not hesitate to use its control of food supplies as a weapon of war and this causes great hardship to the local population.

In West Africa and along the East African coast, Islam is growing again.

In addition to the old missionary influence of Hausa or Fulani traders settling outside their areas of origin, there are now other factors:

1. The influence of a successful Muslim state president on the non-Islamic inhabitants of his country. Cameroon was traditionally religiously divided, but after ten or fifteen years the success in power of President Ahidjo from the Muslim north led to a kind of emanation of the feeling that 'there must be a strong God behind our president, or he would have fallen long ago.'

2. Where Muslim civil servants take over in local government, despite the almost universal constitutional provision for freedom of religion, 'administrative' islamicization takes place here and there. It works very simply. The official refuses to give a 'client' a birth certificate for his child, and this is necessary for obtaining a place in

school; or a hunting or trading licence is refused when the client is not a Muslim or does not want to become one. And people can see whether you are a Muslim or not, because the Muslim wears the long robe called a *bubu*, whereas the non-Muslim wears European clothes.

3. In West Africa, between the Muslim areas which run right from Senegal to Lake Chad along the southern border of the Sahara, and the Christianized coasts, there live an estimated fifty million adherents of African traditional religions. These are the least educated, because among other things Christianity means schools. As uneducated people, they are therefore also the poorest. Their traditional doctors have lost much ground to western health care so that their African traditional religion has no status in their own eyes. They are faced with the choice between Christianity and Islam. In most cases, their choice will be determined by political and economic rather than by religious considerations. They usually weigh the advantages and disadvantages of joining the mosque or the church. They are too poor and powerless to afford the luxury of any other motivation.

Islam is a religion which permeates the whole of society, much as Christianity in the middle ages affected all areas of life and society in Europe.

In its meeting with African society, Islam quickly came to have an African face. It began with the setting up of the so-called brotherhoods among Muslims in Morocco. These brotherhoods were a kind of cross between what Christians call a monastery and what Africans call a secret society. They still play an important part in Moroccan society. In the nineteenth century there arose in Sudan a Mahdi, a kind of long awaited messianic liberator, who was to set Sudan free from the Egyptians and slay the wicked. He first sacked Khartoum, but his successor was killed in 1898. To the south of the Sahara, Islam became African by means of amulets and saints, and with exorcism using Qur'an texts in Arabic which were not understood. The five basic rules of Islam were mixed up with traditions from African religions.

Around 1980 there even arose in northern Nigeria an African Muslim prophet. This man, Mohammed Marvu from Cameroon, was called Maitatsine by his followers, and was seen as a prophet of black Islam. He was killed in a disturbance in Kano.

In the eyes of many Africans, Islam had, and still has, advantages over Christianity. Islam was seen as an African religion, while Christianity came from Europe. However, there are areas in which the Arab slave trader is still not forgotten. Islam has room for the polygamous traditions of many African cultures, while Christianity insists on only one wife. On the other hand, urban Africa is clearly developing in the direction of monogamy, helped by the growing emancipation of women. Islam has simple rules, while the totality of Muslim traditions often remains unknown, because of inadequate knowledge of literary Arabic.

Some doubt whether Islam can really fit in with modern society in which such concepts as human rights, democracy and the emancipation of women are taken seriously. There are scholars who hold that only a heretical form of Islam, such as the Ahmadiyya movement, has an answer to the questions of modern times. On the other hand, there are also Muslims who blame the western world for bringing not only the message of Jesus, but also secularization and godless science.

At the present time, everywhere in the Muslim world, particularly among the intelligentsia, there is an influential movement of return to the old fundamentalist orthodoxy. There are pleas for a return to true Islam, for the reintroduction of the old *sharia* legislation with its harsh penalties, and the abolition of interest on loans. Behind this traditionalism lies a kind of new antithesis, a reaction against westernization. People want western knowledge, science and technology, but reject western decadence, pleasure-seeking and egocentrism in life, culture and the media. In North Africa, this movement is strongest in Algeria. Libya with its 'green revolution' is another story, strongly marked by the personality of Gadaffi. In Egypt, although the El-Azaar University in Cairo is a centre of Muslim thinking for the whole of Islam, the fundamentalists form a minority, because Christian influence on the Nile has always stimulated a liberal form of Islam. In Africa south of the Sahara the influence of the fundamentalists is much smaller, because Islam, particularly in northern Nigeria and north Cameroon, is concerned to rid itself of the image of a religion bound up with the feudal rule of the sultans.

Finally, what appeals to Africa is the fact that Islam, just like the African traditional religions, has to do with the whole of human life, whereas western Christians are more inclined to separate their Sunday faith from what they do during the week.

It is a multi-coloured picture. On a practical level, it can be said that financial support for the propagation of Islam comes from the rich Muslim oil countries. It is used here and there to build mosques; also to offer all radio stations in Africa free long-playing records of the Qur'an. In 1984, a modern printing press was opened in Medina, which will reach an annual production of seven million Qur'ans in Arabic intended for the whole Muslim world. One can ask whether larger distribution of the Qur'an in Africa will have much effect, since despite many Qur'anic schools, knowledge of classical literary Arabic remains limited.

The relationship between European Christianity and Islam is strongly conditioned by the memory of the Crusades, and later statements based on European Christian feeling of superiority. For centuries, the Ethiopian Orthodox Christians have had to maintain themselves over against the Muslims, just like the Coptic Orthodox in Egypt. Important aspects of the Egyptian situation were that the Copts made themselves indispensable by performing functions which the Muslim rulers needed, and also that they became more and more skilled in keeping their place in Muslim society in unofficial ways.

Of course the Coptic Orthodox Christians in Egypt are also influenced by their Muslim neighbours. Egyptian Christians have learnt much from non-figurative Muslim art with its splendid symmetrical designs. Under the auspices of the Bible societies, an interconfessional translation of the New Testament, in the common unvocalized Arabic of the schools, journalism and TV, was published in 1979, but this was criticized, especially by the Copts, because they considered the Bible as a classical text, which should have pointing, just like the Qur'an. The style of the new translation is largely influenced by one of the greatest writers in the Arab world, the Egyptian Christian El-Kaal. Just as the new translation is criticized now for being too modern, so, a century ago, was the Van Dyck translation when it first appeared. Today's Arabic New Testament has been revised; the Old Testament is also finished, and the whole Bible was published in 1994.

The Copts have never really tried to evangelize the Muslims. They have concentrated on maintaining their own communities. Moreover, it is still today administratively impossible for a Muslim to be registered as a Christian. Conversion from Islam to Christianity is administratively impossible; but not vice versa.

When, in the nineteenth century, the modern missionary movement began, efforts were made to preach the gospel to Muslims in North Africa. Protestant teaching, with Jesus as Saviour at its centre, was usually understood as tritheism. Cardinal Lavigerie had his White Fathers dressed in Muslim *bubus* and tried to get African students by opening up orphanages and schools. The results are extremely modest.

In Africa south of the Sahara, Protestant and Roman Catholic missions have avoided mission to Muslims for a long period, after a few failures. Their goal became the followers of traditional African religions, and especially the non-Islamic farmers who lived among the Muslim shepherd peoples often under their power. Nor has there been much reflection on the question of how to present the gospel to Muslims; there was also great ignorance of the Muslim way of life and the religious convictions which went with it.

This changed early in the 1960s with the start, under the auspices of the then International Missionary Council, of the Islam in Africa Project. In cooperation with British, American, French and Dutch missions, a team of experts went to mission workers, pastors and 'ordinary' Christians to tell them how Muslims think and behave, and what convictions underlie their behaviour. The purpose of the project is to help them in their later meeting with Muslims and preaching to them. For some years, African Christian specialists in Islam have been members of the teams working in West and East Africa.

The history of Bible translations intended for mainly Muslim peoples reflects the positions of churches and missions to Islam.

As early as 1516, the Psalms were printed in Arabic in Rome. Soon after its foundation, De Propaganda Fide set itself the task of compiling from extant manuscripts, revising and publishing the text of an Arabic New Testament. This task was completed in 1671.

In 1865 there appeared the still used Van Dyck translation of the Bible, and in 1878 and 1882 were published two Catholic translations; that of the Jesuits in Lebanon became the better known.

The great problem still today (see above) is the question of what kind of Arabic should be used for the Bible. Arabic-speaking Christians are strongly attached to the classical language, because it is used also in the Qur'an. There is also the question of whether, wherever possible, biblical terms should be drawn from the Old Testament or from the Qur'an.

Bible translations in Swahili proceed quickly whether among Protestants or Catholics, but Swahili is seen as a big trade language rather than a typical Muslim language. It took a long time to produce good Bible translations in Muslim languages such as Hausa, Nupe, Fulani and Chad Arabic.

The Bible Societies try in their choice and presentation of biblical books to take account of Muslim thinking.

At the present time, evangelism among Muslims is prohibited throughout North Africa. In a number of countries south of the Sahara, and also in Ethiopia, many people in the next few years will decide between Christ as the way, the truth and the life, or the five Muslim duties of the Qur'an, the book from heaven. Their choice will be primarily pragmatic in response to the question: 'In which great religion can I remain myself and find an answer to my questions?' And secondly: 'Which great religion has the greatest practical advantages?'

38

On Their Way Rejoicing

Old and new messages win thousands in Africa, or try to. Islam claims to be an African religion; it is growing and has won status through the worldwide importance of the Gulf states' oil capital; but its expansion is also limited by collision in southern Sudan with Christian and animist Africa, in the breakdown of Muslim socialism in Algeria, and in the incalculable effects in Libya of Gadaffi's Muslim green revolution.

The western ideologies, in Africa as in the rest of the world, have had their day as a basis for community development. New élitist secret societies such as the Rosicrucians, especially in French-speaking Africa, try to provide a basis for the new upper class, and the second liberation demands democracy and realism.

When westernization in the sense of separating matters of head and heart, belief and thought, feeling and knowledge, succeeds, Africa which has so often been plundered will lose its essential nature, namely the sense of total life and thought in a relationship between the living, the dead and the yet unborn. Yet Africa cannot avoid sharing in world civilization, which means more than wearing jeans. When one thinks of music, rhythm, dance, and also the visual arts, it is clear that Africa has set its stamp on world culture. One may say that Africa is now mortally ill from having shared in world-wide western technology and economics. Modern economics and science, which pretend to be the measure of all things, present Africa in many ways as a sacrificial victim to the neo-colonialist power of the rich countries; but this argument too often serves for Europeans as a kind of compulsory confession of their past sins and for Africans as a too easy excuse for how things are today.

The slaves who long ago were shipped to Africa were cut off from their ancestors and their roots (perhaps even until today), asking the great question: 'Who am I, and where are my roots? Am I an American or an African; do I belong to the western world, or am I a transplanted bit of Africa?' The last word on this was spoken by the Rev. Jesse Jackson: 'We are not negroes. We are not blacks. We are African Americans.'

The African Africans have never understood this problem of their brothers and sisters in America. True, they were colonized by foreign powers; but they were able to remain themselves in their own countries and with their own ancestors. But now African Africans are asking themselves the same question as the African Americans: 'Who am I? If I go back to the roots of my *négritude*, my black consciousness becomes nostalgia and can end in black racism. Moreover, those who rely on vital force from the African traditional religions are the most economically backward and poorest. But I cannot and will not accept the offer which especially the French made to Africa and become a black European.' Yet the strange thing is that where the colonists always failed in their efforts to make Africa a continent of dark-skinned Europeans, superficial westernization and the domainance of western economics and technology seem to be succeeding. In some countries, Islamic fundamentalism is trying to reverse this process, while leaders in a few other countries try to resolve the dilemma through faith in a Marxism which wants to be neither western or African, but universal.

How can one become, or remain, part of world economic and technical developments and still be oneself? How can one progress without cutting the links with the ancestors and with one's own African past?

The search for Africans' own directions and answers is seriously hindered in this respect by the way in which cultural poverty, spreading world-wide through modern advertizing in the mass media, and tending towards a 'bread and circuses' consumer society, manifests itself even in Africa.

In a limited number of African countries there are serious newspapers, but these can only be read where there are railways or airfields to make rapid distribution possible, and also people who can pay for them and who can read them. In many countries, however, there are almost no newspapers, or they are so heavily censored that they are scarcely worth reading.

Through lack of hard currency, misguided customs regulations or lack of technical facilities, the production of books and journals is also poor; so there are bookshops with empty shelves, or only pulp literature to sell. The result is that students and others eager to learn can scarcely obtain the books they need. It is much easier to get novels by African writers in Europe than in Africa itself. Even where bookselling is economically possible, censorship often limits the choice. Of course it is good that the Bible Societies are some of the largest book producers in Africa; but just as one cannot live by bread alone, neither can one live by the Bible alone.

In the area of information, the transmission of music, education and advice, the radio is very important in Africa. Because of national censorship and the lack of resources, world radio transmitters which give more than news, propaganda or religious programmes can make a broad and very significant contribution to the struggle against cultural pauperization of Africa, precisely because they enable Africans to speak for themselves. The BBC World Service in London is the best example of this service.

It can be said that the printed word and even radio belong to yesterday and that the things which matter now are television, the screen, and computers. But in that area the situation is still more pitiful. There have been and still are African countries which have made amazing efforts to provide information and popular education through television. Uganda, for so long a country tearing itself apart, was one of the earliest examples; much has been done also in Gabon, Côte d'Ivoire and Kenya. But television is technically vulnerable and thus expensive to buy and maintain. Here too getting poorer means going backwards. Many countries are now relying on pulp programmes from the West, which means that everything the West is willing to hand over the counter cheaply or for nothing can get on to African television. The result is a lamentable pollution of the airwaves.

As for modern data processing, this requires money and rooms with good air conditioning for the equipment. What is more, if a country like the USSR has difficulty in keeping up with American and Japanese developments in this area, then Africa is in danger of falling so far behind that it can never catch up.

Another risk is that African culture will be turned into mass production products for tourists or plays for western theatres. The only people who seem able to make a contemporary link between African elements and western developments are some African pop artists who have become known all over the world. Cultural poverty is perhaps most clearly seen in the schools where all too often unmotivated teachers struggle day by day with all too few educational materials. And what are the children to learn? A westernizing curriculum? Their own African roots? Or sensible things which teach children to survive in the situation of poverty in which many of them will find themselves tomorrow?

As early as 1920 and 1924, the Phelps-Stokes Foundation, which wanted to improve the situation of black people in the United States and Africa, set up at the request of American and British missions two international committees of experts to research the educational situation in Africa. Their detailed reports, produced after two long journeys, pleaded for education for but also with Africans. Today, the great question is what the content of this education should be. What education does Africa need today, if it is not to become the world's poor back yard, but also in order to remain itself?

It may be argued that the settlement of debts, the growth of local agricultural products, sensible industrialization and a more economic use of land are all important for the future of Africa, but cannot be achieved unless the question of the identity, and thus the motivation and orientation of Africa's people is answered by Africans themselves. It must sadly be said that among those who should take the lead in this respect many are too alienated, westernized and materialistic to be credible. Yet adaptability and flexibility have always been features of African peoples. The Roman writer Pliny said it all: there is always something new from Africa.

The Christian church in Africa is not only very old, but also fully alive, steadily growing, and very African, in both old and new senses of the word.

The oldest church in Africa, the Egyptian church, is again active in a Muslim world; its symbol is the new St Mark's Cathedral in Cairo, but also modern diaconal and development work. The Coptic Orthodox Church has broken out of its isolation to take its place in the world fellowship of churches.

The same is true of the Ethiopian Orthodox Church which has survived atheist Marxist régime.

The ecumenical churches, born of Protestant missions, have had their problems with the many schools, hospitals and other institutions under their control in many countries. They also face the question of whether they must be the Christian conscience of the nation, or whether, like the traditional priests, they should praise the rulers to the skies. In some places, they are going through leadership crises related to status and money.

The churches born of faith missions are specialists in primary evangelization. Because 'their' missions are supposed to be non-clerical, the structural development of a church is harder for them. Their African preachers are now discovering, for example on the edge of the Sahel, that the Bible speaks of more than spiritual salvation. There, common wells are a sign of hope as sources of 'living water'.

The Roman Catholics are, on the one hand, active in the theological and liturgical upbuilding of African churches, and on the other, still too closely linked with western financial and human resources.

The church of the white tribe in South Africa is seeking to learn how to speak prophetically in Christ's name against the sin of apartheid.

Finally, the most quickly growing independent African churches face the choice between various options. How to avoid becoming private enterprises run by enthusiastic individuals? How to avoid the kind of africanization in which the Christ of the Bible disappears from view? How to be the place in which Africans can be themselves, but in which they can still meet the Christ of the Bible?

The Ugandan theologian and philosopher John Mbiti takes the view that the African ancestors knew about God all along, but that the peoples of Africa can now know God in Jesus Christ in his true, saving form. This may in one way or another prove true for Africa. So may

David Barrett's argument that the African way to Christ must run through the world of the Old Testament, which Africa knows and trusts. Otherwise, in the coming years, Christianity in Africa will rust away, will be washed away or will be dried out, like so many products imported from the West.

But Christianity is called to fight one of the greatest hindrances to contemporary development in Africa; something hostile both to human rights and to the biblical command of love, namely tribalism. Placide Tempels, the man who with his *Bantu Philosophy* helped the Africans to further their own thought and feeling about life, once wrote that Africa cannot be converted to Christianity until tribalism is conquered. He is right and what he says applies equally to opposition between peoples and to mixed marriages. By the way, tribalism also tends to weaken every African's struggle against the remnants of apartheid among the still powerful white tribe in South Africa.

But the poverty of the great cities breaks through tribal boundaries. There, one can see the truth in the saying: 'The Christian church is a church of the poor.' The church in Africa today can only be Christian, indeed can only survive, if it is a church of the poor. Linguistically, there is a remarkable contrast here. In order to know God as Father, one needs one's mother tongue; but the Christian conquest of tribalism involves communication which goes beyond the mother tongue.

All Christian families in Africa have this question on their agenda: How can Christianity have a content which fits into the world-wide church of today, but does not cut off its African roots?

In finding an answer to this question, the Bible, the revelation of the Father of our Lord Jesus Christ, both in the vernaculars but also in the (new) big languages of the cities, is as a light on the path, but also as a landmark which can keep people close to the message of Christ, not wandering away into something either purely African or simply fashionable.

That is why it is a serious mistake when each year, the requests from Bible houses in Africa for translating, printing, and distributing the Bible have to be cut back. The churches of the world which want to support all Christians in Africa, not only those who have a historical relation with their own mission, must above all make sure that there is no lack of Bibles, which are the foundation of all Christian witness.

This means, in my view, that fresh priorities must be set for the use of Christian money in Africa.

It is up to the churches and Christians of Africa to decide in what languages they want to have the Bible and in what kind of translations. Relevant factors here include the language policies of governments, people's concern for their own language, and the place of a language in the witness of the church. Certainly, with 1800 languages in Africa, priorities must be set. The nineteenth-century attitude of the BFBS as servant of the churches is still assumed by Bible societies in Africa today. The Wycliffe Bible Translators' principle that the Bible must be translated into the language of each people is not realistic, however sympathetic and Christian that task might sound. Moreover, limitation in the past of their translation work to the New Testament implies for Africans the risk of meeting only a western, spiritualized Christ. The Old Testament is essential in order to make possible an encounter with Christ which is both Christian and African.

The Bible Society movement must also have the courage to be a kind of conscience of the churches and to protest wherever people want to lock the Bible away within the walls of a church. The Bible is still the book which in its own ways brings people into contact with Christ. This can be in the form of a leaflet carrying a Bible story, or a booklet for new readers, or a gospel cassette, or a radio programme in which a Bible story is read. But there must always also be a place for people like the Ethiopian official in Acts, buying a book and reading it on their journey home. That is the moment for the church to ask: 'Do you understand what you are reading?' That is the moment to explain that it is about Christ so that people in Africa (and not in Africa alone) may 'go on their way rejoicing'.

Bibliography

This list includes books read or consulted, and items for further reading.

History and development

Robert Cornevin: *Histoire des peuples de l'Afrique noire*, Paris 1960.
Assoi Adiko and André Clerici: *Histoire des peuples noirs*, Abidjan, n.d.
Cheikh Anta Diop: *The Cultural Unity of Black Africa*, New York 1987.
Catherine Coquery: *La découverte de l'Afrique*, Paris 1965.
A.J. Wills: *The Story of Africa*, 2 vols., London 1971.
Basil Davidson: *Old Africa Rediscovered*, London 1965.
Basil Davidson: *African Kingdoms*, New York 1966.
Basil Davidson: *The Story of Africa*, London 1984.
Ali A. Mazrui: *The Africans: a triple heritage*, London 1988.
Marie-France Briselance: *Histoire de l'Afrique*, 2 vols., Paris 1988.
Jocelyn Murray (ed.): *Cultural Atlas of Africa*, Oxford 1981.
Le dossier Afrique: *Marabout Université*, Yaoundé 1962.
Le nouveau dossier Afrique: *Marabout Université*, Yaoundé, 1971.
E. Mveng and D. Beling-Nkoumba: *Histoire du Cameroun*, Yaoundé 1976.
Elikia M'Bokolo: *Affonso I, le roi chrétien de l'ancien Congo*, Yaoundé 1975.
Ibrahima Baba Kake: *Anne Zingha, première résistante à l'invasion portugaise*, Yaoundé 1975.
Ibrahima Baba Kake: *Donna Béatrice, la Jeanne d'Arc congolaise*, Paris 1976.
Jean-Paul Sartre: *Colonialism et néo-colonialisme*, Paris 1964.
Frantz Fanon: *The Wretched of the Earth*, London 1965.
Basil Davidson: *Which way Africa?*, London 1964.
Yves Benoît: *Idéologies des indépendances africaines*, Paris 1971.
Jean Ziegler: *Sociologie de la nouvelle Afrique*, Paris 1964.
Georges Balandier: *Ambiguous Africa: Cultures in Collision*, New York 1966.
René Dumont: *False Start in Africa*, London, repr. 1988.
René Dumont and Marie-France Mottin: *Stranglehold on Africa*, London 1984.
Lloyd Timberlake: *Africa in Crisis*, London 1985.
Jomo Kenyatta: *Facing Mount Kenya*, London 1938.
Edward Ullendorf: *The Ethiopians*, London 1965.
Solange Thierry: *Madagascar*, Paris 1963.
Simone Lacouture: *L'Egypte*, Paris 1962.

South Africa

James Duffy: *Portugal in Africa*, London 1962.
Brian Bunting: *The Rise of the South African Reich*, London 1964.
  G.J. Schutte: *Nederland en de Afrikaners; adhesie en aversie*, Franeker 1986.
Peter Randall: *South African Minorities*, Johannesburg 1971.
Peter Randall: *The Anatomy of Apartheid*, Johannesburg 1971.
T. Dunbar Moodie: *The Rise of Afrikanerdom*, Berkeley-London 1975.
Marianne Cornevin: *L'apartheid: pouvoir et falsification historique*, Paris 1979.

Ideologies

Placide Tempels: *Bantu Philosophy*, Paris 1959.
Claude Wauthier: *L'Afrique des Africains*, Paris 1964.
Lilyan Kesteloot: *Les écrivains noirs de langue française*, Brussels 1965.
Lilyan Kesteloot: *Négritude et situation coloniale*, Yaoundé 1968.
Thomas Mélone: *De la négritude dans la littérature négro-africaine*, Paris 1962.
Jean-Marie Abanda Ndengue: *De la négritude au négrisme*, Yaoundé 1970.
Marciel Towa: *Essai sur la problématique philosophique dans l'Afrique actuelle*, Yaoundé 1971.
Richard Dogbeh: *Voyage au pays de Lénine*, Yaoundé 1967.

Works by African leaders

Nnamdi Azikiwe: *Renascent Africa*, Accra 1937.
Ndabaningi Sithole: *African Nationalism*, London 1959.
Albert Luthuli: *Let my People go*, London 1962.
Kwame Nkrumah: *Towards Colonial Freedom*, London 1962.
Kwame Nkrumah: *Consciencism*, London 1964.
Tom Mboya: *Freedom and After*, London 1963.
Kenneth Kaunda: *Zambia shall be Free*, London 1962.
Léopold Sédar Senghor: *On African Socialism*, New York 1964.
Julius K. Nyerere: *Freedom and Unity*, Das-es-Salaam 1966.
Eduardo Mondlane: *The Struggle for Mozambique*, London 1969.

African religions

G. van der Leeuw: *Religion in Essence and Manifestation*, Princeton 1986.
Mircea Eliade: *A History of Religious Ideas*, 3 vols., Chicago 1981–88.
Th. van Baaren: *Uit de wereld der religie*, Arnhem 1956.
Claude Lévi-Strauss: *Savage Mind*, Chicago and London 1968.
Paul Radin: *Primitive Man as Philosopher*, New York 1957.
Geoffrey Parrinder: *Religion in Africa*, London 1969.
Geoffrey Parrinder: *West African Religion*, London 1949.
John S. Mbiti: *Concepts of God in Africa*, London 1970.

Islam

J.C. Froelich: *Les musulmans d'Afrique noire*, Paris 1962.
J. Spencer Trimingham: *Islam in West Africa*, London 1964.

Abd-el-Massih: *Au seuil de l'Islam*, Yaoundé 1965.
J. Spencer Trimingham: *Islam in East Africa*, London 1962.

Church and Mission History

Kenneth S. Latourette: *A History of the Expansion of Christianity*, 7 vols.,
  New York 1937–45.
Tim Dowley (ed.): *The History of Christianity*, Berkhamsted, Herts 1977.
David B. Barrett: *World Christian Encyclopedia*, Nairobi 1982.
Stephen C. Neill: *A History of Christian Missions*, London 1964.
Stephen C. Neill: *Colonialism and Christian Missions*, London 1966.
C.P. Groves: *The Planting of Christianity in Africa*, 4 vols., London 1949–59.
G.W. Carpenter: *The Way in Africa*, London 1960.
T.A. Beetham: *Christianity in the New Africa*, London 1967.
Cecil Northcott: *Christianity in Africa*, London 1963.
Walbert Bühlmann: *Missionsprozess in Addis Abeba*, Frankfurt 1977.
Bengt Sundkler: *The World of Mission*, London 1965.
Roland Oliver: *The Missionary Factor in East Africa*, London 1952.
Ralph E. Dodge: *The Unpopular Missionary*, New Jersey 1964.
F.B. Welbourn: *East African Christian*, Nairobi 1965.
Max Warren: *Revival*, London 1954.
Aylward Shorter and Eugene Katara: *Missionaries to ourselves. African
  Catechists Today*, London 1972.
*Ecoles et missions chrétiennes extérieures. Actes de la VIIe session du CREDIC
  à Salamanque*, Lyon 1988.
'Africa: *state-church relations in education*', in: *Exchange. Bulletin of third
  world Christian literature*, 28 April 1981.
John V. Taylor: *The Growth of the Church in Buganda. An attempt at
  understanding*, London 1958.
E.M. Braekman: *Histoire du protestantisme au Congo*, Brussels 1961.
Hans Debrunner: *A Church between Colonial Powers (Togo)*, London 1965.
J. van Slageren: *Les origines de l'Eglise Evangélique du Cameroun*, Leiden
  1972.
Werner Keller: *Zur Freiheit berufen. Die Geschichte der presbyterianischen
  Kirche in Kamerun*, Zürich 1981.
J. van Buitselaar: *Africains, missionnaires et colonialistes. Les origines de
  l'Eglise Presbytérienne du Moçambique*, Leiden 1984.

Independent African churches

David B. Barrett: *Schism and Renewal in Africa*, Nairobi 1968.
Victor E.W. Hayward: *African Independent Church Movements*, London
  1963.
Harold W. Turner: *African Independent Churches*, 2 vols., London 1967.
Bengt Sundkler: *Bantu Prophets in South Africa*, London 1948, 2nd ed. 1961.
Christian G. Baëta: *Prophetism in Ghana*, London 1962.
Jules Chomé: *La passion de Simon Kimbangu*, Brussels 1959.
Marie-Louise Martin: *Kimbangu. An African Prophet and his Church*, Grand
  Rapids 1975.
'And Some Fell on the Ground.' *Risk*, vol. 7, no. 3, Geneva 1971.

African theology

Hans-Werner Gensichen (ed.): *Theologische Stimmen aus Afrika, Asien und Lateinamerika*, 3 vols., Munich 1965–69.
D. Nothomb: *Un humanisme africain*, Brussels 1965.
John S. Mbiti: *African Religions and Philosophy*, London etc. 1969.
John S. Mbiti: *Bible and Theology in African Christianity*, Nairobi 1986.
Kwesi A. Dickson and Paul Ellingworth (ed.): *Biblical Revelation and African Beliefs*, London 1969.
Jean-Marc Ela: *Cri de l'homme africain. Questions aux chrétiens et aux églises de l'Afrique*, Paris 1980.
Marie-France Perin Jassy: *Basic Community in the African Churches*, New York 1970.
Mercy Amba Oduyoye: *Hearing and Knowing. Theological Reflections on Christianity in Africa*, New York 1986.

Apartheid and black theology in Africa

G. Cronjé, E.P. Groenewald and W. Nicol: *Regverdige rasse-apartheid*, Stellenbosch 1947.
A.B. du Preez: *Die skriftuurlike grondslag vir rasseverhoudinge*, Cape Town 1955.
The Future of South Africa, London 1965.
W.A. Landman: *A Plea for Understanding*, Cape Town 1968.
Ras, volk en natie en volkerenverhoudingen in het licht van de Schrift. Rapport van de NG-kerk, Cape Town 1974.
Racism in Theology – Theology against Racism. Report on a Consultation, Geneva 1975.
Theo Sundemeier (ed.): *Church and Nationalism in South Africa*, Johannesburg 1975.
Robert Buis: *Religious Beliefs and White Prejudice*, Johannesburg 1975.
D.J. Bosch: *Black Theology: the South African Voice*, London 1973.
S.P. Govender: *In Search of Tomorrow*, Kampen 1987.
David de Beer (ed.): *Het uur der waarheid. Het kairos document van de Zuidafrikaanse christenen*, Baarn 1986.

Missiology

Hendrik Kraemer: *The Christian Message in a non-Christian World*, London 1938.
David J. Bosch: *Witness to the World*, London 1980.
André Roux: *Missions des églises*, mission de l'église, Paris 1984.
Verstraelen (ed.): *Oecumenische inleiding in de missiologie*, Kampen 1988.
Burton L. Goddard (ed.): *The Encyclopedia of Modern Christian Missions*, New Jersey 1967.

Bible, Bible societies, Bible translation

Oscar Parret: *Die Überlieferung der Bibel*, Stuttgart 1949.
Ernst Würthwein: *Der Text des Alten Testaments*, Stuttgart 1963.
W. Canton: *History of the British and Foreign Bible Society*, 5 vols., London 1904–10.

James Moulton Roe: *A History of the British and Foreign Bible Society 1905–1954*, London 1965.

Henry Otis Dwight: *The Centennial History of the American Bible Society*, New York 1916.

Creighton Lacy: *The Word Carrying Giant*, South Pasadena 1977.

R. Kilgour: *The Bible throughout the World*, London 1939.

G.A. Frank Knight: *The History of the NBSS*, 1809–1900 (unpublished).

Elizabeth Hewat: *Vision and Achievement*, Edinburgh 1960.

A.M. Schenk and J.B. Th. Spaan: *Avontuur met het Woord. 150 jaar NBG*, Amsterdam 1964.

A.O. Smit: *God laat het groei. Geschiedenis fan die Bijbelgenootskapsbeweging in Suider Afrika 1920–1970*, Cape Town 1970.

Johannes Beckmann: *Die heilige Schrift in den katholischen Missionen*, Immensee 1966.

Ludwig Muthe: *Le Bible à Madagascar. Les deux premiéres traductions du Nouveau Testament malgache*, Oslo 1969.

A.M. Chirgwin: *The Bible in World Evangelism*, London 1954.

G.H. Wolfensberger: *Multiplying the Loaves*, London 1968.

G.H. Wolfensberger: *The Indispensable Old Testament*, Amsterdam n.d.

Frank C. Laubach: *Towards a Literate World*, New York 1938.

Eugene A. Nida: *God's Word in Man's Language*, New York 1952.

Eugene A. Nida: *Toward a Science of Translation*, New York 1964.

Eugene A. Nida and Charles R. Taber: *The Theory and Practice of Translation*, Leiden 1969, 2nd ed. 1974.

William L. Wonderly: *Bible Translations for Popular Use*, New York 1968.

Eugene A. Nida and Jan de Waard: *From one Language to another. Functional Equivalence in Bible Translating*, New York 1986.

George M. Cowan: *The Word that Kindles*, New York 1982.

Barbara Grimes (ed.): *Ethnologue. Languages of the World*, 11th ed., Dallas 1988.

Hyatt Moore (ed.): *Pass the Word. 50 Years of Wycliffe Bible Translators*, Huntington Beach 1984.

Periodicals

United Bible Societies Bulletin, biannual.

The Bible Translator, United Bible Societies, quarterly.

Scriptures of the World, United Bible Societies, biennial.

International Review of Mission, special Africa issue, vol. 10, no. 1, 1981.

Abbreviations and special terms

ABS	American Bible Society
Aboena	Spiritual leader of the Ethiopian Orthodox Church
Ancient Churches	Churches in Africa founded before the modern missionary movement, such as the Coptic Orthodox Church in Egypt and the Ethiopian Orthodox Church
Apocrypha	Sometimes used, especially by Protestants, to mean 'deuterocanonical' (see below). More correctly used of ancient books which no Christians recognize as part of the Bible.
BICAM	Catholic Bible Institute for Africa and Madagascar
BMS	(British) Baptist Missionary Society
BFBS	British and Foreign Bible Society
CMS	Church Missionary Society, a British and international evangelical Anglican mission
Colporteur	Someone who sells goods, especially scriptures, from door to door
Cowries	Small shells formerly used as money in many parts of Africa
De Propaganda Fide	A Congregation established in 1622 in Rome to coordinate all Roman Catholic missionary work worldwide
Deuterocanonicals	Books mostly written in the period between the Old and New Testaments, written in Greek, but recognized as part of the Old Testament by Roman Catholics and Orthodox, and as having secondary authority by Anglicans and Lutherans. See also Apocrypha.
Faith missions	Missions in which each missionary is normally responsible for finding his or her own support
IMC	International Missionary Council, now the Division of World Mission and Evangelism of the World Council of Churches
Independent church	A church not founded by a foreign mission
Lambeth Conference	One of the periodical meetings of all Anglican bishops worldwide
LMS	London Missionary Society, originally Congregationalist, now interdenominational and known as the Council for World Mission

LWF	Lutheran World Federation
NBSS	National Bible Society of Scotland
NBS	Netherlands Bible Society
NT	New Testament
NoBS	Norwegian Bible Society
OAU	Organization of African Unity
OT	Old Testament
Saints	Nickname for British Members of Parliament who in the 19th century campaigned for the abolition of the slave trade
SIL	Summer Institute of Linguistics; see WBT
SPCK	Society for the Propagation of Christian Knowledge, set up in the 18th century to distribute Christian literature including Bibles
Syncretism	Mixing of elements from different religions
Theresa taler	Coin bearing the image of the Austrian Empress Theresa. Millions of these coins circulated in Africa as currency.
UBS	United Bible Societies
Union version	A Bible translation in a written language made up of expressions common to two or more dialects
WARC	World Alliance of Reformed Churches
WCC	World Council of Churches
WCFBA	World Catholic Federation for the Biblical Apostolate
WBT	Wycliffe Bible Translators, sister organisation having a common membership with SIL

Appendix

Member societies of the UNITED BIBLE SOCIETIES in Africa

Bible Society in Benin*
Bible Society of Cameroon
Bible Society in Côte d'Ivoire*
Bible Society of Ethiopia
Bible Society of Ghana
Bible Society of Kenya
Malagasy Bible Society
Bible Society of Malawi
Bible Society of Mauritius
Bible Society of Nigeria
Bible Society in Rwanda*
Bible Society of South Africa
Bible Society of Tanzania
Bible Society in Togo*
Bible Society of Uganda
Bible Society of Zaire
Bible Society of Zambia*
Bible Society of Zimbabwe*

There are also Bible society offices in Angola, Botswana, Burundi, the Central African Republic, Lesotho, Liberia, Mozambique, Namibia, Sierra Leone, Sudan, Swaziland and North Africa (Algiers).

Worldwide statistics on translation, production and distribution of the Bible, classified by country and continent, are published annually by the headquarters of the United Bible Societies:

UBS World Service Centre
Reading Bridge House
Reading RG1 8PJ
United Kingdom

* Associate Members

The address of the UBS regional centre for Africa is:

United Bible Societies
P.O. Box 42726
Nairobi
Kenya

The address of the Catholic Bible Centre for Africa and Madagascar is:

BIVCAM/CEBAM
P.O. Box 24215
Karen
Nairobi
Kenya

The address of the central office for Africa of the Wycliffe Bible Translators/
  Summer Institute of Linguistics is:

Summer Institute of Linguistics P.O. Box 44456
Nairobi
Kenya

Epilogue

Ype Schaaf has rendered invaluable service by linking the ancient history of the Bible in Africa with its more recent re-introduction and re-discovery by Africans through the instrumentality of Western Christian missionaries. This is important, because in the corporate African mind it is the more recent Western effort, associated also with the ascendancy of Western economic socio-political and cultural dominance, which seems to have left the more enduring impression. Accordingly, the Bible in Africa may appear to be little more than a reminder of how profoundly Africa has been marked by her contact, for good or ill, with Europe and the West in general. Part of the author's motivation, therefore, is to give to Africans 'the fuller picture'.

In that respect, he has written on a very important subject, one which is of greater significance today than may be generally recognized. He writes as a Westerner conscious that there are dimensions to the story of the Bible in Africa which can only be effectively told by Africans themselves. Nevertheless, he writes with deep passion about Africa; in our time, that is not very common. In Ype Schaaf's own words, 'Africa has become an itch' for him; hopefully, a salutary itch! Elsewhere he has told of how at a conference of the secretaries of African Bible Societies in Ghana in 1967, he conceived the idea of proving to his African colleagues that the Bible did not come to Africa from Europe. He offers his book as that proof .

However, one could also say the book is more than that; and probably the fact of writing such a book is in itself indicative of the larger significance of the subject. When in January 1970, David Barrett published in the *International Review of Mission*, an article with the title, AD 2000: 350 million Christians in Africa, in which he argued, on the basis of his demographic projections, that by the end of the century, Africa might well 'tip the balance and transform Christianity permanently into a primarily non-Western religion' (Barrett, 1970: 50), no textbook on Church History at the time showed any awareness of the idea (Walls, 1976). The suggestion that Africa might be the continent to bring about such a radical transformation of Christianity appeared even less obvious still. However following the publication in 1982, of the *World Christian Encyclopaedia* (Nairobi: OUP), edited by David Barrett, we, may, perhaps, take it for granted that many Christians have now become accustomed to the phenomenon referred to as the modern shift in the centre of gravity of Christianity. The idea that in our time the heartlands of the Christian faith are found no longer in the Western world, but in the non-Western world, not in the northern continents, but in the southern continents of Latin America, Asia and particularly, Africa, sounds less surprising now than it would have done two decades ago. The evidence of a considerable Christian recession in the West, particularly in Europe, occurring in the same period of marked Christian accession in other parts of the world, especially in Africa, may now be taken to demonstrate that Barrett's prognosis has been substantially confirmed. Not only in demographic terms, but in some other respects too, Christianity has become a non-Western religion.

It is important to understand what this means. It is not that Western Christianity has become irrelevant, but rather that Christianity may now be seen for what it truly is, a universal religion, infinitely culturally translatable (Walls, 1981:39) – capable of being at home everywhere without loss to its essential nature. Unlike Islam, Hinduism or Buddhism, Christianity has no one centre: not Jerusalem, nor Rome, nor Geneva, nor Canterbury. The centres of its universality can equally be Kinshasa, Seoul, Rio de Janiero, Manila, Nairobi and Ibadan. It is also important to appreciate how what has taken place in Africa has been a significant part of this process.

The matter has to do with more than the statistics of Christian adherence, and yet the figures are revealing. In 1900 80 per cent of the world's Christians lived in Europe and North America. Today, over 60 per cent of the world's Christians live in Latin America, Asia and Africa. In 1900 it was reckoned, there were 10 million Christians in Africa. Today, it is reckoned, there are well over 250 million and, by AD 2000, there could be between 330 million and 350 million Christians in Africa. By any account then Africa has become one of the heartlands of the Christian faith in our time.

And yet, there is probably only one word which describes the present status of Christianity in Africa as we approach the end of the twentieth century. That word is 'surprise'; surprise quite simply at the fact that Africa has become so massively Christian at all.

For, at the start of this century, in 1910, when the World Missionary Conference met in Edinburgh to consider the 'missionary problems in relation to the non-Christian world', and particularly to seek ways in which the Christian gospel might make a greater impact upon the world's non-Christian religions, it was the traditional (primal) religions of Africa, roundly called 'animism' – a description taken from a

European who was not particularly religious himself and who probably never met any of those to whose religion he gave the term – which caused the most concern. The general feeling was that there was 'practically no religious content in animism', nor was there in it 'any preparation for Christianity'. No one at that time could have foreseen the emergence of a vibrant Christian presence in Africa in the course of the same century. In fact, the official report stated: 'If things continue as they are now tending, Africa may become a Mohammedan continent.' (quoted in Barrett, 1970:39).

Paradoxically, the missionary problem which Africa seemed to raise was the equivalent of the more recent question posed by Lesslie Newbigin regarding the Western world, 'Can the West be converted?', on the grounds that one of the most difficult and intractable mission-fields for the Christian gospel in our time is Western culture (Newbigin, 1986, 1987).

It was not so much that Christian mission had registered more significant advances amid the other non-Christian religions which were identified at Edinburgh for special attention, namely, Chinese religions, religions of Japan, Islam and Hinduism. Rather, of all the non-Christian religions, animism was probably the most difficult for the Western Christian missionary mind to penetrate. Not only was animism devoid of literature and scholars to expound its meanings, animism itself was held to be the 'religious beliefs of more or less back-ward and degraded peoples all over the world' as W. H. T. Gairdner wrote in his account of the conference (Gairdner, 1910:139). The problem was not just with animism, the real stumbling-block was the animist.

It is worth recalling that the modern missionary movement was inheritor, among other things, to the notion of a territorial Christianity which saw Europe and such extensions of its ways of life as existed, as the embodiment of the Christian religion. It is an indication of the success of this modern missionary movement that it has brought about the crumbling of the last vestiges of that notion. The Christian church now resembles what it will look at the end more than it has ever done before – people from every nation, tribe, people and language (Revelation 7:9). However, it would be misleading to conclude from this that the missionary enterprise set out to abolish a Eurocentric Christendom. The sense of confidence in the Christian culture of Europe was too strong to permit such a self-critical perspective. Even the Edinburgh 1910 Conference spoke in terms of 'fully missionized lands' (which included Europe) as against 'not yet fully missionized lands' (largely outside of Europe, with the possible exception of Roman Catholic Latin America). And yet, it was because for several decades prior to 1910 many saw the world precisely in those terms and decided to do something about it, that we have the new Christian world we now see.

It follows, then, that the present global transformation of Christianity cannot be understood apart from the modern missionary movement from Europe and the West generally. However, unlike the earlier missionary history of northern and western Europe, and to the credit of the modern missionary enterprise, the more recent missionary history of Africa, and of the non-Western world as a whole, can justly be regarded as the history of Bible translation (see Stine (ed.), 1990). It came to be recognized early that for effective communication of the faith, converts should have access to the original Christian sources in their mother-tongues. The *possibility* of vernacular Christian Scriptures as the functional equivalent of the original source-materials in itself demonstrated that the Christian faith is 'culturally translatable'. Unlike, for example, Islam, where the word of Allah is fully heard only through the medium of Arabic, in Christianity the perception of the word of God is achieved in our own mother-tongues (Act 2:11). This recognition and its impact on missionary action also had the effect of loosening the grip of any 'Western possessiveness' of the faith that there may have been. (See Cragg 1968:15–28). Whenever Western missionaries or a missionary society made the Scriptures available to an African people in that people's own language, they weakened, by the same token, whatever Western bias might have characterized their presentation and prescription of the gospel.

Therefore, well before the dismantling of the European empires and their association with Christianity in Africa, the Western value-setting for the Christian faith was already being discarded as a result of the Western missionary enterprise itself. It is hardly surprising that in the study of the so-called Independent Churches of Africa, it was the availability of the Scriptures in African mother-tongues, that was frequently the crucial factor in the rise and formation of many of the movements (Barrett, 1968). The Bible had become an independent yardstick by which to test, and sometimes to reject, what Western missionaries taught and practised, whilst it also provided the basis for developing new, indigenous forms of Christianity. The spectacular rise of these churches, far from being the mark of a peculiar African 'syncretism', may, in fact, be an indicator of how much Africans seem to 'feel at home' in the gospel of Jesus Christ. African Christians, with access to the Bible in their mother-tongues, can truly claim to hear God speaking to them in their own language. It amounts to the realization that God speaks our language too.

The possession of the Christian Scriptures in African languages became thus probably the single most important element of the Western missionary legacy. In some cases, the Scriptures became the foundation for a new literacy culture which did not exist previously, and ensured that there did take place an effectual rooting of the Christian faith in African consciousness. This, in turn, ensured that a deep and authentic dialogue would ensue between the gospel and

African tradition, authentic in so far as it would take place, not in the terms of a foreign language or of an alien culture, but in the categories of local idioms and world-views. Africa in modern times was experiencing the reception of the word of God in ways and at levels which the crucial formative generations of Christians of northern and western Europe, who received Christianity through the medium of a special ecclesiastical language, Latin, may never have known.

And yet, only gradually did it become more widely acknowledged that the Independents signified how deeply the Christian gospel had 'had a liberating effect [in Africa], setting man free, free from fear, fear of witches and the power of darkness, but above all, conferring a freedom from an inner dependence on European tokens of grace or favour, to aim for higher things and a higher sensitivity'. (Sundkler, 1976:318–319). To that extent, the wider significance of the Independents is that they pointed in the general direction that African Christianity as a whole, was developing.

It may even be suggested, therefore, that it is in modern Africa that Christianity's essential character as an 'infinitely culturally translatable' faith (Walls, 1981:39) has been most notably demonstrated in more recent Christian history. In Africa, the continent of language and languages, the significance of this has been far-reaching. For, as Lamin Sanneh has graphically put it, the import of Scripture translation and its priority in missionary work is an indication that 'God was not disdainful of Africans as to be incommunicable in their languages' (Sanneh, 1983:166). This, Sanneh goes on, not only 'imbued African cultures with eternal significance and endowed African languages with a transcendent range'; it also 'presumed that the God of the Bible had preceded the missionary into the receptor-culture'. As, through the very process of Scripture translation, 'the central categories of Christian theology – God, Jesus Christ, creation, history – were transposed into their local equivalents, suggesting that Christianity had been adequately anticipated', they created, in indigenous languages, resonances far beyond what the missionary transmission conceived (Sanneh, 1983:166; also Sanneh, 1989).

Through these local equivalents, Jesus Christ the Lord had shouldered his way into the African religious world, and could be discovered there through faith by all those who 'approach the spiritual world with requests for guidance and help in difficulties', even where these requests are 'formulated in traditional terms' (Jenkins, 1986:68). This process is entirely consistent with what is reported to have taken place in New Testament times as in Acts 14:15–18. For the centrality of Scripture translation points to the significance of African pre-Christian religious cultures, not only as a 'valid carriage for the divine revelation', but also as providing the idiom for Christian apprehension, as anyone who knows the origins of African Christian names for God will understand. In contrast, for example, to what had happened in the earlier evangelization of Europe, in Africa the God whose name had been hallowed in indigenous languages in the pre-Christian tradition was found to be the God of the Bible, in a way that neither Zeus, nor Jupiter, nor Odin could be. Onyankopon, Olorun, Ngai, Nkulunkulu are among the names of the God and the Father of Jesus Christ; Zeus, Jupiter and Odin are not. In this respect, and perhaps in others too, the African experience takes 'Christian theology into new areas of life, where Western theology has no answers, because it has no questions' (Walls, 1991:147f), precisely because the formative Western missionary encounter with the Christian faith was different. What has happened to the Christian religion in Africa in the present century may, perhaps, be taken to suggest that we are now to consider the continent's persisting Primal Religions as its 'old' religions and to regard Christianity as its 'new' religion.

However, since the impact of the West upon Africa is part of the more recent history of the Bible in Africa, the comparison of their missionary histories may be worth pursuing a little further still. If Lamin Sanneh is right that in the African field,

'The enterprise of Scriptural translation with its far-reaching assumptions about traditional religious categories and ideas as a valid carriage for the revelation and divine initiative that precedes and anticipates historical mission, concedes the salvific values of local religions' (Sanneh, 1983:170),

then what has happened in the process of the transmission of Christianity in Africa may hold some relevance for understanding the same process outside the African field.

It is worth mentioning that when the Edinburgh Conference of 1910 concluded that the primal religions of Africa contained no 'preparation for the gospel', the realization that the primal religions of the world have, in fact, provided the religious background of the faith of the majority of Christians in the twenty centuries of Christian history, including the Christians of Europe, still lay in the future (Turner, 1977; Walls, 1978; for an African view, see Mbiti, 1973). In this connection one may recall Paul Bohannan's observation that 'African culture shares more of its traits, its history, its social organization with Europe that Asia shares with Europe, and certainly more than the North American Indians share with Europe' (quoted in Robin Horton, 1967:263). In relation to our present discussion, what is important is the fact that Europe shares with Africa a pre-Christian primal religious heritage. But it is in Africa (as in some other parts of the non-Western world) that the significance of the primal religions in the history of Christianity has been seen for what it is. In the case of Europe, Christian mission appears to have proceeded on a basis of substitution to such an extent that the primal traditions were virtually completely wiped out.

What this has done to the total Western religious memory may probably never be fully recovered. In the light of the European story, one might be forgiven for thinking that the old primal religions of Europe quickly became a spent force. Yet, the fact that Christians continued to name the days of the week after pre-Christian deities, that pre-Christian elements and notions made their way into the celebration of Christian festivals, and in several other ways too, must be indicators that the old beliefs had not entirely lost their hold upon people's minds. It may well be that in Africa, the opportunity which was lost in Europe, for a serious and creative theological encounter between the Christian and primal traditions, can be regained.

Curiously, the fact that the early flowering of African Theology at its formative stage in the immediate post-missionary era focused on the theological interpretation of the African pre-Christian religious heritage may also be the sign that such an encounter might be possible. For the African theologian, the primal religions, even though they constitute his or her past, are of the nature of an 'ontological' past; and so, together with the profession of the Christian faith, they give account of the same entity, namely, the history of the religious consciousness of the African Christian. The theological investigation of the pre-Christian religious heritage therefore became also a quest for what Bishop Kenneth Cragg has called 'integrity in conversion: a unity of self in which one's past is genuinely integrated into present commitment, so that the crisis of repentance and faith that makes us Christian truly integrates what we have been in what we become' (Cragg, 1980). In this regard the prime concern of the formative stage of African Theology has been about the nature of African Christian identity. (On this subject, see Bediako, 1992). Wrestling with the question of African Christian identity entailed not only confronting constantly the problem of how 'old' and 'new' in African religious consciousness could become integrated in a unified vision of what it meant to be Christian and African. The issue also forced the theologian to become in himself/herself the point of intersection of this struggle for integration through an inner dialogue which had to be infinitely personal and intense, if it was to be authentic African Theology, therefore, by becoming 'something of a dialogue between the African Christian scholar and the perennial religions and spiritualities of Africa' (Adrian Hastings, 1976:50), was thereby also a struggle for an appropriate Christian discourse which would account for and hold together the 'total religious experience of Africans in a coherent and meaningful pattern' (see E. Fasholé-Luke, 1975:267–268).

An indication that this early concentration by Africa's Christian theologians on the African pre-Christian primal heritage was appropriate, is the fact that a later generation of African Theologians, while exploring other themes, has been able to do so by taking off from genuinely African categories. This is most markedly so in relation to christological discussion, which was rather conspicuously minimal or absent in earlier writings. But the current christological explorations revolve around such categories as Christ as Healer, as Master of Initiation and as Ancestor – all of which are derived directly from the world-view and from the apprehension of reality and the Transcendent within African primal religions; (for examples of this development, see Bediako, 1984, 1990; Nyamiti, 1984, Pobee, 1979 and the collection of African christological essays, *Faces of Jesus in Africa,* edited by Robert J. Schreiter, 1991).

It could be argued however, that in the process, African theology has gained rather than lost. For, having been forced to do theology in the interface of their Christian faith and the perennial spiritualities of the African primal traditions of their own backgrounds, as well as having to internalize that dialogue within themselves, African theologians have recaptured the character of theology as Christian intellectual activity on the frontier with the non-Christian world, and hence as essentially communicative, evangelistic and missionary. It is this character of African theology which Dutch theologian and missiologist, Johannes Verkuyl, recognized when he wrote:

> 'African theology does all the things which theology in general does, but in African theology (as in Asian) all these other functions are embraced in the missionary or communicative function. It is not primarily an intra-ecclesiastical exercise, but a discipline whose practitioners keep one question central: How can we best do our theology so that the Gospel will touch Africans most deeply?' (J. Verkuyl, 1978:277)

But, perhaps even more significant in this African effort has been the underlying argument that space had to be made for a positive pre-Christian religious memory in the African Christian consciousness, on the basis that 'religion informs the African's life in its totality' (Dickson 1984:29). Memory is integral to identity; and without memory, none of us knows who we are. As Dickson further explains, the theologian who fails to:

> recognise the structures of religion as revealed by the historian of religions . . . may not notice the absence of religion from his theology. In the context of Africa, Christian theology must of necessity take account of that understanding of religion which bears the stamp of an authentic African contribution [that means, the primal religions]. (Dickson, 1984:46).

To the extent that the African endeavour has achieved a measure of success, it may hold promise for a Western theology which is now also asking seriously how the Christian faith may be related, in a missionary sense, to Western culture.

It is this re-location of African primal religions 'at the very centre of the academic stage' (Hastings, 1976:50), which may prove a benediction to Western Christian theology as it also seeks to be communicative, evangelistic and missionary in its own context. For the African vindication of the theological significance of African primal religions, if it has validity, also goes to affirm that the European primal heritage was not illusory, to be consigned to oblivion as primitive darkness. The nature of the meeting of Christianity with European primal religions may hold more significance for understanding the modern West than it may have been assumed. A serious Christian theological interest in the European primal traditions and some of the early forms of Christianity which emerged from the encounter with those traditions, could provide a fresh approach to understanding Christian identity in Europe too, as well as opening new possibilities for Christian theological endeavour today. And the primal world view may turn out to be not so alien to Europe after all, even in a post-Enlightenment era.

For the signs of what appears to be a post-modernist rejection of the Enlightenment in the West can be seen partly in the resurgence of the phenomenon of the occult as well as in the various 'quests' for spiritual experience and wholeness – even if without explicit reference to God – all bearing the marks of elements of a primal world view. These are sufficient indicators that a primal world-view, suppressed rather than encountered, purged and integrated, rises to haunt the future. In this connection, the viability of a Christian consciousness which retains its sense of the spiritual world of primal religions, as well as the theological encounter between the primal world view and Christian faith that is evident in African Christianity – all these are an implicit challenge to the notion that humanity can be fully defined in exclusively post-Enlightenment terms. It seems then, that the world's primal religions, in Europe as in Africa and elsewhere, the religious traditions which have been most closely associated with the continuing Christian presence historically in the world so far, may yet again point the way into the Christian future. If this expectation proves right, the African contribution will have been an important one.

Some readers may object to my use of African Theology on the grounds that Africa's Christian theologians have not followed the logic of the translatability of their faith into a full-blown recourse to African indigenous languages. In 1979, John Pobee of Ghana stated in his book, *Toward an African Theology*, which though written in the main in English, nevertheless makes an ample use of Akan wisdom-concepts and proverbial sayings:

> 'Ideally, African theologies should be in the vernacular. Language is more than syntax and morphology; it is the vehicle for assuming the weight of a culture. Therefore, this attempt to construct an African theology in the English language is the second best, even if it is convenient if it should secure as wide a circulation as possible'.

But perhaps the more perceptive response has been stated by Cameroonian theologian, Father Engelbert Mveng:

'When the objection is made that this theology is not written in native languages, we reply that it is lived in native languages, in the villages and in the neighbourhoods, before being translated into foreign languages by its own rightful heirs, the African theologians' (L. Boff & V. Elizondo (eds.) 1988).

Mveng's answer, though stated somewhat polemically, is nonetheless a pointer to the impact that a 'translatable faith', apprehended by and large through the medium of mother-tongues, has come to live in Africa. It arises from the realization that the emergence of a significant African theological tradition in the twentieth century, even if it is articulated predominantly in 'foreign languages', is itself an indication that in African Christian life, there is a substratum of vital Christian consciousness, and a sufficiently deep apprehension of Jesus Christ at the specific level of religious experience, itself of a theological nature, which can be seen to be the only real basis for a viable activity of academic theology. It is this essential ingredient for the 'birth of theology' (von Allmen 1975) that the translated Bible has provided in Africa.

According to the Book of Acts, the Ethiopian official, after understanding the message of the Bible, 'went on his way rejoicing' (Acts 8:39). Future developments in African Christianity will test the depth of the impact that the Bible has made upon Africa.

Kwarne Bediako

REFERENCES

Allmen, Daniel von (1975) The birth of Theology – Contextualisation as the dynamic element in the formation of New Testament Theology, in *International Review of Mission,* vol. 64, January 1975:37–52.

Barrett, David B. (1968) *Schism and renewal in Africa – An analysis of six thousand contemporary religious movements,* Nairobi: Oxford University Press.

—— (1970) AD 2000 – 350 million Christians in Africa, in *International Review of Mission,* Vol. LIX, no. 233, January 1970:39–54.

—— (1982)*World Christian Encyclopaedia,* Nairobi: Oxford University Press.

Bediako, Kwame (1984) Biblical Christologies in the context of African traditional religions, in Vinay Samuel & Chris Sugden (eds.) *Sharing Jesus in the Two-Thirds World,* Grand Rapids: Eerdmans, 81–121.

—— (1990) *Jesus in African Culture – A Ghanaian perspective,* Accra: Asempa Publishers.

—— (1992) *Theology and Identity – The impact of culture upon Christian thought in the second century and modern Africa,* Oxford: Regnum Books.

Boff, L. & V. Elizondo (eds.) (1988) *Third World Theologies – Convergences and differences,* (Concilium 199), Edinburgh: T. & T. Clark.

Cragg, Kenneth (1968) *Christianity in World perspective,* London: Lutter-worth Press.
—— (1980) Conversion and convertibility with special reference to Muslims, in John R. W. Stott & Robert Coote (eds.) *Down to Earth – Studies in Christianity and Culture,* Grand Rapids: Eerdmans, 193–208.
Dickson, Kwesi A. (1984) *Theology in Africa,* London/New York: Darton, Longman & Todd/Orbis Books.
Fasholé-Luke, E. (1975) The quest for an African Christian theology, in *Ecumenical Review,* vol. 27, no. 3, 1975, 259–269.
Gairdner, T. H. W. (1910) *Edinburgh 1910 An Account and Interpretation of the World Missionary Conference,* London: Oliphant, Anderson & Ferrier.
Hastings, Adrian (1976) *African Christianity – An essay in interpretation,* London: Geoffrey Chapman.
Horton, Robin (1967) Philosophy and African Studies, in David Brokensha & Michael Crowder (eds.) *Africa in the wider world,* Oxford: Pergamon Press, 261–291.
Jenkins, Paul (1986) The roots of African Church History – some polemical thoughts, in *International Bulletin of Missionary Research,* vol. 10, no. 2, April 1986 67–71.
Mbiti, John S. (1973) African Indigenous Culture in relation to Evangelism and Church Development, in R. Pierce Beaver (ed.) *The Gospel and Frontier Peoples,* Pasadena: William Carey Library, 79–95.
Newbigin, Lesslie (1986) *Foolishness to the Greeks – The Gospel and Western Culture* Geneva: World Council of Churches.
—— (1987)Can the West be converted? in *International Bulletin of Missionary Research,* vol. 11, no. 1, January 1987:2–7.
Nyamiti, Charles (1984) *Christ as our Ancestor – Christology from an African perspective,* Gweru: Mambo Press.
Pobee, John S. (1979) *Toward an African Theology,* Nashville: Abingdon Press.
Senneh, Lamin (1983) The horizontal and the vertical in mission – An African perspective, in *International Bulletin of Missionary Research,* vol. 7, no. 4, October 1983: 165–171
—— (1989) *Translating the message – the missionary impact on culture,* New York: Orbis Books.
Schreiter, Robert (ed.) (1991) *Faces of Jesus in Africa,* London: S.C.M. Press.
Stine, Philip (ed.) (1990) *Bible Translation and the Spread of the Church – the last 200 years,* Leiden: E. J. Brill.
Sundkler, Bengt (1976) *Zulu Zion and some Swazi Zionists,* London: Oxford University Press.
Turner, Harold W. (1977) The Primal Religions of the world and their study, in Victor Hayes (ed.) *Australian Essays in World Religions,* Bedford Park: 27–37.
Verkuyl, Johannes (1978) *Contemporary Missiology – An introduction* (ET), Grand Rapids: Eerdmans.
Walls, Andrew F. (1976) Towards understanding Africa's place in Christian history, in J. S. Pobee (ed.) *Religion in a pluralistic society* (Essays presented to Professor C. G. Baëta), Leiden: E. J. Brill:180–189.

—— (1978) Africa and Christian Identity, in *Mission Focus,* vol. 6, no. 7, November 1978:11–13.

—— (1981) The Gospel as the prisoner and liberator of culture, in *Faith and Thought,* 108 (1–2), 1981: 39–52.

—— (1991) Structural problems in Mission Studies, in *International Bulletin of Missionary Research,* vol. 15, no. 4, October 1991:146–155.